ScottForesman Science

Discover the Wonder

Series Consulting Author

David Heil
Associate Director,
Oregon Museum of Science & Industry
Portland, Oregon

Consulting Authors

Maureen Allen
Science Resource Teacher/Specialist
Irvine Unified School District
Irvine, California

Dr. Timothy Cooney
Professor of Earth Science & Science Education
Earth Science Department
University of Northern Iowa
Cedar Falls, Iowa

Dr. Angie L. Matamoros
Science Curriculum Specialist K–12
Broward County Schools
Ft. Lauderdale, Florida

Dr. Manuel Perry
Manager, Educational Programs
Lawrence Livermore National Laboratory
Livermore, California

Dr. Irwin Slesnick
Professor of Biology
Biology Department
Western Washington University
Bellingham, Washington

 ScottForesman

A Division of HarperCollins*Publishers*

Editorial Offices: Glenview, Illinois
Regional Offices: Sunnyvale, California • Tucker, Georgia
Glenview, Illinois • Oakland, New Jersey • Dallas, Texas

Content Consultants

Dr. Linda Berne
University of North Carolina
Charlotte, North Carolina

Dr. Kurt Brorson
Laboratory of Cellular and Molecular
Immunology
National Institutes of Health
Bethesda, Maryland

Dr. Bonnie Buratti
Jet Propulsion Laboratory
California Institute of Technology
Pasadena, California

Dr. Michael Garcia
Department of Geology and Geophysics
University of Hawaii
Honolulu, Hawaii

Dr. Norman Gelfand
Fermi National Accelerator Laboratory
Accelerator Division
Batavia, Illinois

Dr. Roger Pielke
Department of Atmospheric Science
Colorado State University
Fort Collins, Colorado

Dr. Harrison H. Schmitt
*Former Astronaut (Apollo 17) and
    United States Senator
Geologist and Science and Technoiogy
    Consultant*
Albuquerque, New Mexico

Dr. Richard Shippee
Department of Biology
Vincennes University
Vincennes, Indiana

Dr. David Stronck
Department of Teacher Education
California State University at Hayward
Hayward, California

Dr. Merita Thompson
Department of Health Education
Eastern Kentucky University
Richmond, Kentucky

Dr. Antonio Garcia Trejo
Arizona Department of Environmental
    Quality
Chandler, Arizona

Dr. Lisa Wagner
Department of Biology
Georgia Southern University
Statesboro, Georgia

Multicultural Consultants

Dr. Thomas Crosby
Department of Biology
Morgan State University
Baltimore, Maryland

Dr. Frank Dukepoo
Department of Biology
Northern Arizona University
Flagstaff, Arizona

Dr. Amram Gamliel (Ben-Teman)
*Educational Consultant/Professional
    Writer*
Newton Center, Massachusetts

Dr. Hilda Hernandez
Department of Education
California State University at Chico
Chico, California

Dr. Luis A. Martinez-Perez
College of Education
Florida International University
Miami, Florida

Safety Consultant

Dr. Jack A. Gerlovich
*Science Education Safety
    Consultant/Author*
Waukee, Iowa

Reading Consultant

Dr. Robert A. Pavlik
Professor of Reading/Language Arts
Reading/Language Arts Department
Cardinal Stritch College
Milwaukee, Wisconsin

Activity Consultant

Mary Jo Diem
Science/Educational Consultant
Croton-on-Hudson, New York

Math/Science Consultant

Catherine R. Ney
Teacher
Blacksburg, Virginia
1994–95 Christa McAuliffe Fellow,
State of Virginia

Acknowledgments

Photographs Unless otherwise acknowledged, all photographs are the property of
ScottForesman. Page abbreviations are as follows: (T)top, (C)center, (B)bottom, (L)left,
(R)right, (INS)inset.
Cover Design Sheldon Cotler + Design
Cover Background: Richard Pharoah/INTERNATIONAL STOCK PHOTO.   Inset: George
K. Bryce/ANIMALS, ANIMALS   Magnifying Glass: Richard Chesnut
Page iv(T) C. Allan Morgan   **iv(B)** David Muench   **v(T)** Don & Pat Valenti/f/Stop
vi(T) Milt & Joan Mann/Cameramann International, Ltd.   **viii(B)** Courtesy Pittsburgh
Plate Glass   **x(T)** Visuals Unlimited   **x(B)** Dave B. Fleetham/Tom Stack & Associates
xiii AP/Wide World Photos   **xiv(BR)** Tony Freeman/Photo Edit   **xv(R)** Dwight R. Kuhn

Illustrations Unless otherwise acknowledged, all computer graphics by Ligature, Inc.
Page vii Karen Kluglein   **viii** Blanche Sims   **ix** Hank Iken   **xiii** Susan Spellman
xiii(R) Ron Lipking   **xiv(T)** Ron Becker   **xiv** John Burgoyne

Acknowledgments continue on page 31.

About the Cover

Even though this desert habitat is called
Death Valley, it is teeming with life. The
soldier beetle is only one of many organisms
that live in the desert. The background
photograph was taken in Inyo County,
California, which contains part of Death
Valley.

Reviewers

Habitats

Gardening

CHAPTER

3 Good Food!

Finding Shelter

CHAPTER 3 Machines in Building

Sounds All Around

CHAPTER

3 Louder Sounds

Protecting the Earth

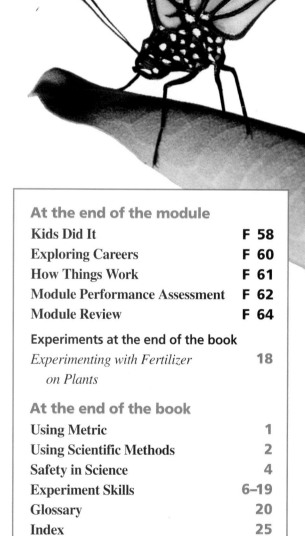

Habitats

Habitats

What do deserts, forests, and cities have in common? They're all habitats—places where plants and animals live. The desert is home to lizards and cactuses, the forest to trees and rabbits, the city to people and pets. Each of these habitats is special in its own way. In this module, you'll read about different habitats and discover what makes each one special.

CHAPTER

1 Into the Desert

Could you live inside a cactus?
If you could, you'd have lots of company. Birds, mice, and many other desert animals live inside these prickly plants.

2 Changes in the Desert

What happens when the desert gets wet? When rain comes to the desert, plants and animals must take in water quickly.

CHAPTER

3 Into the Forest

Let it snow. The plants and animals of the cold northern forests survive the winter in many different ways.

In this module

At the end of the book

Into the Desert

I made a sand castle at the beach one time... it dried out really fast!

Discover Activity

Which dries faster?

Use a hand lens to take a close look at some sand and some soil. Compare the sand and the soil. Which do you think will dry out faster? Think of a way to find out. Then try it.

For Discussion

1. *Which dried out faster, soil or sand?*
2. *What kind of plants would grow best in sand?*

1.1 *Lands of Little Rain*

▶ *What kind of place is this?*

If you could step into the picture below, what would you find? Everywhere you look, it's hot, dusty, and dry. You're wearing a hat to shade your eyes from the bright sun. But nothing can stop the sun's scorching heat. Your clothes are wet with sweat, and your throat is burning. You need a drink of water! "Where am I?" you ask yourself.

You're in the Sonoran Desert in the southwestern United States. You have a pretty good idea that it would be hard to live in this place. But what kind of place is this, and what does it take to survive the heat and the dryness?

▼ The mesquite tree is an example of the kind of trees that survive in the Sonoran Desert.

Dry Places

You may have thought of deserts as sandy and hot. Some deserts are all sand, but others are covered with dry soil, loose gravel, large rocks, or even ice. Most deserts are hot, but some are cold. But whatever the differences might be, every desert is very, very dry.

A **desert** is a place that gets less than 15 centimeters of rain a year. Most places on the earth get much more rain. For example, over 100 centimeters of rain falls each year in the southeastern United States. That's why there are no deserts in the southeastern states.

Find the Sonoran Desert on the map. How are this desert and all the other deserts alike? The answer: They are all very dry places.

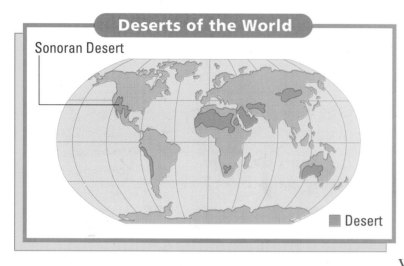

Deserts of the World

Sonoran Desert

■ Desert

▼ The Sonoran Desert gets its name from Sonora, a state in northern Mexico.

The Sonoran Desert

Take a look at the picture of the Sonoran Desert. Are you surprised to see so many plants growing in such a dry place? In spite of the heat and dryness, an amazing number of plants and animals live in the Sonoran Desert. Saguaro (sə gwär′o) cactuses and creosote (krē′ə sōt) bushes dot the landscape. Lizards, jackrabbits, and dozens of other animals also live in the desert.

All these living things are at home in the desert habitat. A **habitat** is the place where an animal or plant lives. Desert plants and animals need water to live, but their habitat gets little rain. As you learned in the Discover Activity, sand dries out quickly. So when it does rain, the sandy soil in the desert dries out quickly. How do desert plants and animals survive on so little water? To solve this mystery, you will have to keep reading.

Checkpoint

1. What do all deserts have in common?
2. Describe the plant and animal life in the Sonoran Desert habitat.
3. **Take Action!** Saguaro cactuses grow to be about five meters tall. Cut a string that length. Compare it to your height.

How Dry Is Dry?

All deserts get some rainfall. But remember none get more than 15 centimeters of rain per year. For example some places in Baja California in Mexico might go four or five years without a drop of rain. A desert in Chile holds the record for the longest period without rain—14 years!

The graph below shows the annual yearly rainfall for 3 different cities.

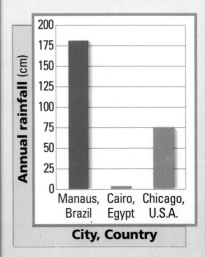

City, Country

What Did You Find Out?
1. *Which city gets the most rainfall? Which city gets the least?*
2. *Which city is in a desert? How did you know?*

Make a Desert Habitat

Deserts are places that get little rainfall. Try planting a desert garden and see what kinds of plants can grow in it.

Picture A

Picture B

Picture C

Gather These Materials

clear plastic 2-liter bottle   sand

scissors   paper towel

aquarium gravel   cactus

aquarium charcoal   coleus

potting soil   water

Follow This Procedure

1. Make a chart like the one on the next page. Record your observations in your chart.

2. Cut off the top of a plastic 2-liter bottle just where the neck starts to curve in. Your teacher will help by making the first cut with the scissors. (Picture A)

3. Mix small amounts of aquarium gravel and aquarium charcoal together. Form a layer at the bottom of the bottle.

4. Add a layer of potting soil.

5. Cover the soil with a layer of sand. (Picture B)

6. Carefully dig a small hole in the soil. Plant the coleus in the hole.

Record Your Results

	Day 1	Day 2	Day 3
Coleus			
Cactus			

7 Fold a paper towel and wrap it around a cactus so that you can hold the cactus. Plant the cactus in the soil with the coleus. (Picture C) Add a few drops of water around the plants.

8 Draw what each plant looks like.

Predict: *Will the cactus or the coleus grow better?*

9 Place the bottle in a sunny spot. Do not water them again. Observe your plants for a few days. Draw what the plants look like each day.

State Your Conclusions

1. What happened to the cactus?
2. What happened to the coleus?
3. Which plant would grow better in a desert?

Let's Experiment

Now that you've seen how the plants in your desert habitat grew, what would happen if you watered the habitat every day?

1.2 *The Struggle to Survive*

> *How can living things find water in the desert?*

▼ *Gila woodpecker*

The gila woodpecker gets food and water by eating insects that live in the saguaro cactus. Notice the sharp bill on the gila woodpecker pecking a hole in the saguaro. This red-headed bird will nest in the hole. After a year, the woodpecker moves out and makes a new hole.

Gila woodpeckers aren't the only desert animals that depend on the saguaro. For example, elf owls and mice move into holes left by the woodpeckers. Over time, the saguaro becomes like a busy apartment building, with many different animals rushing in and out. All these animals have body parts and ways of acting that help them survive the dryness of their desert habitat. Desert plants, like the saguaro cactus, also have parts that help them survive.

Typical Desert Plants

In the Sonoran Desert, it may rain only once or twice a year. So when the rain comes, the saguaro cactus is ready. The saguaro has long, shallow roots, which spread out in all directions from its stem.

The roots soak up rainwater soon after it falls and carry the water to the stem. The fleshy stem soaks up water from the roots like a giant sponge. The stem swells up when it stores water.

The stem of the saguaro has a hard, waxy covering that keeps the plant from drying out. You might think of that covering like the plastic covering that keeps your lunchtime sandwich from drying out. The leaves of a saguaro are actually sharp spines. These spines don't let water escape into the air as other leaves do. The spines also help keep hungry animals away from the cactus.

But the spines can't stop all the animals. For example, insects crawl inside the saguaro to feast on the juicy pulp. When the insects crawl back out of the saguaro, insect eaters are just waiting to snap them up. Who could those insect eaters be?

▲ *Because the saguaro grows very slowly and stores much water, it can flower each year—even when it doesn't rain.*

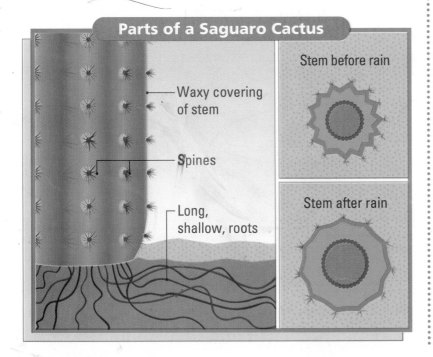

Parts of a Saguaro Cactus

Waxy covering of stem

Spines

Long, shallow, roots

Stem before rain

Stem after rain

Into The Field

***How can living
things in your area
survive?***

*Observe and describe
a plant or animal that
lives in your area.
What body parts or
ways of acting help it
survive?*

➤ *Spiny lizards often
climb trees to find insects.*

▼ *These insects are just a
few of the kinds of insects
that desert lizards eat.*

Typical Desert Animals

Slurp! A spiny lizard, such as the one shown below, has just eaten another insect. The insect isn't just food for the lizard. The bodies of insects also contain a lot of water, so lizards get all the water they need by eating insects. In fact, lizards in the desert never need to drink water, which helps them survive. What would you have to do to survive without taking a drink of water?

Now you know how spiny lizards get the water they need. But how do they survive the hot days in the desert? Spiny lizards often lie on rocks in the hot desert. They're not lazy— they just need to warm up their bodies. When it gets too hot, the lizards crawl under rocks in search of shade.

The spiny lizard also has body parts that help it survive in the desert. Notice the sharp, spiny scales that cover the long body of the spiny lizard in the picture. This thick, scaly skin helps keep the lizard from losing water through its skin.

The spiny lizard's eyes have "built-in sunglasses" that cut down on the sun's bright rays. With its sharp eyes, the spiny lizard can spot insects from far away. The lizard can then catch insects it needs for food and water.

◄ *The western banded gecko comes out of hiding to hunt for food at night.*

The spiny lizard is just one of many kinds of lizards that live in the Sonoran Desert. Notice another kind of lizard in the picture above. This western banded gecko hides in rocks or under fallen limbs during the heat of the day and comes out at night.

Desert Animals Find Shelter

Desert animals choose shelters that help them survive.

It is midday and a hot sun beats down on the desert. The desert is a tough place to live, but these animals find ways to survive.

To avoid the heat, a desert tortoise stays in an underground shelter it digs with its powerful front legs. Sometimes, a tortoise crawls into a ready-made opening in rocks or soil.

Nearby, some bats hang from the wall of a cave. They sleep upside down in a cave during the heat of the day. At sunset, the bats will fly off to hunt for food.

Desert Tortoise
The desert tortoise may dig shallow tunnels up to 9 meters long under the earth's surface.

Western Pipistrelle Bat
This bat often flies before dark and is usually the first bat to be seen in the evening.

Antelope Ground Squirrel

Ground squirrels dig burrows in rocky places that other animals can't get to.

Kangaroo Rat

The kangaroo rat may hollow out a shallow "dish" near the opening to its burrow to store seeds.

A ground squirrel sits on the ground and seems to be washing its face. First the squirrel licks its paws and then rubs them on its head. The squirrel isn't really washing, it's trying to cool off. The ground squirrel also makes a shelter in a tunnel underground.

At sunset, after a long day's sleep, a kangaroo rat leaves its burrow shelter. With tiny front legs, it pushes soil from the tunnel opening it closed up earlier to keep hot, dry air out.

When it's hot, the temperatures are cooler underground than they are aboveground. What kind of shelter would you build if you lived in the desert? Where would you build your shelter?

Night Life in the Desert

The hot sun has set and it's nighttime. Now a whole new set of animals comes out of their hiding places to hunt for food.

Sleeping during the heat of the day helps these animals survive in the desert. The animals that hunt at night have body parts that help them find their food.

Notice the large eyes and sharp bill of the elf owl in the picture. These tiny owls can see as well at night as you can in daylight. Their sharp bills help the owls snap up insects.

Kangaroo rats, such as the one in the picture, pop up from underground tunnels where they stay out of the hot desert sun. The rats use their front feet to stuff seeds, grass, and cactus bits into pouches inside their cheeks. When the pouches are full, the rats hop back to their burrows. Like lizards, the kangaroo rats never drink water. Instead, they get all their water from the food they eat.

Another night hunter, the kit fox, comes out of its underground den. Notice the huge ears on the kit fox in the picture. The fox loses heat through its ears and this helps its body stay cool.

▼ The elf owl can live in holes made in the saguaro by a gila woodpecker because it is the smallest American owl—only about 13 to 15 centimeters tall.

▲ The kangaroo rat stays in its burrow on nights when the moon is bright. Why might the rat stay hidden on moonlit nights?

◄ *Instead of digging its own burrow, sometimes the kit fox just makes the burrows of ground squirrels or kangaroo rats larger.*

Kit foxes have excellent hearing. When a kit fox hears an animal such as a kangaroo rat hopping by, the fox dashes after it at top speed. Sometimes the kit fox wins and sometimes it loses.

When morning comes, all these nighttime animals will return to underground hiding places or to their nests until the sun goes down. By staying underground or inside of a cactus, these animals keep the dry air from drying out their skin. This way of living helps many desert animals survive.

Checkpoint

1. Where do saguaros store water?
2. How do spiny lizards get water?
3. How does staying underground during the day help desert animals?
4. **Take Action!** Invent your own desert animal. Make a model of it. Tell how it survives in the desert.

How Fast Does It Dry Out?

What helps keep cactuses from drying out in the hot sun? Find out in this activity, using paper towels as your "stems."

Picture A

Picture B

Picture C

Gather These Materials

3 paper towels
water
plastic tray

sheet of waxed paper
paper clips

Follow This Procedure

1 Make a chart like the one on the next page. Record your observations in your chart.

2 Wet each paper towel with water so that it is damp but not dripping.

3 Flatten out one of the paper towels, and place it on the plastic tray.

4 Roll up the next paper towel. Set it down on the tray next to the flat one. (Picture A)

5 Roll up the third paper towel. Cover the towel completely with a sheet of waxed paper. Use paper clips to keep the waxed paper in place. (Picture B) Place it on the tray next to the second paper towel. (Picture C)

6 Put the tray in the sunlight.

Predict: Which paper towel will dry out the fastest? Why?

7 Feel the paper towels a few hours later. Compare how much they have dried out.

8 Record your observations.

State Your Conclusions

1. Which paper towel dried out faster, the flat one or the one that was rolled up?

2. How did the waxed paper affect whether the paper towel dried out?

3. Which paper towel was the most like a cactus stem? Explain.

Record Your Results

	Paper Towel: Wet or dry?
.Flat	
Rolled up	
Rolled up and covered with waxed paper	

Let's Experiment

Now that you've learned about how cactus stems hold water in the desert, what do you think would happen if the air was damp? How does damp air affect the rate of drying out? Use what you know about scientific methods to find out.

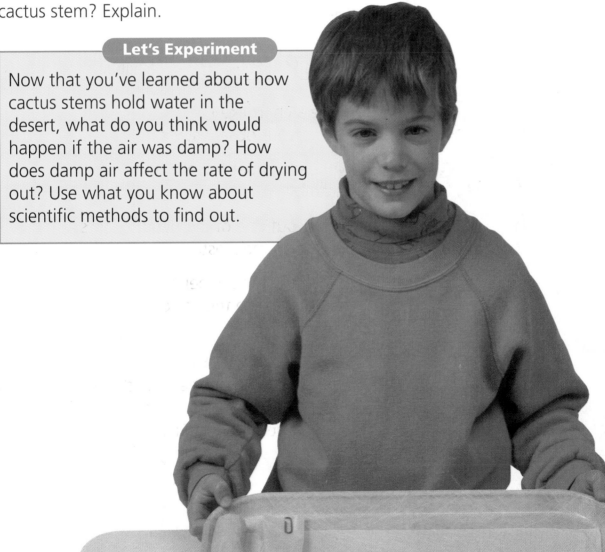

Chapter Review

Reviewing Words and Concepts

Write the letter of the word or phrase that best completes each sentence.

1. A _____ is a place that is very dry.
2. Creosote bushes and _____ are plants that grow in a desert.
3. A _____ is the place where an animal or plant lives.
4. The long, shallow _____ of the saguaro cactus soak up rainwater.
5. The stem of the saguaro has a hard, waxy _____.
6. The thick, scaly _____ of a spiny lizard helps keep the lizard from losing water.
7. Many desert animals stay _____ during the day.
8. Kangaroo rats get all their _____ from the food they eat.
9. The tiny _____ can see as well at night as you can during the day.
10. A _____ loses heat through its large ears.

a. covering
b. water
c. cactuses
d. skin
e. kit fox
f. desert
g. elf owl
h. roots
i. underground
j. habitat

Connecting Ideas

1. Copy the concept map. Use the terms at the right to complete the map to show how living things get water in the desert.

lizard   rain

insect

A. _____ — B. **cactus** — C. _____ — D. _____

2. Write a sentence or two about the ideas shown in the concept map.

Interpreting What You Learned

1. Name three characteristics of the Sonoran Desert.
2. How does a saguaro cactus survive in the desert?
3. How is the saguaro cactus like a busy apartment building?
4. How do some animals find shelter from the desert heat?

Performance Assessment

Which lizard heats up quickest?

Materials • 3 thermometers • cutout lizard • scissors • paper • construction paper (black, white, and green) • lamp (optional) • pencil

Collecting Data

1. Using the cutout lizard your teacher gives you, trace two lizards on each color of construction paper.
2. Cut out the lizards you traced.
3. Place one cutout lizard of each color on top of a table in the sunlight. Use a lamp if there is no sunlight.
4. Place a thermometer on top of each cutout. Make a chart and record the temperature on each thermometer. Then cover the thermometer with the other cutout of that color. Make sure each thermometer is entirely covered. Wait 10 minutes.

5. Lift the cutout off each thermometer. Read the temperature carefully on each thermometer. Record each temperature in your chart. Wait longer if the temperatures have not changed.

Analyzing Data

How might a lizard's color affect its survival in the desert?

Changes in the Desert

Alright—my water is already two degrees hotter than yours!

Discover Activity

How hot can it get?

How hot can you make a cup of water using only sunlight as a source of heat? Start with one cup of water at room temperature. Think of what you can use to make the cup of water heat up faster. Then try it. Let the water sit in the sunlight for 30 minutes. Take the temperature of the water every 10 minutes.

For Discussion

1. What was the temperature after 30 minutes?

2. Explain how you made your water heat up.

2.1 *Desert Heat*

How does the sunlight make the desert such a hot place?

If you could take a walk through the desert you would know what makes it so hot—the sun. Few clouds are ever seen above the desert. Day after day, the sun beats down on the sand, plants, and animals.

Remember how you tried to heat water in the Discover Activity? The sun heated the water in the cup. Also, think about when you left your bicycle or a ball in the sun for a couple of hours. How did these objects feel when you touched them? Think about it. Sure, the sun is a very bright light, but what does light have to do with heat? Why do things that the sun shines on get hot?

◄ *The sun shines brightly over the desert almost every day.*

Heating Up!

Everything you can see and touch is made of **matter**. Anything that takes up space is matter. Water, sand, schools, and books are made of matter. When the sun shines, light energy hits objects on the earth that are made of matter. If these objects absorb—or take in—light energy, the light energy is changed to heat. Sand, cars, houses—all things made of matter—can be warmed by sunlight.

Notice the arrows in the picture showing what happens when the sun's light energy hits the lizard and the rock. The lizard and the rock absorb light energy and become warmer than the air around them. Then these warm objects give off heat and warm the air. The same thing happens when the sun shines on other objects. They become warm and give off heat because heat moves from hot objects to cooler ones.

▼ *The collared lizard becomes warm when it absorbs light energy.*

Light Energy

Heat

Look at the picture of the children. Which child would feel warmer in the sun—the one wearing the white shirt or the one wearing the black shirt? Shiny and light-colored objects reflect, or bounce back, much of the sun's light. On the other hand, dark-colored or dull objects absorb a lot of light. As a result, dark-colored objects become warmer than light-colored objects. If you were going for a walk in the desert in the picture, would you rather wear black or white clothing?

If the girl was in this desert, what might she be watching through the binoculars?

As night falls in the desert, the sun no longer beats down on things. The sand and rocks cool down because they are no longer absorbing light energy that warms them. When these objects become as cool as the air, they no longer give off heat. Everything in the desert cools off after the sun stops shining.

Measuring Temperature

The measure of the hotness or coldness of an object or place is called **temperature**. A **thermometer** is a tool that measures temperature. Hot objects or places have a high temperature, while cold objects or places have a low temperature.

During summer in the Sonoran Desert, the early morning temperatures range between 15 degrees Celsius and 23 degrees Celsius (°C). The temperature of your classroom is probably about 23°C.

▼ *Early in the morning, the temperature in the Sonoran Desert begins to rise. The highest temperature is reached in the late afternoon.*

Early Morning

Late Afternoon

Notice the thermometers beside the pictures of the desert places. To read the thermometers, count two degrees for each line on the thermometer. What is the difference between the temperature at five o'clock in the morning and at four o'clock in the afternoon?

In the afternoon, the temperature in the desert is usually about 36°C. The hottest summer days in many places in the United States reach this temperature. But at times in the desert, the temperature in late afternoon rises to 50°C or higher! No wonder most desert animals look for a shady place or go underground during the day. Even daytime animals are only active early in the morning and in the early evening—after the sun goes down.

January in the Sonoran Desert sometimes brings temperature readings of about 4°C. But the cold temperatures in the desert don't last very long. Think for a minute though of the wide range of temperatures in the desert. From a high temperature of 50°C to a low temperature of 4°C. That's a big difference. Still, plants and animals in the desert can survive these temperature changes.

Checkpoint

1. What makes the desert so hot?
2. What is the range of temperatures in the Sonoran Desert?
3. **Take Action!** Go out into the school yard. Find colored things that are in the sun. Which things are the warmest? coolest?

Measuring High and Low

How much does the temperature change during the day? Let's investigate.

What to Do
A. Find a spot outside that stays sunny for the whole day.
B. Put a thermometer in that location. Take a temperature reading early in the morning. Record it on a chart like the one below.
C. Take and record another reading around midday and again late in the afternoon.
D. Find the difference between the high and low temperatures. Record the results.

Record Your Results

Time	Temperature
Early morning	
Midday	
Late afternoon	
High/low difference	

What Did You Find Out?
1. *Why do you think the temperature changes during the day?*
2. *Why might the readings be different if the day were cloudy?*

Which Heats Up the Quickest?

The sun shines on many different surfaces on the earth, including the desert sand. How fast does the sand in the desert heat up? Try this activity to find out.

Picture A

Picture B

Picture C

Gather These Materials

sand	3 identical, plastic
soil	containers
water	3 thermometers

Follow This Procedure

1. Make a chart like the one on the next page. Record your observations in your chart.

2. Fill one plastic container about one-half full of sand. (Picture A)

3. Fill the second container with the same amount of soil.

4. Fill the third container with the same amount of water.

5. Put a thermometer in each container so that the bulb of the thermometer is buried in the material in the container. (Picture B)

6. Read and record the starting temperature in each container. (Picture C)

7. Put all three containers in a sunny location.

Predict: *Which material will heat up the fastest?*

Record Your Results

Time	Temperature		
	Sand	Soil	Water
Starting temperature			
15 minutes			
30 minutes			
45 minutes			
60 minutes			
Total change from start to finish			

8 Read and record the temperature in each container every 15 minutes for one hour.

9 Find the temperature change from start to finish for each container.

State Your Conclusions

1. Which material heats up quickest?
2. Which material heats up slowest?
3. On a sunny day, which will heat up faster, a sandy desert or a large body of water?

Let's Experiment

Now that you have discovered how fast sand, soil, and water heat up, do you think that all three cool at the same rate? Use what you know about scientific methods to find out.

2.2 *Rain in the Desert*

▶ *What changes does a rainstorm cause in the desert?*

It's another hot, dusty day in the desert. Or is it? You look around and see dark clouds rising over the mountains. Soon the sky grows dark and thunder roars in the distance. Suddenly, the rain comes pouring down! You begin to wonder. What happens when it does rain in the desert?

Desert Rainstorm

Most rainstorms, such as the one in the picture, come during the spring in the Sonoran Desert. A storm usually lasts no longer than an hour and brings between 5 and 8 centimeters of rain.

▼ *Notice how dark the desert gets during a rainstorm.*

The sudden downpour hits the desert with great force. The sand soaks up only part of the rainwater. The rest of the water runs off digging deep ditches in the desert sand as it rushes downhill. Puddles become ponds and new streams begin to look more like rivers. As the water moves, it carries sand, small rocks, and dry grass to lower places. In some low places, the rushing water may completely cover the sand in a very short time.

Animals that have been hiding under the ground from the heat and dryness come alive. Find the spadefoot toad in the picture. These toads hear the sound of the thunder and the pouring rain. They crawl up to the surface and lay eggs in the new puddles. The rain cools the desert only briefly. The toads hunt for a hearty meal of insects and return underground while it is still cool. One meal is all the toads need to keep them alive until the next rainstorm. And that might not be for another year. Would you be able to live on one meal for a year?

Remember from Chapter 1, how the stem of the saguaro cactus swells up when it soaks up rain. Other desert plants also quickly absorb the rain that seeps into the ground. Meanwhile, seeds hidden in the sand begin to sprout and grow. The rain brings many new plants to life.

▲ The eggs of the spadefoot toad may hatch within 36 hours.

Into The Field

How much rain falls near your home?

Make a rain gauge. Use it to measure the rain that falls outside your home. Compare your results to your local weather rain report.

Plants That Grow After Rainstorms

Some plants survive in the desert by growing only after heavy rains.

One of the plants that grows in the Sonoran Desert, the lupine, also grows in other places that have much more rain. The lupine blooms every year in other places, but the desert lupine only blooms in years when there is enough rainfall for it to complete its short life cycle—the stages in the life of a plant or animal. During years when there is not enough rainfall, the lupine seeds lie in the ground and don't sprout—sometimes for ten years!

Plants Bloom The lupine plants bloom from late February to early April.

Plants Grow After a rainy winter, the lupine plants grow quickly.

Seeds Form After blooming for less than three months, the plants die and begin to drop their seeds.

Seeds Sprout Lupine seeds lie in the ground until enough rain falls for them to sprout.

After the Rainstorm

Even though the storm is over, you can see the rainwater gushing through the desert. Then the flow of water finally stops and puddles begin to form. The wet rocks glisten in the sunlight. You might wonder, "With all that water, how do deserts get dry so quickly after rainstorms? Where does all the water go?"

The storm clouds move on and the sun shines brightly. Sunlight beats down on the desert again. But now, in addition to shining on the sand and the rocks, the sun shines on the puddles of water, too. The light energy heats the water. As the water gets warmer, it begins to **evaporate** (i vap′ə rāt′), or change from a liquid into a gas. Notice in the bottom picture that the water is disappearing. As the water evaporates, the puddles dry up.

Water that becomes a gas is called **water vapor** (vā′pər). Water vapor disappears into the air. You can't see it or touch it. Some water vapor stays near the ground and some moves high into the air.

At night in the desert, everything cools off. After a rainstorm, some water vapor that stays near the ground touches cool leaves or rocks. Sometimes, the water vapor may cool and **condense** (kən dens′), or change from a gas into a liquid. The drops of water that form on leaves and rocks are called dew. A few insects may be lucky enough to get a drink from the water that condenses. However, in the desert, the dew evaporates very quickly when the sun comes out the next morning.

▲ This flooded arroyo in the Sonoran Desert looks like a stream that flows all the time. But the water evaporates quickly after a rainstorm.

A few days pass and all the puddles have dried up. During that time, the eggs the spadefoot toad laid in the puddles hatched. The tadpoles grew into toads and ate a few insects. Then they dug themselves into the ground while it was still wet and soft. The toads will stay underground until the next rainstorm. Imagine that! From eggs to tadpoles to adult toads in just a few days.

Remember those seeds that started to grow when the rainstorm began? Wildflowers bloomed soon after the rainstorm. For about four to six weeks, the desert will be blanketed with flowers of all colors. Notice the picture of the wildflowers with the mountains in the background. Soon the blooms will be gone, and then the plants will dry up and die. The seeds will lie in the sand until another rainstorm.

▲ The bright desert poppies are one of the wildflowers that grow in the Sonoran Desert.

Checkpoint

1. How is the spadefoot toad able to survive in the desert?
2. How does having a short life cycle help some desert plants survive?
3. How does water evaporate?
4. **Take Action!** Find three things that measure 5 to 8 centimeters—the amount of rain that usually falls during a desert rainstorm.

Activity

Which Will Dry Out Faster?

You know that water dries up faster in hot weather. What else affects the rate of evaporation? Try this activity to find out.

Picture A

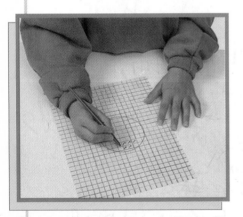

Picture B

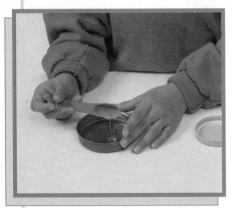

Picture C

Gather These Materials

metric ruler	small jar lid
paper	paper towel
pencil	spoon
large jar lid	water

Follow This Procedure

Part A

1. Make a chart like the one on the next page. Record your observations in your chart.

2. Use a metric ruler to draw a 10 cm by 10 cm square on a sheet of paper. Then, mark off every centimeter to form a grid of 100 squares that are each 1 square centimeter. (You can use graph paper if it is the correct size.)

3. Repeat step 2 to make a second grid.

4. Place a large jar lid on one grid and a small jar lid on the other. (Picture A)

5. Use a pencil to trace the outline of the lids on the grids. Then, take the lids off the paper. The number of squares in each circle is the surface area of that lid in square centimeters.

Predict: *Which lid will have the greater surface area?*

6 Count the number of squares inside each circle, including the parts of squares. Record your results. (Picture B)

Part B

1 Place a paper towel on a flat surface where it will not be disturbed. Place the two lids on the towel. Then, pour a spoonful of water into each lid. (Picture C)

> **Predict: *From which lid will the water dry up faster?***

2 Observe the amount of water in the lids the next day. Record your observations.

State Your Conclusions

1. From which lid did the water evaporate faster?
2. How does surface area affect the rate of evaporation?
3. A thick barrel cactus has much less surface area than a bean plant of the same size. From which plant will water evaporate faster?

Let's Experiment

Now that you have found out how surface area affects evaporation, what else do you think affects it? Use what you know about scientific methods to find out.

Record Your Results

	Large lid	Small lid
Surface area of lid (sq. cm)		
Amount of water after 1 day		

Chapter Review

Reviewing Words and Concepts

Write the letter of the word or phrase that best completes each sentence.

1. Anything that takes up space is _____.
2. Warm objects on the earth give off heat and warm the _____.
3. The measure of the hotness or coldness of an object is called _____.
4. The tool that is used to measure temperature is a _____.
5. The spadefoot toad escapes the desert heat and _____ by hiding under the ground.
6. When water _____, it changes from a liquid to a gas.
7. Water that becomes a gas is called _____.
8. Light _____ from the sun heats matter in the desert.
9. When water vapor _____, it changes from a gas to a liquid.
10. Spadefoot toad _____ grow into adult toads within a few days.

a. thermometer
b. air
c. dryness
d. water vapor
e. temperature
f. energy
g. condenses
h. matter
i. tadpoles
j. evaporates

Connecting Ideas

1. Copy the concept map. Use the terms at the right to complete the map to show how sunlight changes water.

water vapor   **condense**
evaporate

sunlight ——→ A. **water**

B. _____

C. _____

D. _____

2. Write a sentence or two about the ideas shown in the concept map.

Interpreting What You Learned

1. Explain what matter is and how it becomes warm.
2. Describe the temperature changes during a day in the desert.
3. Explain how a desert rainstorm affects a spadefoot toad.
4. How do some plants, such as the lupine, grow in a desert?
5. Explain how water evaporates and condenses.
6. How are dew and water vapor alike? different?

Performance Assessment

How does a spadefoot toad get food?

Materials • cutout toad • construction paper (2 pieces) • straw • tape • stapler • hole punch • plastic cup with water

Collecting Data

1. Using the cutout toad your teacher gives you, trace a toad on each piece of construction paper.
2. Cut out the toads you traced. Place one cutout toad directly on top of the other. Staple the sides together.
3. Starting at the back of your toad, push the straw between the sheets of paper and toward the toad's mouth. Push until the straw sticks out of the toad's mouth. The straw represents the toad's tongue.
4. Make a loop of tape with the sticky side out. Attach the loop to the end of the straw.
5. Use the hole punch to punch out ten circles from the construction paper. Spread out the circles on the table. The circles represent insects.
6. Move the toad and use its "tongue" to pick up as many circles as you can. Record your results.
7. Punch out ten more circles from the construction paper and spread them on top of the table.
8. Remove the tape from the straw. Dip the tip of the straw in water. Move the toad again and pick up as many circles as you can. Record your results.

Analyzing Data

How does a sticky tongue help a spadefoot toad get food?

Into the Forest

Discover Activity

Where are the hot spots?

Think about places in your classroom that might be hotter or colder than other places. Put a thermometer in one of the places. After 10 minutes, record the temperature. Then find the temperature in some of the other places.

For Discussion

1. Which spots were the hottest and coldest?

2. What caused one spot to be hotter? colder?

3.1 Lands of Much Rain

▶ **What are some other habitats in the world like?**

You are seated under a giant tree with its branches gently swaying in the breeze. The only sounds are the quiet rustling of leaves and the water in a nearby stream flowing over some rocks. Suddenly a little gray squirrel darts across a log and up a nearby tree. "How different from the hot, dusty desert!" you say to yourself. Where might you be?

You might be in a place like the forest shown here. How is a forest different from a desert?

Kinds of Forests

What makes a forest different from a desert? The most important difference is the amount of rain! Remember, deserts get very little rain, but forests get a lot of rain. Some forests get ten times as much rain as a desert. When you look at the picture of the forest, the first thing you may see are the trees. **Forests** are places that get plenty of rain and have many trees.

▼ *Wildflowers often grow among the trees in a Wisconsin forest.*

There are different kinds of forests. Some forests have trees, such as firs and pines, with stiff green needles for leaves. The needles do not all fall off at once, so the trees stay green all the time. The needles are waxy like the hard covering on cactus stems and help keep the trees from losing water. Find the needle-like leaves in the picture.

United States

Wisconsin

▾ Lakes in the forests of northern Wisconsin provide water for many living things.

Other forests have trees, such as maples and oaks, with broad leaves. These trees lose their leaves each fall and grow new ones in the spring. Without leaves, the trees lose less water during the winter when it doesn't rain. Losing their leaves or having needles helps trees live through the winter.

A Wisconsin Forest

The picture shows a northern Wisconsin forest with both kinds of trees. Find Wisconsin on the map of the United States. In such forests, oaks and maples shade the forest floor along with firs and pines.

In warm weather, Wisconsin forests get rain about every eight to twelve days each month. During the winter months, snow falls on about the same number of days. About 79 centimeters of rain and snow fall each year. As the snow melts in the spring, plants get plenty of water to begin growing.

The temperatures in these forests are also different from those in the desert. The temperatures range from a high of about 37°C in summer to as low as 40 degrees below freezing in winter. The forest is not nearly as hot as a desert in summer. But it is much, much colder than a desert in winter. Animals and plants must survive the cold winter in the forest, instead of the heat and dryness of the desert. But before learning about how plants and animals survive in the winter, you will learn about them in summer.

▲ The leaves are from maple, oak, and pine trees.

Checkpoint

1. What are two kinds of forests?
2. What are two ways a Wisconsin forest is different from a desert?
3. **Take Action!** Draw pictures of the trees near where you live.

Activity

Make a Forest Habitat

What plants and animals might you see in one of the many forest habitats? In this activity make one of the habitats.

Picture A

Gather These Materials

clear plastic 2-liter bottle
scissors
pebbles
aquarium charcoal
soil
large spoon

woodland plants
rocks
tape
pieces of wood
water
plastic wrap

Follow This Procedure

1 Make a chart like the one on the next page. Record your observations in your chart.

2 Cut the top off a clear plastic 2-liter bottle where the neck begins to curve in. Be careful when using the scissors. Have your teacher help you get started. (Picture A)

Picture B

3 Put a layer of pebbles at the bottom of the bottle. Cover the pebble layer with a layer of aquarium charcoal. These layers will allow water to drain from the soil so it doesn't stay too wet.

4 Add a layer of soil on top of the layer of charcoal. (Picture B)

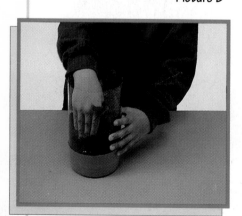

Picture C

5 Choose a few woodland plants for your habitat. Arrange them in a natural, attractive way. Cover the roots with soil. (Picture C) Add rocks or pieces of wood to complete the habitat.

6 Sprinkle a small amount of water around each plant. Then, tape some plastic wrap to the top of your woodland habitat. Keep the habitat away from heat. Place it where it will get only indirect light.

> **Predict: *What changes might occur in your habitat?***

7 Record your observations of the habitat over the next few weeks.

State Your Conclusions

1. What does your habitat look like in a week? in two weeks?
2. How is your forest habitat similar to a desert habitat? How is it different?
3. What kinds of animals do you think could live in your habitat?

Record Your Results

Date	Observations

Let's Experiment

Now that you have made a forest habitat, what would happen if you left out the layer of soil? Use what you know about scientific methods to find out.

3.2 Forest Plants and Animals

> ## How do living things survive in a forest?

Just as in a desert habitat, plants that live in a forest habitat need water and sunlight. Also, animals that live in a forest need food, water, and shelter. Let's find out how some plants and animals survive in a forest.

A Summer Day in the Forest

Forests have a variety of habitats where many different plants can live. Remember in the Discover Activity, you found different temperatures in different parts of the room. Different habitats in the forest also have different temperatures.

The large ferns in the pictures need a cool, damp habitat to grow in. Ferns grow in the shady, cool parts of the forest. Along the edges of the forest, you see plants such as blueberry bushes and goldenrods that need a lot of sunshine. Plants such as water lilies fill the shallow waters of ponds and lakes.

▼ Deer usually come out to the edge of the forest for food at a time when they aren't easily seen—at dawn and at dusk.

Many deer live in Wisconsin forests. During spring and summer, deer find plenty of grass and small plants to eat in the forest. The deer and other animals can drink water from the lakes, ponds, and streams. Frogs also live near the water where they can find insects to eat.

Notice the picture of the rabbit nibbling on some grass. As it eats, the rabbit often looks around and listens. It knows that a hungry fox may be looking for a rabbit to eat.

Farther ahead, a chipmunk comes up from a hole in the ground. This little animal is probably hunting for some acorns to store in its underground nest. With so many oak trees in the forest, the chipmunk can easily find acorns.

A woodpecker loudly taps away on a nearby tree. The tapping helps the woodpecker find holes in the tree where insects might be hiding. When the woodpecker finds an insect hole, it sticks its long bill into the hole. Then the woodpecker uses its long, sticky tongue to pull the insect out of the hole.

Usually in summer, animals can find plenty of food, water, and shelter in forest habitats. But when winter comes, many changes take place in a forest. The lakes and ponds are covered with ice and much of the food is covered with snow. What do animals find to eat during the winter?

▼ *Rabbits eat many kinds of green leafy plants, such as grass and clover.*

▲ *The part of the fern that is underground remains alive all winter, but a new set of leaves grows each year.*

▲ In a snow covered Wisconsin forest, the woodpecker and the deer need to find food to survive.

Winter in the Forest

Back in the desert, you learned how liquid rainwater changed into water vapor, a gas. In the forest, the winter is so cold that water in the lakes and ponds freezes and becomes ice, a solid. That's right. Water can have three forms in nature—a liquid, a gas, or a solid. These forms are known as the different **states of matter.** But the animals in the forest can't drink water in its solid form—ice.

Notice the blanket of snow that covers the forest in the pictures during the winter. Find the deer in the picture digging under the snow for grass to eat. It gets a "drink" from the snow that melts in its mouth. When the snow gets too deep for the deer to find grass, it eats twigs and buds from bushes.

Besides the water in the forest being frozen, many of the plants have died or are covered by snow. Many of the insects and small animals that provided food for other animals have died or are underground.

With temperatures below freezing, the animals also need to find shelter to keep warm. The deer stay in the thicker parts of the forest out of the cold wind. The deer and other animals also grow thicker fur in winter. The chipmunk stays in its underground nest and eats acorns it stored during the summer.

Like the spadefoot toads in the desert, frogs in the forest can go a long time without food. They spend the winter buried in the mud at the bottom of a lake or pond. Of course, in the winter, the frogs are hiding from the cold—not the heat and dryness.

Notice the woodpecker pushing its bill into the hole in the tree. The insects that bore into trees stay there during the winter, so the woodpecker can still find food.

The rabbit has dug a hole in the snow beneath a bunch of logs. The hole may be lined with dry grass and leaves for warmth. During the winter, the rabbit can't find green grass, so it has to eat other food.

INVESTIGATE

Furry and Warm?

Does a covering help hold in heat? Let's investigate.

What To Do
A. Fill two paper cups with the same amount of warm water. Think of the cups as the bodies of two animals of the same size.
B. Take the temperature of each cup of water. Record it on a chart like the one shown below.
C. Wrap one of the cups in a towel.
D. Wait 15 minutes. Take and record the temperature of each cup again.

Record Your Results

	Temperature	
	Starting	Ending
Wrapped cup		
Unwrapped cup		

What Did You Find Out?
1. *Which cup stayed the warmest?*
2. *Which cup is like an animal with fur? without fur? Give reasons for your answer.*
3. *Why do you think some animals that live in cold places have thick fur?*

Who Lives Where?

Each living thing is well-suited to its habitat.

Think about the living things pictured here as game pieces that you can move to their habitat. Where do you think each living thing belongs?

Use these clues to help you decide:
• A **cactus** can live for long periods of time without rain.
• A **fern** needs shade and lots of water.
• A **beaver** builds its lodge in the water.
• A **roadrunner** gets most of the water it needs from eating small animals.
• A **rattlesnake** is often eaten by hawks and roadrunners.
• For the **child**, think about yourself—for which habitat are you well-suited?

Rattlesnake

Fern

Child

Beaver

Roadrunner

Cactus

Into The Field

Is everything in my home needed for survival?

Look around your home and list things that are needed for your family to live. Explain why each thing is needed.

Your Habitat

Deserts and forests are only two of the many kinds of habitats in the world. Notice the city habitat in the picture. What is the habitat like where you live?

The ways that people survive in their habitats are different from the ways that other animals survive. People can change habitats and build their own shelters. Most people can change the temperature of their habitats. They can heat their homes in winter and cool them in summer. People can also wear cool clothing during summer. In winter, people can't grow thicker fur as animals do. But people can wear warm clothing and maybe a scarf and gloves such as the ones shown.

The boy in the picture is drinking from a fountain. People bring water from lakes, rivers, or streams to their homes. People use trucks, planes, or railroad cars to carry food hundreds of miles. Food that is grown or produced in one part of the world can be shipped to other places. Therefore, most people can have foods besides those grown near their habitat.

► *Outdoor drinking fountains provide water for people when they are away from home.*

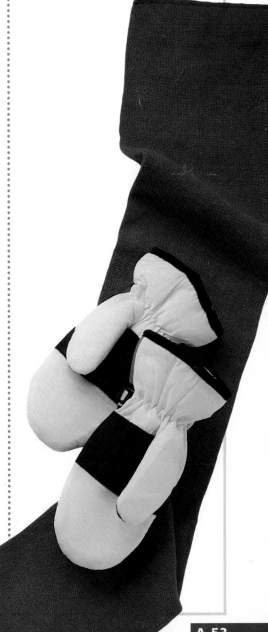

◄ Many people live in city habitats, such as San Francisco.

▼ Would you be more likely to need a scarf and gloves in a desert or in northern Wisconsin?

People and other animals do have different ways of surviving in their habitats. But both need food, water, and shelter. People and other animals also share many habitats. For example, people live in or near deserts and forests as do other animals. Living things also share many of the other habitats of the world. Each kind of habitat has different conditions such as heat, cold, or dryness. Living things have different ways of surviving in each of the many different habitats.

Checkpoint

1. What do forest animals eat in summer?
2. How does winter affect the feeding habits of animals in the forest?
3. Why don't beavers live in the desert?
4. How are the ways that people and other animals survive different?
5. Take Action! Make a map to show where the milk your family uses is produced.

Activity

Does Ice Float or Sink?

In winter, lakes in northern forests may be covered with ice. Do this activity to see how ice can float on water.

Picture A

Picture B

Picture C

Gather These Materials

50 mL plastic
  graduated cylinder
water

freezer
large pan or baking
  dish of tap water

Follow This Procedure

1 Make a chart like the one on the next page. Record your observations in your chart.

2 Pour 25 mL of water into a 50 mL plastic graduated cylinder. (Picture A)

3 Place the graduated cylinder in a freezer overnight.

Predict: **What will happen to the water in the cylinder?**

4 The next day, observe the space taken up by the ice. Is the water level still at the line marking 25 mL? How many mL of ice have formed? Record your observations in your chart.

5 Place the graduated cylinder into a large dish of tap water. What happens? After about one minute you will be able to slide the ice out of the graduated cylinder. (Picture B) Watch to see whether the ice sinks or floats.

6 Your dish of water is like a northern lake. Move the dish to create some "waves" around the edges of the dish. (Picture C) Observe any changes in the ice.

Record Your Results

	Water: Volume in mL
Before freezing	
After freezing	

State Your Conclusions

1. Does the water take up the same amount of space once it is frozen?

2. Did the ice sink or float in the dish of water? Explain why you think this happened.

3. Using your observations of the ice being struck by "waves," where do you think ice would form faster, in still water or in moving water?

Let's Experiment

Now that you have seen what happens when fresh water freezes, what do you think will happen to salt water if you freeze it? Use what you know about scientific methods to find out.

Chapter Review

Reviewing Words and Concepts

Write the letter of the word or phrase that best completes each sentence.

1. Places that get plenty of rain and have many trees are _____.
2. Firs and pines are trees with _____ for leaves.
3. Maples and oaks are trees with _____ leaves.
4. A forest is much _____ than a desert in winter.
5. During summer, forest animals have plenty of food and _____.
6. Liquid, solid, and gas are known as the three _____.
7. In winter, some animals get water by eating _____.
8. When the grass is covered with snow, some animals eat _____.
9. Frogs spend the _____ buried in the mud at the bottom of a lake or pond.
10. Deserts and forests are only two of the many kinds of _____ in the world.

a. colder
b. snow
c. needles
d. habitats
e. water
f. twigs
g. broad
h. winter
i. forests
j. states of matter

Connecting Ideas

1. Copy the concept map. Use the terms at the right to complete the map about a forest habitat.

   ferns pine trees forest
   oak trees

   A. **habitat**
   B.
   C.
   D.
   E.

2. Write a sentence or two about the ideas shown in the concept map.

Interpreting What You Learned

1. Describe a northern Wisconsin forest.
2. How do forest animals get water in summer?
3. Describe the three forms that water has in nature.
4. What are some ways forest animals find shelter in winter?
5. Why can some plants live in deserts and others in forests?
6. Name some ways in which people can change their habitats.

Performance Assessment

How can you stay warm in your habitat?

Materials • 2 large self-sealing plastic bags • 2 small self-sealing plastic bags • 2 thermometers • very warm water (about 200 mL) • marker • various materials (cloth, foil, cotton, feathers, and so on) • tape

Collecting Data

1. Line the inside of one of the large plastic bags with material such as cloth, foil, cotton, or feathers. Use tape and a marker to label this bag *Wearing a jacket.* The other large bag will remain empty. Label this bag *Not wearing a jacket.*
2. Place one thermometer in each of the small plastic bags. Then pour about 100 milliliters of very warm water into each of the small plastic bags. Seal the bags.
3. Wait one minute, then look at the thermometers in the small sealed bags. Read and record the temperature on each thermometer.
4. Place one small bag containing water into each of the large plastic bags. Be sure the material in the bag labeled *Wearing a jacket* covers the bag of water. Seal the large bags.
5. After 15 minutes, remove each of the bags of water from the large plastic bags. Do not open the bags of water. Look at the thermometers in the bags and record the temperatures.
6. Repeat steps 4 and 5.

Analyzing Data

How does wearing different kinds of clothing help you survive in your habitat?

Kids As Caretakers

Thirteen-year-old Michelle Bianchi has had many encounters with hawks like the one below. Michelle also encounters snakes and other wild animals. No, she doesn't live in the woods. She's a teenage volunteer at the San Francisco Children's Zoo.

Like many other children, Michelle is helping to care for wild animals. For two days a week during the summer, she works as a guide along the zoo's nature trail. Michelle's work gives kids a chance to meet animals that usually live in the wild.

Many animals in the program were once pets.

Along the nature trail are several stations. At each one, pairs of volunteers exhibit some of the animals and tell visitors about the animals' behavior and eating habits. Many of the animals in the program were once pets. Others are wild animals that were injured and brought to the zoo to be taken care of.

To prepare for their work at the zoo, the volunteers go through a special three-day training program. In the program, students learn information about the animals. The students also learn how to safely handle each of the animals at the zoo.

Like many of the other volunteers, Michelle plans to continue working with animals. She's interested in a career as a veterinarian. Some other volunteers have gone on to become animal keepers or work with animal-related organizations.

▲ *He's a California Desert Tortoise who was rescued by Ms. McKinnon's students.*

In Goldendale, Washington, Grandpa Joe is a special guest in Ms. McKinnon's fourth grade class. He's not a relative. He's a California Desert Tortoise who was rescued by Ms. McKinnon's students.

Three years ago, two students spotted the tortoise as he walked along a busy road. They brought him to class. Somehow the tortoise had either been abandoned or strayed from his natural habitat.

The students named the tortoise Grandpa Joe and made him the class pet. In order to care for him, the students learned as much about tortoises as possible.

From their research they learned that Grandpa Joe is a member of an endangered species. That means that there are very few of these tortoises left in the world.

Now every group of fourth graders looks forward to caring for Grandpa Joe. He is one guest that has moved right in.

On Your Own

Visit a children's zoo or a nature trail to find out more about wild animals. What are their habitats? What might you do to help wild animals that live near you?

Forest Ranger

Occupation: Forest Ranger
Hobbies: Fishing and hiking

Duane Resere

I f you and your family ever go camping in Logan Canyon, Ranger Duane just might visit you at your campsite. That's his job. As a forest ranger, Duane spends a lot of his time talking to campers, telling them about things to do and see in the canyon. He also reminds them how to take good care of the forest and to be careful with fires.

Are all fires bad?

"Fires can be helpful—they can cook your dinner or light your way.

But they can also be dangerous. Wildfires, fires that are out of control, can cause a lot of damage to the forest." So Duane spends part of each day driving his truck through the canyon, looking for fires. Usually Duane and the other rangers can put the fire out. If it's a big fire, teams of fire fighters are called in to help.

What do you like best about your job?

"It includes a little bit of everything." That's one reason Duane's glad he learned everything he did in school. "With this job, sooner or later you're going to need it."

"When I started college, I first thought about jobs where I could make a lot of money. But then I tried to figure out how to work at something I really liked doing. Being a forest ranger uses my skills and keeps me where I want to be."

What do you do for fun?

"I go to the forest. When I was little, I liked the feeling I had of being 'on my own' in the forest. On my day off, I take my family to the forest, to fish or hike, just like my parents took me."

Thermometer

*Knowing how to read a thermometer can help you
know if you need to wear a coat or not when
you go outside.*

4 Temperature is measured in degrees Celsius (°C).

3 The numbers along the tube show the degrees. Each mark below the °C is for 1°C.

2 When the alcohol gets warmer, it takes up more space and rises in the tube. When the alcohol gets cooler, it takes up less space and moves down in the tube.

5 To read a thermometer, you find the top of the alcohol in the tube.

1 Colored alcohol is in the round bulb at the bottom of a thermometer.

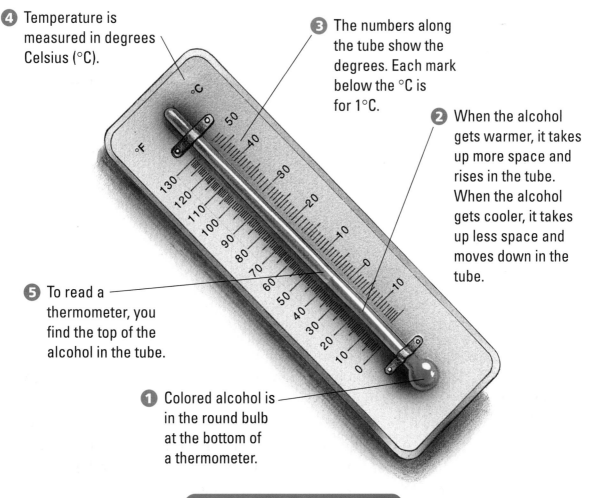

Find Out On Your Own

Record the outdoor temperature each day for three days.
Make a chart to show the temperature readings.
How much did the temperature change?

Module Performance Assessment

Habitat Day

Using what you learned in this module, help prepare a Habitat Day display for your school. Complete one or more of the following activities. You may work by yourself or with others in a group.

Drama

Plan a puppet show in which you act out one day in the life of desert or forest plants and animals. Make puppets for the different plants and animals.

Writing

Imagine that you are an animal that lives under the ground in a forest or a desert. Write a story or a skit to show what your life might be like.

Art

Paint a picture of either a desert landscape or a forest. You might show a variety of plant and animal life as well as landforms, such as hills and gullies, or bodies of water, such as lakes and streams.

Conservation

For people who live in the desert, saving water is very important. Sometimes, other communities must also save water. Find out if your community needs to save water, and make a list of ways you and your classmates can help.

Investigation

Measure three dry sponges of different sizes. Record the length, width, and height of each sponge in a chart. Wet the sponges and measure them again. Record their measurements in your chart. Leave the sponges in the open air overnight. What happens? Explain in what ways the sponges are like the stem of a cactus.

Module Review

Reviewing Words and Concepts

Write the letter of the word or phrase that best completes each sentence.

1. Many animals in the _____ get water by eating insects.
2. Different plants and animals live in different _____.
3. The most important difference between a _____ and a desert is the amount of rain.
4. Everything you can see and touch is made of _____.
5. Cooling causes water vapor to _____.
6. In the afternoon, the _____ in the desert is much higher than in the morning.
7. The three forms of water in nature are examples of the different _____.
8. To find the temperature of the air, you would use a _____.
9. Water in the form of a gas is called _____.
10. Warming causes water to _____, or change from a liquid to a gas.

a. temperature
b. desert
c. evaporate
d. thermometer
e. forest
f. condense
g. states of matter
h. water vapor
i. habitats
j. matter

Interpreting What You Learned

1. Give three examples of some changes that might take place in a desert after a rainfall.
2. How does life change in winter for animals living in a forest?
3. How are the covering of a cactus and tree needles alike?
4. Explain how desert animals get and keep enough water to live.

Applying What You Learned

1. How are the needs of desert plants and forest plants alike?
2. How does desert air become hot in the daytime and cool at night?
3. List all the animals you can think of. Sort them into groups according to where they live. What groups did you think of?
4. Group plants in the same way. What groups did you think of?

Gardening

Gardening

Soil, seeds, sun, and water—these are all the ingredients you need to start a garden. By working with nature, you can grow your own food and eat a healthful diet. In this module, you'll find out how plants grow from seeds, how soil and water help plants grow, and how your body digests food.

CHAPTER

2 Soil and Water

Water the soil, grow a plant. By choosing the right soil and using the right amount of water, you can help seeds grow into big, healthy plants.

CHAPTER

1 Plants and Energy

How is a plant like a powerhouse? Both plants and powerhouses change energy so that it can be used. Animals of all kinds—including people— depend on the energy found in plants.

3 Good Food!

What makes good food good?

The nutrients in plants and other foods are good for your body, and they taste good too. Healthy bodies depend on healthful foods.

Plants and Energy

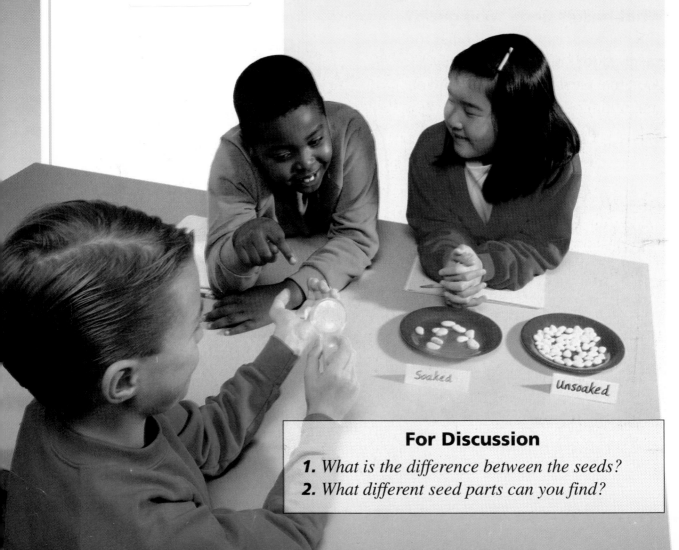

Discover Activity

What's in a seed?

You've planted them and probably even eaten them. But have you ever examined one with a hand lens? There's more to seeds than meets the eye. Compare a soaked and an unsoaked seed. Then, take them apart to see what's inside.

Soaked

Unsoaked

For Discussion

1. *What is the difference between the seeds?*
2. *What different seed parts can you find?*

1.1 *How Your Garden Grows*

How do plants live and grow?

Imagine you are standing on the rooftop in the picture. The sun is shining brightly and the air is warm. It is here on your rooftop that you decide to grow a tomato plant. First, you open a packet of seeds. You poke the tiny seeds into a pot of soil, soak the soil with water, and place the pot in the sun. Images of juicy tomatoes fill your thoughts. How can you get large, red tomatoes from tiny seeds?

▼ *Plants can grow from seeds.*

What Seeds Need to Grow

A seed is the beginning—a powerhouse of life waiting to burst into action. In the Discover Activity, you saw some parts of a seed. Look at the drawing of the bean seed. The seed has a thin, outer cover called a seed coat. Find the **embryo** (em′ brē ō), the tiny part of the seed that can grow into a new plant. The rest of the seed contains stored sugars that the embryo can use to grow and develop. What else might a seed need?

To start growing, a seed needs three things: the right amount of water, the proper temperature, and enough air. Too much water or too little water can keep a seed from growing. Temperatures that are too hot or cold also can keep it from growing. Most seeds develop well in loose, light soil. This kind of soil holds the right amount of air and allows water to reach the seed.

Parts of A Seed

Embryo

Stored Sugars

Seed Coat

▼ *Germinating bean seed*

Suppose a seed has all the things it needs. What happens next? The seed **germinates** (jėr′ mə nāts), or starts to grow and develop. The pictures below show how a bean seed germinates. First, the seed soaks up water and swells until it splits the seed coat. Next, a sprout begins to grow from the embryo. At about the same time, roots begin to grow from the embryo down into the ground. Notice that the leaves start to develop.

The seedling, or young plant, uses the stored sugars in the seed to grow a little each day. What happens when the plant uses up the sugars stored in the seed? The plant still needs sugars to live and grow. Where will those sugars come from now?

INVESTIGATE

Take Off Your Coat

Will seeds grow without a seed coat? Let's investigate.

What To Do
A. Soak 20 red kidney bean seeds overnight in water.
B. Carefully remove the seed coats from 10 seeds.
C. Wrap these 10 seeds in a moist paper towel. Slide the towel into a self-sealing sandwich bag. Wrap the other 10 seeds in a moist towel and place them in another sandwich bag.
D. Check your seeds each day for 5 days. Record how many are growing. A seed is growing if a small root grows from it.

Record Your Results

Day	No Seed Coat	With Seed Coat

What Did You Find Out?
1. *Was growth affected by removing the seed coat?*
2. *What is the job of a seed coat?*

Green Power

Green plants use energy from the sun to make sugars.

The leaves of green plants make most of the sugars a plant needs. The way plants make sugars is called **photosynthesis**. Here's how it works.

The plant's roots take in water from the soil. Water goes through the stems to the leaves. Carbon dioxide, a gas in the air, goes into tiny openings in the leaves. The green material in the leaves, chlorophyll, traps energy from sunlight. Plants use the energy to change water and carbon dioxide into sugars and oxygen. The oxygen goes into the air. Plants use the sugars to live and grow.

Photosynthesis

Plants get energy from sunlight.

Plants release oxygen into the air.

Plants get carbon dioxide from the air.

Plants make sugars in the leaves.

Plants get water from the soil.

Sugars and Starches in Storage

Suppose your tomato plant cannot take in enough energy from the sun to make the sugars it needs. How will it live? Most plants store sugars to provide for times when the leaves can't make enough. Plants change some sugars and store them as starches. The sugars and starches can be stored in the roots, stems, and leaves of plants. They also can be stored in fruits and seeds.

Many foods, such as those shown here, come from plants. When you eat a carrot, you are eating a root. Asparagus and potatoes are stems. Tomatoes are fruits. Even peanuts and beans are plant parts. They are seeds. When you bite into a crispy lettuce salad, you are eating leaves. Now here's something to think about. When people and animals eat different parts of plants, they are eating the sugars and starches stored in the plants.

▼ *These foods contain stored sugars and starches.*

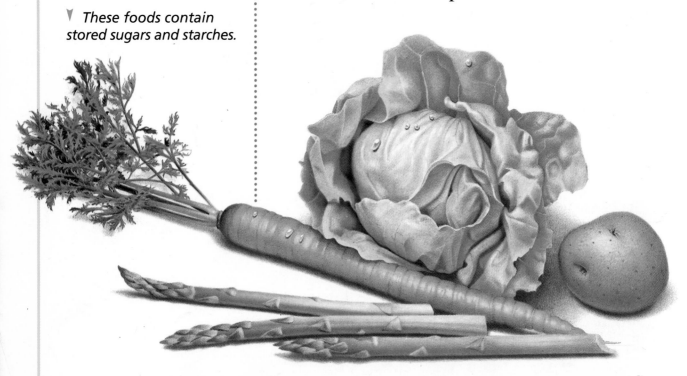

Seeds to Plants

What would you see if you sliced into a tomato? You probably know that you'd see many small seeds. Can these seeds grow into new tomato plants? The answer, of course, is yes. If conditions are right, these seeds can germinate.

Many other plants grow and develop the same way tomato plants do. You might have seen an acorn like the one shown here. The acorn is the seed of an oak tree. How can a huge oak tree like the one in the picture grow from something as small as an acorn? It happens just the way a tomato plant grows from a tiny seed. A seed grows into a new plant that forms seeds. Then the whole cycle begins again.

▼ *A tiny acorn can grow into a tall oak tree.*

Checkpoint

1. Explain how a seed germinates.
2. How do plants make sugars?
3. Where do plants store sugars and starches?
4. How does an acorn grow into a tree?
5. **Take Action!** Find a newspaper advertisement for foods. Identify the foods that come from plants.

Activity

The Secret Lives of Plants

Most flowers bloom for only a short time. But even though blossoms fade, they help plants live on. Try this activity to find out how.

Picture A

Picture B

Picture C

Gather These Materials

fresh-cut marigold in bloom

paper

pencil

hand lens

tape

marigold with blossom that dried naturally

Follow This Procedure

1 Make a chart like the one on the next page. Record your observations in your chart.

2 Look closely at a fresh-cut marigold. Does the marigold look like it is alive? What colors are the different parts? Use a hand lens to examine the blossom. (Picture A)

3 Examine the features of the dried marigold blossom. Record your observations. (Picture B)

4 Draw a picture of each marigold to show their similarities and differences.

Predict: *The dried marigolds contain seeds. Where might the seeds be?*

5 Find the thick portion of the stem just below the parts of the dried blossom. Peel this part away from the base of the blossom. You have just opened the part of the marigold that has seeds.

Record Your Results

Blossom	Does blossom look like it is alive?	Colors of Parts	Other observations
Fresh-cut marigold			
Dried marigold			

6 Choose one of the structures you see. In marigolds, each yellow "petal" is a flower. The black part at the bottom is the seed. Hold the flower firmly and pull off the seed. (Picture C)

7 Pull 5–10 more seeds apart from their flowers. Tape the seeds to a piece of paper, and label them as seeds.

8 Tape the flowers to the same piece of paper, and label them as flowers.

State Your Conclusions

1. How do fresh-cut blossoms differ from dried blossoms?
2. How does a flower help a plant to produce new plants?

Let's Experiment

What do marigold seeds need to sprout and grow into new plants? Use what you know about scientific methods to find out.

1.2 *Food for Energy*

▶ **How do animals get energy?**

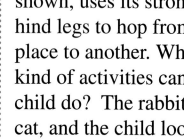

A cat, like the one in the picture, can scamper and leap and even scoot up trees. A rabbit, such as the one shown, uses its strong hind legs to hop from one place to another. What kind of activities can this child do? The rabbit, the cat, and the child look and behave differently from one another. Yet they have something in common. They all need energy to live and grow. Do people and animals get energy the same way plants do?

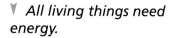

▼ *All living things need energy.*

Getting Energy

All living things need energy to live. But plants and animals get energy in very different ways. Think about how a tomato plant uses energy to carry out photosynthesis. Plants are called **producers** (prə dü′ sərs),

because they use energy from the sun to produce, or make, the sugars they need. Look at the pictures of the living things shown on these two pages. Which of these pictures show producers? If you named the clover and carrots, you gave the right answer.

Can a child, a rabbit, and a cat get all the energy they need directly from sunlight? Can these living things produce the food they need through photosynthesis? You probably know that the answer to each of these questions is no.

People and other animals get the energy they need from the food they eat. They are called **consumers** (kən sü′ mərs) because they must consume, or eat, food. Point to the consumers in the pictures. Did you pick the child, rabbit, and cat? Did you choose the bird too? The child and the other animals shown here are consumers because they get their energy from food produced by plants.

What kinds of food do these consumers eat? Some consumers eat only plants and some eat only animals. Others eat both plants and animals. As a consumer, which of the foods in the pictures would the rabbit eat? A rabbit is a consumer that eats only plants. The carrot and clover would be the rabbit's choice. Would the cat also eat plants? No, it would not. Cats eat other animals, such as the bird. What would the child eat? What different kinds of foods do you eat to get the energy you need?

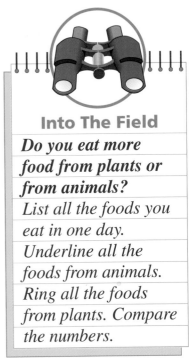

Into The Field

Do you eat more food from plants or from animals?
List all the foods you eat in one day. Underline all the foods from animals. Ring all the foods from plants. Compare the numbers.

▲ People get energy from food they eat.

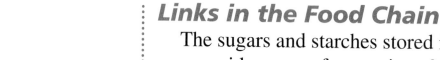

A food chain

Links in the Food Chain

The sugars and starches stored in a plant can provide energy for a series of consumers. The picture shows a small worm near the plant. This tomato hornworm feeds on the tomato plant and uses the plant's stored sugars as food. A blue jay, like the one shown here, might spot the hornworm and eat it for lunch. Then suppose a hungry cat enters the picture, stalks the blue jay, and eats it.

The tomato plant uses energy from the sun to make sugars. The energy passes from the sugars in the tomato plant, to the hornworm, to the blue jay, and finally to the cat. The passing of energy from the sun through a series of living things is called a **food chain**.

You can find food chains on land, in the soil—even in water. Think about an ocean food chain. It begins with living things called algae (al′ jē), a group of producers that live in water. Algae take in light energy from the sun to make sugars. A small fish gets energy by eating the algae in the water. Then a larger fish swims over and eats the small fish. Before long, a hungry seal dives deep into the ocean. The seal eats the large fish to get the energy it needs. Energy passes from the sun, to the algae, to the small fish, to the large fish, and finally to the seal.

Every living thing is a link in a food chain. Food chains begin with producers. All animals, or consumers, depend on producers in some way for their energy. Some animals eat plants. Some animals eat other animals. In this way, all living things are connected to one another and to the sun.

Checkpoint

1. How are producers and consumers alike and different?
2. Explain how producers are important to every food chain.
3. **Take Action!** Find and cut out pictures of different animals and plants. Arrange your pictures to make a model of a food chain.

Making a Model of a Food Chain

How can you make a model of a food chain? Try this activity to find out.

Picture A

Picture B

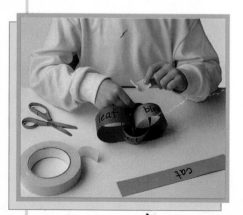

Picture C

Gather These Materials

strips of paper   crayons
tape

Follow This Procedure

1 Make a chart like the one on the next page. Record your observations in your chart.

2 Choose at least 4 names of different plants and animals that make a food chain. (Picture A)

3 Write the name of each of your living things on a separate strip of paper.

4 Lay the strips out in front of you in the correct order for a food chain.

Predict: How can you show how living things are linked in a food chain?

5 Carefully cut several pieces of tape. Tape the first strip in the food chain into the shape of a circle. (Picture B)

6 Loop the second strip in the food chain through the first strip and tape it into the shape of a circle. (Picture C)

Record Your Results

Food chain
_____ $\longrightarrow$ _____ $\longrightarrow$ _____ $\longrightarrow$ _____

7 Add the other strips one at a time to make a chain of loops.

8 Record the names of living things you used in your food chain on your chart.

State Your Conclusions

1. Explain how the living things you chose make up a food chain.

2. How does your food chain compare with those of your classmates?

3. Explain why two producers cannot be in the same food chain.

Let's Experiment

What would happen to a food chain if one of the links disappears? Use what you know about scientific methods to find out.

Chapter Review

Reviewing Words and Concepts

Write the letter of the word or phrase that best completes each sentence.

1. The part of a seed that can grow into a new plant is the _____.
2. A seed needs water to _____, or start to grow and develop.
3. The way plants make sugars is called _____.
4. Plants are called _____ because they use energy from the sun to make the sugars they need.
5. The passing of energy from the sun through a series of living things is called a _____.
6. People and other animals are called _____ because they get energy from the food they eat.
7. The covering of a seed is called the _____.
8. Sugars are made in the _____ of green plants.
9. Plants store _____ and starches in their roots, stems, leaves, fruits, and seeds.
10. A plant embryo uses the stored sugars in the _____ to grow.

a. consumers
b. leaves
c. producers
d. seed coat
e. germinate
f. sugars
g. seed
h. embryo
i. food chain
j. photosynthesis

Connecting Ideas

1. Copy the concept map. Use the terms at the right to complete the map about food chains to show how energy passes through them.

fox   producer
consumers   rabbit

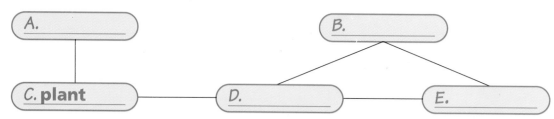

A. _____

B. _____

C. plant

D. _____

E. _____

2. Write a sentence or two about the ideas shown in the concept map.

Interpreting What You Learned

1. Explain how an embryo can grow into a plant.
2. What three things does a seed need to germinate?
3. Describe what a plant does during photosynthesis.
4. Name some foods that come from roots, stems, and leaves of plants.
5. Explain how grass, a cow, and a person can form a food chain.
6. Explain how all food chains are alike.

 ## Performance Assessment

What are producers and consumers?

Materials • old magazines • scissors • 2 index cards • marker • 2 pieces of yarn (each 1 meter long)

Collecting Data

1. Look for pictures of producers and consumers in old magazines. Cut out at least five pictures of producers and five pictures of consumers.
2. Arrange each piece of yarn to make a large circle.
3. Write *producers* on one index card and place the card in a yarn circle. Write *consumers* on the other index card and place the card in the other yarn circle.
4. Place each of the cutout pictures in the correct yarn circle.

5. To record your results, draw your yarn circles on a piece of paper. Write words telling about the pictures you put in each circle.

Analyzing Data

What is similar about the consumers you found? What is similar about the producers?

Soil and Water

Anybody want a drink?

Discover Activity

What is soil made of?

Put a handful of soil on a piece of paper. Sort through the soil and separate all the materials you find in it. Place some soil in a jar of water. Screw the lid on and shake the jar. Set it aside and watch what happens.

For Discussion

1. What did you find in the soil?

2. How did the soil look after it settled?

2.1 *Planting a Garden*

Where is the best place for my garden?

Suppose you could grow vegetables and fruits in your very own garden. You might be able to grow some of your favorite foods. Where would the best place for your garden be? Would you plant it on the gravel driveway? That doesn't sound like a very good idea. Your plants need soil to grow. What would you think about planting your garden under the shade of a big oak tree? True, there is soil there. But your fruit and vegetable plants would not get enough sunlight. How about finding a place in the sunlight that has plenty of dark soil? Yes, that's just the spot you're looking for!

The tomato plant can live and grow in soil.

You reach down and grab a handful of the soil. You squeeze the soil in your hand. You let it sift through your fingers. How does the soil feel? Does it look like the soil you observed in the Discover Activity? Now imagine that you're almost ready to plant your garden. You use a shovel to dig deep into the soil in the picture. What might you find? You can find out by reading the next two pages.

The Good Earth

What's going on down under?

Welcome to the underground world of the tomato plant. This plant grows in rich, dark soil.

Over many years, rocks break apart and form soil. Soil also contains air, water, and **humus**, the decayed remains of dead plants and animals.

Humus adds **nutrients** to the soil. A nutrient is a material that plants and animals need to live and grow.

What kinds of living things do you see in this soil? Earthworms and insects dig tunnels in the soil. The tunnels allow air, water, and nutrients to reach plants' roots.

Kinds of Soil

Think about the soil in your garden. Is the soil easy to dig? Is it wet and squishy? Does it have big chunks or tiny pieces? Which kind of soil did you imagine digging?

Compare the three kinds of soil shown in the picture. **Clay soil**, shown in the first pot, is tightly packed soil with tiny grains. If you could touch it, you would notice how smooth it feels. Clay soil has some nutrients. If you water this pot of soil, water might overflow the pot. The grains in clay are so close together that water cannot soak into clay soil easily.

Sandy soil, like that in the center pot, is loose and has large grains. It contains few nutrients. What happens when you pour water into sandy soil? Water runs quickly through this kind of soil. Sandy soil does not hold water well.

▼ Clay soil, sandy soil, and loam

Loam, shown in the third pot, is a mixture of clay, sand, and humus. Loam holds water well and has many nutrients. Loam is lighter and looser than clay soil.

The Right Soil

Seeds were planted at the same time in the three pots in the picture. The seeds in the clay soil could not grow. This kind of soil has few air spaces. It is not easy for roots to push through the tightly packed grains in clay soil. Remember that seeds need air to germinate and grow.

Compare the plants in the sandy soil and the loam. Why might plants not grow well in sandy soil? You can see that the plant in the loam looks healthy. Why do plants in this kind of soil often grow well?

Look at the plants in the picture to the right. They are growing in dark, rich soil. This soil would be just right for your garden!

▲ Plants grow well in this soil.

Checkpoint

1. Describe the three kinds of soil.
2. Which kind of soil is best for growing plants? Explain your answer.
3. Take Action! Soak a plastic sponge in water. What do the holes and soft parts of the sponge compare to in soil? How is the sponge like loam?

The Great Soil Contest

What type of soil is best for growing tomato plants? Try this activity to find out.

Picture A

Gather These Materials

3 flower pots	hand lens
marker	pencil
masking tape	tomato seeds
clay soil	water
sandy soil	metric ruler
loam soil	

Follow This Procedure

1 Make 3 charts like the one on the next page. Record your observations in your charts.

2 Give each of the 3 flower pots one of the following labels: *clay*, *sand*, and *loam*. Label your charts with the same names as the pots. Fill each pot with the type of soil on its label. (Picture A)

Picture B

3 Examine each soil with a hand lens. Notice its color, how it feels, and if it contains dried leaves or seeds or other materials. Write your observations on a sheet of paper.

4 Use a pencil to poke a hole in the soil in each pot. Make each hole about 1 cm deep and 2 cm wide. (Picture B) Drop 3 tomato seeds into each hole. (Picture C) Cover the holes with soil. Add just enough water to make the soil damp. Place the pots in a warm, sunny place.

Picture C

Predict: *Which type of soil do you think will be best for growing tomato plants?*

5 Observe your pots every day for 2 to 3 weeks. Lightly water the soil if it becomes dry. On your charts, note the date when a tomato sprout first comes up in each pot. Also note how many sprouts come up.

6 Use a metric ruler to measure the height of each plant every day. Count the number of leaves it has. Record this information on the proper chart. If a pot has more than one tomato sprout, remove the smaller sprouts.

Date when sprouts appear:		
Date	Height of plant	Number of leaves

State Your Conclusions

1. Which type of soil was best for growing tomato plants? How could you tell?

2. Which types of soil were not good for growing tomato plants? How could you tell?

3. What do you think makes some types of soil better than others for growing tomato plants? Use the observations you made in step 3 to help you answer this question.

Let's Experiment

Now that you've found out how tomato plants grow in different types of soil, how do you think cactus plants would grow in these soils? Use what you know about scientific methods to find out.

2.2 *Water on Earth*

▶ **When is it going to rain?**

A rainstorm is just what your plants need! Notice how the clouds in these pictures are changing. If you saw these clouds, would you want to get out your umbrella or boots? You might. Dark clouds often bring rain.

Raining and Sleeting

Water vapor rises into the cool air high above the earth. Then the water vapor condenses on invisible bits of dust and salt in the air, forming droplets. Clouds are made of billions of these tiny droplets.

What happens to water droplets high in the air where temperatures are below freezing? If you said that water droplets freeze into bits of ice, you're right.

▼ *Clouds often get dark before a storm.*

Water droplets keep freezing onto the ice bits, making them larger and larger. The bits of ice become too heavy to float in the air. Then these bits of ice fall down through the clouds. They fall to the ground as snowflakes.

Water in any form that falls from clouds is called **precipitation** (pri sip′ ə tā′ shən). Snow is one kind of precipitation that you may have seen.

Suppose the air temperatures near the ground are above freezing. Would snowflakes fall? You probably figured out that warm air makes ice melt. That's right. In warmer temperatures, the bits of ice that fall from the clouds melt into raindrops. Rain is another kind of precipitation.

Suppose raindrops pass through a thick layer of very cold air close to the earth. These raindrops freeze before they can fall. This kind of precipitation is called sleet. You can even hear sleet rattle when it hits the ground!

How Big Is a Raindrop?

In the tropics, near the Equator, the air is very warm. So most clouds in the tropics are made of tiny water droplets, but not bits of ice. A drop of water in a cloud is very tiny, but not as small as a speck of dust.

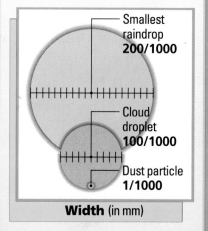

Smallest raindrop
200/1000

Cloud droplet
100/1000

Dust particle
1/1000

Width (in mm)

Rain will only fall if the cloud droplets join and become at least as large as the small raindrop shown above. The average raindrop is much bigger and is made of many cloud droplets.

 What Did You Find Out?
1. *How wide is a cloud droplet?*
2. *Do you think you could see one cloud droplet? Why?*
3. *How many times wider is the small raindrop than the cloud droplet?*

The Water Cycle

The rainstorm finally is over. You see puddles of water everywhere. You might even feel like splashing in a puddle like this child is doing. The sky looks clear now. Suddenly, the sun begins shining brightly. Later, you notice that the puddles have disappeared.

➤ *What might happen to this puddle?*

Into The Field

What do clouds look like?

Go outside and observe clouds once a day for two weeks. Record what you see. Describe how the clouds are alike and different.

What happened to the water in the puddles? Let's review what you learned in Module A. Light energy from the sun causes the water to evaporate. The water vapor can condense into water droplets, forming clouds. These water droplets can freeze. What happens when bits of ice in clouds become too heavy to stay in the air? You already learned the answer to that question. Precipitation falls from the clouds.

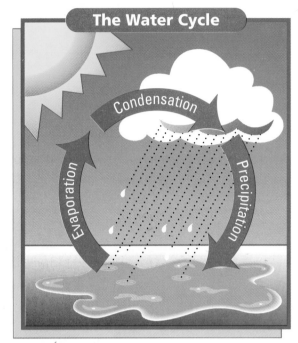

The Water Cycle

Condensation

Evaporation

Precipitation

The process of evaporation, condensation, and precipitation is called the **water cycle**. Trace the three steps of the water cycle shown in the picture. The entire water cycle keeps repeating itself over and over again.

Think back to the garden you planted. Loam provided the best soil for your plants. Plenty of rain has fallen. How well have your plants grown? Well, if the pictures on this page give a hint, the rain and the right soil helped make your tomatoes grow well. Look at them! They look ripe, juicy, and good enough to eat.

▼ *Fully grown tomatoes*

Checkpoint

1. How do rain and snow form?
2. What are the steps in the water cycle?
3. **Take Action!** Place a small mirror into a freezer for a few minutes. Remove the mirror and breathe on it. What forms on the mirror? Explain why.

Activity

How Do Clouds Form?

Water really moves around on a rainy day. How do clouds form? Make this model to find out.

Picture A

Picture B

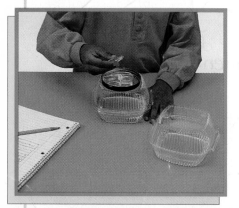

Picture C

Gather These Materials

2 clear plastic
   containers with lids
metal lid

warm water
ice cubes

Follow This Procedure

1. Make a chart like the one on the next page. Record your observations in your chart.

2. Fill each of two clear plastic containers about one-third full of water. (Picture A)

3. Close the lids on both containers. Observe what happens inside the containers for 1 minute. Record your observations in your chart. (Picture B)

4. Place a metal lid upside down on top of one of the containers. Fill the lid with ice cubes. (Picture C)

Predict: *What do you think will happen in the containers over time?*

5. After 5 minutes, remove the metal lid with the ice cubes from the top of the container. Observe the inside of both containers. Record your observations.

Record Your Results

	Container without ice on top	Container with ice on top
At the start		
5 minutes		
10 minutes		
15 minutes		

6 Replace the metal lid with the ice cubes on the top of the same container. Continue to observe the inside of the containers every 5 minutes for 15 minutes. Record your observations.

State Your Conclusions

1. What did you observe in each container?

2. How can you explain what you saw?

3. The movement of water in your container serves as a model for the water cycle. What do the water on the bottom of the container and the water on the lid of the container each represent in nature?

Let's Experiment

Now that you've learned how the water cycle works, how could you make water evaporate faster in your model? Use what you know about scientific methods to find out.

Chapter Review

Reviewing Words and Concepts

Write the letter of the word or phrase that best completes each sentence.

1. The decayed remains of dead plants and animals in the soil are called _____.
2. Materials that plants and animals need to live and grow are _____.
3. Tightly packed soil with tiny grains is _____.
4. Water runs quickly through _____ because it is loose and has large grains.
5. Water in any form that falls from clouds is called _____.
6. Soil that is a mixture of clay, sand, and humus is _____.
7. Earthworms dig tunnels in soil that allow air, water, and nutrients to reach plant _____.
8. The process of evaporation, condensation, and precipitation is called the _____.
9. Precipitation that falls as frozen rain is _____.
10. Clouds are made of billions of tiny water _____.

a. clay soil
b. roots
c. water cycle
d. nutrients
e. sleet
f. sandy soil
g. loam
h. humus
i. droplets
j. precipitation

Connecting Ideas

1. Copy the concept map. Use the terms at the right to complete the map about the water cycle.

evaporation   condensation
precipitation   snow
sleet

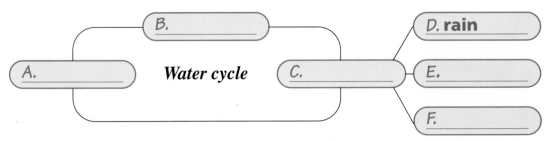

2. Write a sentence or two about the ideas shown in the concept map.

Interpreting What You Learned

1. How are the nutrients humus adds to the soil important?
2. Explain why many plants do not grow well in clay soil and sandy soil.
3. How is loam different from sandy soil and clay soil?
4. Explain how precipitation is formed.
5. Why does precipitation fall in different forms, such as snow and sleet?
6. Explain how the water cycle is important to plants.

 ## Performance Assessment

How does precipitation change?

Materials • crushed ice • 2 jar lids

Collecting Data

1. Place several pieces of crushed ice in each of the jar lids. The pieces of ice represent bits of ice in the clouds.
2. Lean over so that your mouth is next to one jar lid. Breathe on the ice pieces in one jar lid for two minutes. Your breath is like warm air that ice pieces pass through as they fall to the ground.
3. Look at the ice pieces after you breathe on them for two minutes. What kind of precipitation do they look like now? Record your observations.
4. Compare the ice pieces in the lid you breathed on with the ice pieces in the other lid. Record your observations.

Analyzing Data

How does air temperature affect the kind of precipitation that falls?

Good Food!

Discover Activity

What's in your cereal?

You will need a box of breakfast cereal that is labeled "Iron Fortified." Place a handful of this cereal in a sandwich bag. Crush it to a fine powder, and add the powder to a glass of water. Stir this mixture with a bar magnet. After about 5 minutes, take a close look at your magnet.

For Discussion

1. What did you find on your magnet?

2. Why might this material be put in cereals?

3.1 Getting Hungry

▶ What do I need to eat?

You might sometimes hear your stomach rumbling before a meal. That noise probably means you are hungry. Suppose someone in your family needs to shop for food before dinner. The first step might be to write a grocery list like the one in the picture. What kinds of foods would you put on your list?

You first might think of foods that taste especially good to you. But that's not all you need to think about! You need to think about foods that are good for you.

Remember what you learned about foods in the Discover Activity. Foods have nutrients that your body needs to stay healthy. Different nutrients give you energy and help your body grow bigger and stronger. The nutrients in your food help all the parts of your body work properly. Can foods that have nutrients still taste good? What do you think? To learn more about foods that are good for you, let's go on an imaginary shopping trip. Come along.

▼ A list of healthful foods

- GROCERY LIST -

MILK
EGGS
RICE
LETTUCE
BOK CHOY
CHICKEN
TORTILLAS
APPLES
TOMATOES
PASTA

Fruits and Vegetables

What colorful fruits and vegetables fill the bins at the grocery store! Which ones look tasty to you? Are they good for you, too?

Fruits and vegetables come from plants. Look at the roots, stems, leaves, and fruits in the picture. These plant parts contain many kinds of nutrients. You already learned that sugars and starches are stored in plants. These sugars and starches are nutrients called **carbohydrates** (kär′ bō hī′ drāts). Here's an interesting fact. You probably get most of your energy from carbohydrates.

Fruits and vegetables also provide you with other important nutrients. **Vitamins** are nutrients that help keep all the parts of your body working properly and help fight disease. Fruits and vegetables contain many different vitamins, but they are especially rich in vitamins A and C. Find some dark green vegetables in the picture. Find some yellow and orange vegetables and fruits. These foods are high in vitamin A. You need vitamin A for healthy skin and hair and good eyesight.

▲ Fruits and vegetables contain nutrients.

Look at the juicy orange shown in the picture. Citrus fruits, such as oranges and grapefruits, are high in vitamin C. Green peppers and green, leafy vegetables have some vitamin C, too. Vitamin C helps your body fight infections. Every day, you need to eat foods rich in vitamin C. What other fruit has a lot of vitamin C? The answer might surprise you. It's the tomato!

Fruits and vegetables contain **minerals**, too. Minerals are nutrients that help your body grow. Calcium is one mineral found in many fruits and vegetables. It helps build strong bones and teeth. What foods might provide you with calcium? Dark green vegetables such as broccoli and turnip greens would be good choices.

Fruits and vegetables also contain water. Water helps carry other nutrients to all the parts of your body. You can see why water is so important to your health!

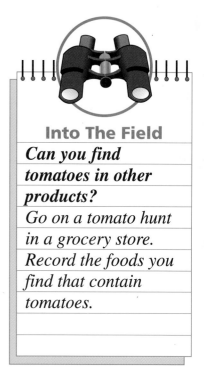

Into The Field

Can you find tomatoes in other products?

Go on a tomato hunt in a grocery store. Record the foods you find that contain tomatoes.

◄ Oranges contain vitamin C.

Breads and Cereals

Look at the foods shown below. Be sure to put many of these in your grocery cart! These foods contain carbohydrates. As you know, carbohydrates provide most of the energy your body needs.

These foods are rich in vitamins, such as B vitamins, that are important for good health. These foods also contain different minerals. Many breads and cereals have iron, a mineral that helps keep your blood healthy.

All the foods shown here come from grains. These grains are seeds from plants such as wheat, barley, oats, rice, and corn. Bran is the outer covering of a grain. Bran has **fiber**, a kind of carbohydrate. Why is fiber important? It helps food move through the parts of your body that digest food. You will learn more about these body parts when you read Lesson 2.

▼ *Foods which are high in carbohydrates, vitamins, and minerals*

Meats and Milk Products

The foods shown on this page contain a nutrient called **protein.** Your body needs protein to grow and stay healthy. Which of these foods do you especially like to eat?

Meat, poultry, fish, eggs, milk, and cheese are protein foods that come from animals. These foods also contain other nutrients, such as vitamins and minerals. Red meats are rich in iron. Why do you need iron in your diet?

Milk has other nutrients, too. It contains vitamin D and calcium. These nutrients work together. Vitamin D helps your body use calcium. Both the vitamin D and the calcium in milk help build strong bones and teeth. Milk also has vitamin A. How does vitamin A help you stay healthy?

Why are beans, peas, and nuts in the picture? These foods come from plants. They are rich in protein and iron. In fact, many people in the world get most of their protein from soybeans.

▼ Foods which are high in proteins, vitamins, and minerals

You Are What You Eat

How can you choose healthful foods each day?

Which foods do you like to eat? The U.S. Department of Agriculture has developed a Food Guide Pyramid that divides foods into five food groups. The table on the next page shows how many daily servings from each group are recommended.

Plan different meals for the plates on the right. Choose any healthful foods you like. Be sure to provide the proper number of daily servings from each food group. Then tell about the nutrients in the foods you chose.

Macaroni

Milk

Broccoli

Chicken

Beans

Bread

Spinach

Tortillas

Apple

Cereal

Yogurt

Beans

Carrot

Cheese

Bok choy

Egg

Pepper

Orange juice

Hamburger

Watermelon

Bagel

Okra

Yam

Tomato

Crackers

Corn

Fish

Hot cereal

Potato

Cheese

Strawberries

Today

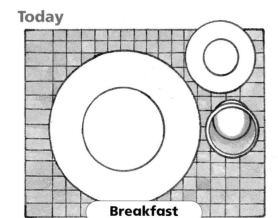
Breakfast

Lunch

Dinner

Tomorrow

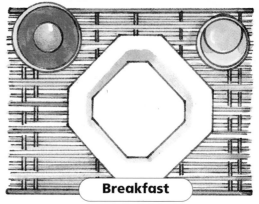
Breakfast

Lunch

Dinner

A Guide to Daily Food Choices
Recommended Daily Servings

Food Group	Number of Servings
Bread, cereal, rice, pasta	6-11
Vegetable	3-5
Fruit	2-4
Milk, yogurt, cheese	2-3 (Teen-agers need 3 servings)
Meat, poultry, fish, dry beans, eggs, nuts	2-3
* Use fats, oils, and sweets sparingly	

Healthful Eating

During the shopping trip, you learned about nutrients in many foods. You probably noticed something about nutrients. You cannot get all the nutrients you need from just one kind of food. The key to healthful eating is eating different kinds of foods each day. That way, you can get all the nutrients your body needs.

Eating the right foods will give you energy and help keep you healthy. Eating these foods in the right amounts can help you stay at a healthy weight.

➤ *Preparing a healthful meal*

Eating foods that are low in fat, sugar, and salt is another part of healthful eating. **Fat** is a nutrient that gives you energy. It also helps carry some vitamins through your body. Milk, butter, cheese, meats, and nuts contain fat. Limiting fatty foods in your diet can help keep your heart healthy. It also can help you keep the right amount of body fat.

Soft drinks, sweetened cereals, candy, cookies, and cake are some foods that have large amounts of sugar. Eating too much sugar can harm your teeth. Limiting the amount of sugar in your diet also can help you stay at a weight that is right for you.

Limiting salt in your diet can help keep your body healthy. Fresh foods contain all the salt your body needs. Not adding extra salt to your food is a healthful practice. Staying away from salty snacks is a wise practice, too.

Now it's time to prepare a meal like the one in the picture with plenty of vegetables, fruits, and grain products. That's the healthful way to eat!

Checkpoint

1. What nutrients do fruits provide?
2. What nutrients are in breads?
3. Name five foods high in protein.
4. How many servings from the milk group do you need each day?
5. What foods need to be limited?
6. Take Action! Check the label on a cereal box. List the vitamins and minerals in the cereal.

Activity

Passing the Fat Test

Do your favorite snack foods contain fat? Can they pass the fat test? Do this activity to find out.

Picture A

Picture B

Picture C

Gather These Materials

clean brown paper bag
scissors
permanent marker

pat of butter
carrot stick
assorted snack foods

Follow These Procedures

1. Make a chart like the one on the next page. Record your observations in your chart.

2. Cut a square from a brown paper bag. Draw several circles the size of a dime on the paper.

3. Label one circle Butter-5. Rub butter over the whole circle. Hold the paper up to the light. (Picture A) Butter is almost all fat. The fat makes a clear, greasy spot on the paper. Also, the fat will spread outside your circle.

4. Label the next circle Carrot-1. Rub the carrot over the whole circle. If the carrot makes a wet spot, let the spot dry. Hold the paper up to the light. A carrot has very little fat, so you won't be able to see through its spot. (Picture B)

5. Label the other circles with the other foods you will test.

Predict: Which foods do you think have the most fat? the least fat?

Record Your Results

Food	Size of clear spots	Greasiness of spots	Ranking of amount of fat
Butter	large	very greasy	5
Carrot	none	not greasy	1

6 Test the snack foods for fat by rubbing them into the labeled circles. Compare each spot with the spots the butter and the carrot made. Observe the size of the spot and how clear each spot is. (Picture C)

7 If the food seems to have as little fat as the carrot, give the food a 1. If it seems to have as much fat as butter, give it a 5. If the fat in the food is between that in butter and the carrot, give it a 2 or 3 or 4, depending on how big and clear the spot is. Record the numbers on your chart. *CAUTION: Do not taste any of the foods.*

State Your Conclusions

1. Which of the snack foods had the least fat?
2. Which of the snack foods had the most fat?

Let's Experiment

How would you plan and prepare a low-fat snack treat? Use what you know about scientific methods to plan recipes.

3.2 *Yum! Dinnertime!*

▶ *What happens to the food you eat?*

The family in the picture gathers at the table. Finally, it's time to eat! Would you like to eat a meal like this one? You might find it quite tasty. What do you notice about this meal? You might notice that it has many different kinds of foods. You might point out foods with different nutrients. You might even find some of your favorite foods.

What happens when you eat food? How do the nutrients in your food reach all the parts of the body? It's an interesting story.

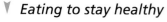

▼ *Eating to stay healthy*

The First Step

The girl in the picture crunches into a juicy apple. Then her body gets to work. It begins to **digest** the food. When your body digests food, it changes the food into a form the body can use. Here's how it happens.

Chewing is the first step. Your teeth cut and grind your food into tiny pieces. Saliva is a juice in your mouth. Your tongue helps your saliva mix with your food. Saliva begins to digest some food. It also helps make the food soft enough to swallow.

What happens when you swallow soft pieces of food? A long food tube connects your mouth with your stomach. Muscles in this food tube squeeze the food along. It only takes a few seconds for your food to reach your stomach.

◄ Digestion begins in the mouth.

INVESTIGATE

Protein Digestion

What happens when proteins are digested? Let's investigate.

What To Do
A. Make gelatin following the package directions.
B. Fill two plastic foam cups a quarter full of liquid gelatin. Cool for 30 minutes.
C. Add fresh pineapple to one cup.
D. Let the cups cool overnight. Observe them the next day. Record what you see in each cup.

Record Your Results

	Observations
Gelatin	
Gelatin + pineapple	

What Did You Find Out?
1. Gelatin is protein. What happens when gelatin protein cools?
2. A substance in pineapple digests protein. What happens when digested gelatin protein cools?
3. Where in your digestive system might such changes take place?

How is this apple digested?

► *The parts of your body that digest food*

Digestion

The picture below can help you understand more about digestion. Trace the path your food follows from your mouth to your stomach. Juices in your stomach mix with foods and digest them further. Stomach muscles churn your food around. After a while, your food looks like a thick liquid.

Soon your stomach squeezes out the thick liquid food into your small intestine. Here's a surprise. The small intestine is not really small! It is a long, narrow tube that is curled up inside of you. Find it in the picture.

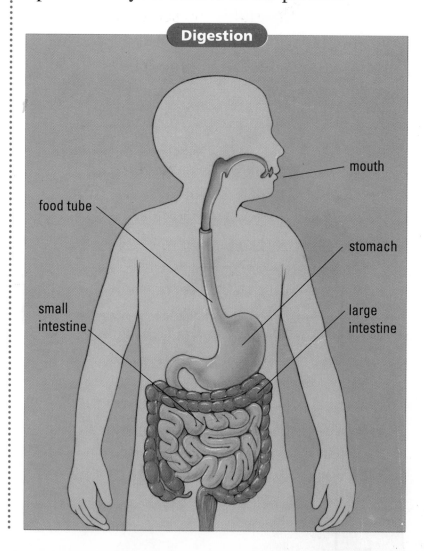

Digestion

mouth

food tube

stomach

small intestine

large intestine

Juices in your small intestine finish digesting your food. Muscles in your small intestine keep squeezing the food along. The liquid food has now been digested and is in a form your body can use. What happens next to the nutrients in the digested food?

Your small intestine is lined with many tiny blood vessels. Nutrients pass from your small intestine into these blood vessels. Then your heart pumps the nutrient-rich blood to all the parts of your body.

Your body cannot use some parts of the food you eat. For example, your body can't digest fruit skins and some seeds. The food your body does not use moves from your small intestine into your large intestine.

In your large intestine, water is absorbed into your blood vessels. The parts of food that are left are wastes. They are stored in the large intestine until they leave your body.

The next time you swallow food, think about how it will be changed. The way your body digests food truly is amazing!

Checkpoint

1. How is food changed in the mouth?
2. What happens in the small intestine?
3. Take Action! Place a sugar cube in a cup of water. Place a crushed sugar cube in another cup of water. How is crushing the sugar like chewing? How does the size of food affect the time it takes to change the food?

Activity

Observing Changes in Milk

How do different substances change milk? Try this activity to find out.

Picture A

Follow This Procedure

1. Make a chart like the one on the next page. Record your observations in the chart.

2. Put on your cover goggles.

3. Use masking tape to make labels for 4 plastic cups. Label the cups: 1, 2, 3, and 4. Put 3 spoonfuls of milk into each cup. (Picture A)

Picture B

4. Put cup 1 aside. This cup is the control in this activity.

5. Take a clean spoon. Add 2 spoonfuls of water to cup 2. Stir. (Picture B)

6. Take another clean spoon. Stir 2 spoonfuls of vinegar into cup 3.

7. Take another clean spoon. Stir 2 spoonfuls of meat tenderizer into cup 4.

Picture C

Record Your Results

Whole milk	Observations after 1 minute	Observations after 1–2 hours
1. Milk with nothing added		
2. Milk and water		
3. Milk and vinegar		
4. Milk and meat tenderizer		

Predict: *How will the milk in each cup look after 1 minute? after 1 hour?*

8 Cover all 4 cups with plastic wrap. Use a rubber band to hold the plastic in place. (Picture C)

9 After 1 minute, observe the milk in all the cups. Record your observations on your chart.

10 After 1 hour, observe the milk again. Record your observations on your chart.

State Your Conclusions

1. What was the purpose of observing a cup of plain milk with nothing added?

2. How did each of the substances that you added change the milk?

Let's Experiment

Now that you have learned how different substances change whole milk, how do you think they would change skim milk? Use what you know about scientific methods to find out.

Chapter Review

Reviewing Words and Concepts

Write the letter of the word or phrase that best completes each sentence.

1. Sugars and starches are nutrients called _____.
2. Nutrients that help keep your body working properly and help fight disease are called _____.
3. Nutrients, such as calcium, that help your body grow are called _____.
4. Bran has a kind of carbohydrate called _____ that helps move food during digestion.
5. Meat, poultry, fish, and eggs are _____ foods that come from animals.
6. A nutrient that gives you energy and helps carry some vitamins through your body is _____.
7. When your body _____ food, it changes the food into a form you can use.
8. Oranges are high in _____, which helps your body fight infection.
9. In your mouth, _____ begins to digest food.
10. The mineral _____ helps build strong bones and teeth.

a. fat
b. fiber
c. saliva
d. vitamins
e. minerals
f. vitamin C
g. calcium
h. protein
i. digests
j. carbohydrates

Connecting Ideas

1. Copy the concept map. Use the terms at the right to complete the map about foods to show the different nutrients they contain.

carbohydrates   vitamins
minerals   vegetables

A. **fruits**

B.

C.

D.

E.

2. Write a sentence or two about the ideas shown in the concept map.

Interpreting What You Learned

1. Why are carbohydrates important to your health?
2. Name some foods that contain fat.
3. Why is water important to your health?
4. Name four kinds of food that contain protein.
5. Explain how food is digested.
6. How does vitamin D help your body build strong bones and teeth?

Performance Assessment

How much juice is in an orange?

Materials • cover goggles • orange • plastic knife • plastic cup • small measuring cup

Collecting Data

1. Put on your cover goggles. Use the plastic knife to carefully cut the orange in half.
2. Hold one half of the orange over the plastic cup. Squeeze the orange so juice drips from the orange into the cup. Squeeze until no more juice drips from the orange.
3. Hold the other half of the orange over the plastic cup. Squeeze the orange so juice drips from the orange into the cup. Squeeze until you remove all of the juice.
4. Pour the juice from the plastic cup into the small measuring cup.
5. Find out how many milliliters of juice you collected. Read the number on the small measuring cup next to the surface of the juice. Record your results.

Analyzing Data

Use your results to estimate how many oranges you would need to fill a 100-milliliter cup.

The Fine Art of Buying Cereal

How do you choose a cereal to buy? There are several things you need to think about.

Needs and Goals

To choose a cereal, think about these three things:

- Nutrition: Does the cereal provide the nutrients you need?
- Cost: How does it compare with other cereals in cost?
- Taste: Do you like it?

Gathering Information

Every cereal has a label that gives nutrition information. Notice the labels on the cereal boxes pictured.

Today, many stores also use shelf labels, like those in the picture. Shelf labels show the price of the item and the unit cost—how much the food costs per ounce. This information helps you compare prices.

Taste is something only you can decide on. You might try several cereals to see which you like best.

To choose a cereal, think about these three things: nutrition, cost, and taste.

Possible Alternatives

There are many different cereals in supermarkets. Of course, comparing all of them would be impossible. But suppose you are trying to choose from among only three cereals. The cereals are called Crunchos, Shreddos, and Loopies. The pictures of the labels can help you compare these cereals.

Evaluating Alternatives

Copy the table shown. Record the information given in the pictures. Fill in the Taste column as you choose.

Making the Best Choice

Suppose you like a cereal that contains very little protein. If you eat another food, such as yogurt, that contains protein, you need less protein in your cereal. Making a decision is often based on many factors. You can put information in a table to help you make a decision.

Crunchos

Nutrition Information

Serving size:
1 oz. (28.4 g, about ¾ cup)
Servings per package: 10

	cereal	with ½ cup vitamins A&D skim milk
Calories	110	150
Protein, g	1	5
Carbohydrate, g	26	32
Fat, Total, g	0	0
unsaturated, g	0	
saturated, g	0	
Cholesterol, mg	0	0
Sodium, mg	200	260
Potassium, mg	25	230

$2.85
28.5¢ per oz.

Shreddos

Nutrition Information

Serving size:
1 oz. (28.4 g, about 1 cup)
Servings per package: 10

	cereal	with ½ cup vitamins A&D skim milk
Calories	110	150
Protein, g	2	6
Carbohydrate, g	25	31
Fat, Total, g	0	0
unsaturated, g	0	
saturated, g	0	
Cholesterol, mg	0	0
Sodium, mg	290	350
Potassium, mg	35	240

$2.69
26.9¢ per oz.

Loopies

Nutrition Information

Serving size:
1 oz. (28.4 g, about ⅔ cup)
Servings per package: 16

	cereal	with ½ cup vitamins A&D skim milk
Calories	90	130
Protein, g	3	7
Carbohydrate, g	22	28
Fat, Total, g	0	0
unsaturated, g	0	
saturated, g	0	
Cholesterol, mg	0	0
Sodium, mg	220	280
Potassium, mg	160	360

$2.48
15.5¢ per oz.

Comparing Cereals

Cereal	Taste	Cost	Nutrients
Crunchos			
Shreddos			
Loopies			

Now You Do It

1. How do the three cereals compare in cost? How do they compare in nutrition?

2. Suppose that you like all three cereals. Which one appears to be the best choice? Explain your answer.

3. *On Your Own* Choose several real cereals that you like. Visit a supermarket and gather information about cost and nutrition. Use the skills you practiced here. Which cereal is the best choice?

4. *Critical Thinking* When making decisions about buying food, many people also think about how different food products are packaged. How might this show concern for the environment?

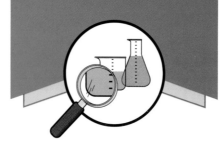

It All Starts With a Seed

Cliff Zenor

Occupation: Urban horticulturist
Challenge: Saving neighborhoods
Favorite saying: Plant a seed, grow a community, harvest good health.

Cliff Zenor is a man who likes his work. When he was growing up, he thought it might be fun to be a gardener or a scientist or maybe a teacher. Today Cliff is all those things and more. Cliff Zenor is an urban horticulturist. He works with neighborhoods to plan and plant gardens in empty city lots.

Where do you find enough space for a garden?

"You would be surprised how many empty lots there are in a city. Sometimes people move away, leaving their homes behind. Sometimes an empty house burns down. Then people start dumping trash in the yard."

How do you make a garden?

"The first step is cleaning up the lot and choosing the plants. Then the fun begins! People of all ages begin to work together. Before long, the neighbors get to know each other. People who had never met become good friends. It turns out that neighborhood gardening is really more about neighborhoods and people than it is about gardening."

What do you like about your job?

"The most fun is being with people when they put their hands in the dirt. Things start happening. A garden is one of the first steps in changing a neighborhood for the better. It brings people together. And it's fast—in six months you have something to show, and people have something to be proud of. The garden shows everyone that people really care about a neighborhood. Then people start taking care of their neighborhood, and each other."

Plant Medicine: A Peppermint Cure

For many years, people have used plants to make medicine. About one-fourth of today's medicines come from flowering plants. For example, oil from peppermint plants is used to make poison ivy medicines. Here's how people get peppermint oil.

1 Flowering peppermint plants are put into a tank. Steam is piped into the tank. Heat changes water from inside the plants into water vapor.

2 The water vapor and oils from the plants are piped to a cool tank. Here the water vapor condenses, or changes to a liquid.

4 The pale, yellow peppermint oil is stored in a sealed tank.

3 Oil and water do not mix. The water flows into separator tanks.

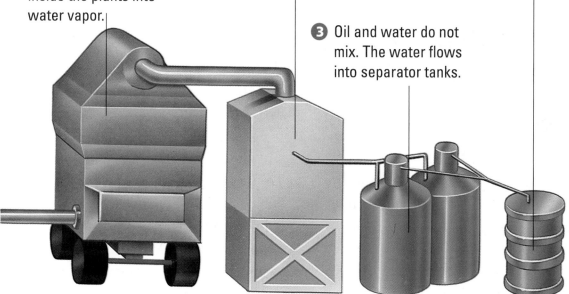

Find Out On Your Own

Add a spoonful of vegetable oil to a glass of water. Stir them together. Draw a picture of what happens.

Module Performance Assessment

Television Special

Using what you learned in this module, help prepare a television special on Healthful Foods and Food Chains to present at a school assembly. Complete one or more of the following activities. You may work by yourself or with others in a group.

Art

Make a poster of a food chain that includes people. You may draw pictures of the members of the food chain or cut pictures from old magazines.

Drama

Prepare a commercial for a healthful snack food. Explain how the food is healthful.

Investigation

Find out what types of fruits and vegetables are grown in your area. Then find out what vitamins are found in these foods. Make a chart to report your findings.

Environment

What if your town decided to clear wooded land to build a shopping center? How might this affect the food chain on the land? Write a television news brief reporting the plans and what changes might take place.

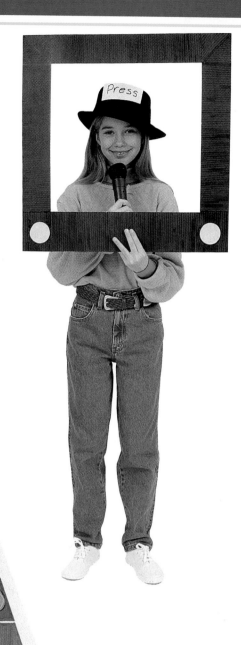

Health

Make a poster showing the food groups from the Food Guide Pyramid. Cut pictures from magazines or from empty food cartons to use on your poster. Write about how each food group helps your body work properly.

Module Review

Reviewing Words and Concepts

Write the letter of the word or phrase that best completes each sentence.

1. A plant _____ uses the stored sugars in the seed to grow and develop.
2. The sun's energy is used by _____ to make sugars.
3. Plants change water and carbon dioxide into sugars during _____.
4. Seeds need the right amount of water and the proper temperature to _____.
5. Loam has many nutrients because it is made partly from _____.
6. Snow and rain are kinds of _____.
7. The mineral _____ helps build bones and teeth.
8. Saliva in the mouth begins to _____ some foods.
9. Water moves from puddles to clouds and back to the earth through the _____.
10. People probably get most of their energy from sugars and starches called _____.

a. germinate
b. humus
c. calcium
d. digest
e. water cycle
f. photosynthesis
g. precipitation
h. embryo
i. producers
j. carbohydrates

Interpreting What You Learned

1. Explain how energy from the sun gets into the foods you eat.
2. Explain how every living thing is a link in a food chain.
3. To which food group do turkey, beef, and peanuts belong?
4. Explain why the water cycle would not be possible without energy from the sun.
5. How do different types of precipitation form?

Applying What You Learned

1. If you plant a seed in freezing temperatures, what will happen to the seed?
2. Make a diagram of an ocean food chain using the following living things: small fish, algae, seal, large fish.
3. Draw a diagram that shows the movement of a water drop through the water cycle.
4. Plan a healthful menu for breakfast, lunch, and dinner.

Finding Shelter

Finding Shelter

Where do you go when the rain falls and the wind blows? If you know what's good for you, you head for shelter. Animals of all kinds protect themselves by building or finding shelters. Your home is a shelter, and so are the nests of birds and the dens of bears. In this module, you'll find out how different animals build shelters.

CHAPTER

1 Shelters

Where do shelters come from?
People and other animals build shelters from resources found in nature.

CHAPTER

2 Heat on the Move

Brrr! It's time to turn on the heat. Well-insulated houses keep heat on the inside and cold on the outside. They also save fuels.

CHAPTER
3 Machines in Building

Beavers bite and build. Both beavers and people use machines to build shelters. But the beavers' machines are parts of their bodies.

In this module

Shelters

How can you build a shelter?

Imagine that your family is taking a hike in a forest and gets lost. It is getting late. You are going to have to spend the night in the forest. You need a shelter of some kind. Make a model of the kind of shelter you might build.

For Discussion

1. Why do you need a shelter?

2. What could you use to build your shelter?

1.1 Resources in Shelters

▶ Why do people need shelters?

In the early morning, this family watched storm clouds gather overhead and listened to the low rumble of thunder. Now, rain soaks their clothing and turns their cereal and toast into a mushy mess.

Would you like to join the family in the picture for breakfast? Your answer most likely is, "No way!" When rain comes or when snowflakes fall, what do you do? You probably head for a **shelter**—something that covers and protects.

From early times, people have built shelters to protect themselves from the weather and from danger. In this lesson, you will find out what materials people use to build shelters.

◄ This family could use a shelter to keep the rain off themselves and their food. Even the dog is under the table out of the rain!

▶ *Lumber is often used to build the framework of a house.*

Building Shelters

Remember what you decided you might use to build your shelter in the Discover Activity? Was it the materials you could find in the forest? For hundreds of years, people have built shelters of materials they can get easily. Some people still use materials found near where they live, but many people use materials that are produced far away.

What material was used to build the framework for a house in the picture? Yes, it's lumber. But do you know how lumber is made? Let's find out.

From Forest to Lumberyard

Trees are cut down, branches are trimmed off, and logs are loaded onto trucks.

Trucks haul the logs to a lumber mill to be cut into different sizes and made smooth.

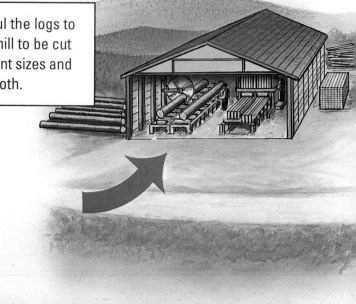

Lumber is made from wood, and wood comes from trees. Like clay, stone, and many other materials people use to build shelters, trees are a natural resource. A **natural resource** is a material that comes from the earth and can be used by living things. Most of the trees now used to make lumber grow in the southeastern United States and along the Pacific coast of North America. However, trees, like many natural resources, usually are not used as they are found in nature.

Look at the pictures that show the steps between cutting down trees and lumber arriving at the lumberyard. Over the years, many changes have taken place in the way lumber is made. More and better machines are being built to produce lumber.

Of course, lumber is only one of the materials you need for a house. Imagine having a house without windows or a foundation to hold it up! So you need glass and concrete. Also, you may want to use brick for the outside walls.

Trucks haul finished lumber to a lumberyard to be sold.

INVESTIGATE

Which Is Softer?

How can you find out how soft wood is without pounding a nail into it? Let's investigate.

What To Do
A. Fill a metal pan or dish with water.
B. Place a 3-centimeter cube of balsa and of pine in water.

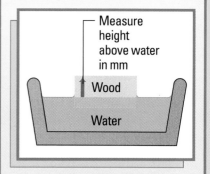

Measure height above water in mm

Wood

Water

C. Measure the height in millimeters that each cube sticks above the water. Record it in a chart such as the one shown below.

Record Your Results

Wood	Height Out of Water
Balsa	
Pine	

What Did You Find Out?
1. *The higher the wood floats in water, the softer it is. Which wood is softer?*
2. *Which wood would be better for building a house? Why?*

Sources of Building Materials

Natural resources are the beginning of many materials.

Look around! The chair that you sit on and the pen you're holding are made from natural resources. What materials from the earth went into these objects? Find other things in your classroom—the chalkboard and chalk perhaps—and name the natural resources used to make them.

The building materials in homes and schools often are made from natural resources. For example, the bricks and glass in a building are made from natural resources.

How Glass Is Made

Step 1: A large amount of sand is heated with small amounts of lime (from limestone) and soda (from salt or another mineral).

Step 2: The mixture is then cooled and shaped into glass.

How Bricks Are Made

Bricks are made from the natural resources clay and rock (shale).

Step 1: The ground clay and shale are mixed with water into a stiff paste. The paste is formed into blocks by machines. Then the blocks are cut into bricks.

Step 2: The bricks are baked in ovens, or kilns, at high temperatures.

Keeping It Together

Lumber, bricks, and glass are materials you can use to build a house. But that's not all you need. You can't just stand the lumber on end and have it stay in place. You need something to hold the lumber together—such as a nail. Nails are made of steel, and steel is made from iron ore, another natural resource. But notice how different the nails and the iron ore in the pictures look. Let's find out how to get steel nails from iron ore.

The open-pit mine in the picture is huge. Miners use power shovels to scoop up the ore from the pits. Trucks, ships, and railroads carry the ore to steel plants. At the steel plant, iron is separated from the ore in huge furnaces—higher than a ten-story building! The melted iron collects in a pool at the bottom of the furnace.

Remember that nails are made from steel, not iron. So, how is iron made into steel? Melted iron is heated to a very high temperature with a small amount of carbon. The melted iron and carbon combine to form liquid steel, which is poured into molds. The liquid steel hardens in the molds. Giant rollers squeeze the steel into long narrow strips of wire.

▼ Steel nails are made from iron ore, which comes from iron mines such as this open-pit mine in Minnesota.

At a nail factory, machines cut the wire and shape the point of the nail at one end. At the same time, the machine hammers the other end of the nail to make the head. One machine can make over 500 nails in a minute!

Now, if the outside walls of the house are bricks, nails won't help. To hold bricks together, you need cement—made of two natural resources, limestone and clay. Limestone comes from a gravel pit such as the one in the picture. Dry cement, shown in the picture, is mixed with water and sand to make a thick paste, or mortar. The mortar, shown on a trowel in the picture, is then placed between bricks with a trowel. When the mortar hardens, it will keep those bricks in place for years!

▲ Limestone comes from a gravel pit and is used to make cement. A trowel is used to put mortar between bricks.

Checkpoint

1. Where do natural resources come from?
2. What natural resources are used to make bricks and glass?
3. What natural resources are used to hold building materials together?
4. Take Action! Look around one room of your house and list all the building materials that come from natural resources.

Activity

Observing Different Building Materials

Building materials differ in many ways. Observe some materials to find out how they are different.

Picture A

Picture B

Picture C

Gather These Materials

brick	pebbles
burlap	rock
concrete	sticks
leaves	thick, clear plastic
mud	wood

Follow This Procedure

1 Make a chart like the one on the next page. Record your results on your chart.

2 Look closely at the building materials that are displayed on the table. (Picture A) What do you think these materials might be used for?

3 Pick up one of the materials. What do you think it is? Observe how it feels—rough or smooth, what it looks like, how big it is, and how heavy it is. (Picture B)

Predict: If the pieces were the same size, which materials would be heaviest?

4 Record your observations of the building material.

5 Repeat steps 3 and 4 for each of the other materials. (Picture C)

State Your Conclusions

1. Which material feels rough? smooth?

2. Imagine you have equal-sized pieces of each material. Which material do you think would be lightest? heaviest?

3. Think about what you have learned about natural resources. What natural resource might each of these materials be made from?

Let's Experiment

From your observations of these materials, which of them do you think would be best to use for the roof of a shelter if you lived where there was a lot of rain? Use what you know about scientific methods to find out.

Record Your Results

Material	Description	Use

Into The Field

What kinds of shelters do animals use?

Observe animal shelters in your neighborhood. Draw or describe each shelter.

➤ *A gray squirrel has built a nest in a hollow tree to shelter its babies in the picture on the next page.*

1.2 Using Resources Found Nearby

▶ *What natural resources do animals use for shelters?*

A small gray squirrel sits at the base of an oak tree eating an acorn. Every few seconds its head turns from side to side, its beady eyes on the lookout for danger. Suddenly, the wind starts to blow and it begins to snow hard! What happens next? The squirrel races up the tree and dives into its nest.

Animal Shelters

Like people, animals need shelter. They need protection from the rain, snow, heat, cold, and from other animals. They need a safe place in which to raise their young. Many animals find shelter in hollow trees, under logs, or in other places. Other animals build their own shelters or add natural resources to the shelters they find.

Now, from the squirrel's point of view, the ideal nest is a hole high up in a large tree or in a hollow tree trunk. Finding a hole means less work for the squirrel. It has only to clean out any rotten wood and make a nest. For the nest, the squirrel might use grass, leaves, pieces of bark, and twigs. A nest, such as the one in the picture, keeps the baby squirrels safe, dry, and warm.

Like squirrels, beavers use trees—that great natural resource—to build shelters. They build lodges at the shore or in the middle of a pond or river. The dome of the lodge will rise from a meter to twelve meters above the water line. Notice what the beaver lodge in the picture looks like.

How do beavers build such a huge lodge? It's really quite simple—if you're a beaver. Notice in the picture how the beaver uses its strong front teeth to cut down trees. Beavers also use their teeth to peel the bark and branches off the trees.

A beaver then holds a branch, or even a log, tightly between its teeth. With the branch in its mouth the beaver swims back to the place it has chosen for its lodge. The beavers pile up the branches and weave them together to make a lodge.

▼ *Beavers need to be good "lumberjacks" to cut down enough trees to build their lodges.*

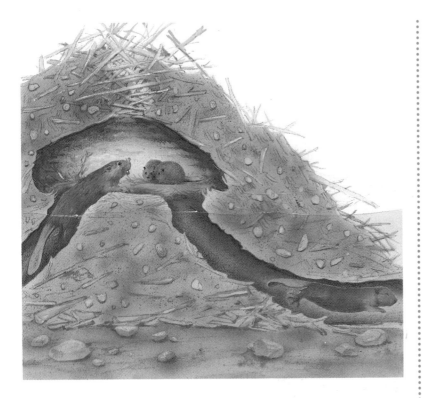

◄ *The entrances to the tunnels leading to the beavers' lodge are underwater.*

▲ A beaver carries a branch in its mouth and swims back to the lodge it is building.

Using their teeth, the beavers tunnel up from the bottom of the pond. They gnaw through the bottom of the lodge and hollow out a den. Find the two tunnels leading to the lodge in the picture. Beavers use these tunnels to get in and out of the lodge.

While the lodge is quite comfortable in warm weather, the loose tangle of sticks and branches wouldn't keep out cold winter winds. So before ice forms on the pond, the beavers plaster the outside of the lodge. A beaver uses its paws to scoop up rotted leaves and mud from the bottom of the pond. Then the beaver pats and punches the wet material into spaces between the sticks. It leaves a small opening at the top of the lodge to let in air. When the weather gets cold, the mud freezes solid. Like the squirrels in their nest, the beavers will be safe and warm.

Shelters in Early America

Native Americans who settled in the woodlands of North America made houses of wood covered with bark. Later, European settlers also built their homes of wood. Look at the picture of the log cabin. The settlers filled the spaces between the logs with mud and moss. As settlers moved westward, they found many kinds of shelters built by Native Americans. Each tribe of people made houses with materials they could find easily.

On the Great Plains, only a few trees grew along the riverbanks. Native Americans who lived there built earth lodges made of logs thickly covered with hard-packed grass and dirt. The settlers, who had plows and spades, cut sod into blocks, such as those shown in the picture. They piled the blocks one on top of the other to form the walls of the house. Notice in the picture that the roof of the house was also made of logs and sod.

In the Southwest, Native Americans built homes with the resources they had nearby—stone and mud. They built flat-roofed rooms and placed them side by side and on top of one another. The buildings looked somewhat like apartment houses of today.

▲ This log cabin is typical of those built in America by early European settlers.

▼ In 1892, many people in Nebraska lived in houses made of sod blocks.

These Mexican women are building a house of adobe brick. Finished houses often looked like the one shown below.

In lowland parts of the Southwest, Native Americans made houses of adobe—a mixture of sandy clay, water, and straw. They shaped the mixture into lumps. When the lumps hardened, the people used the same mixture to plaster lumps together into thick walls. The walls kept out both heat and cold.

Later, people who moved up from Mexico also made their homes of adobe. But they shaped the adobe into bricks. Notice the bricks and the adobe houses in the pictures. Before long, Native Americans were also making their houses out of bricks. Even today, the kind of shelters that people build depends on where they live and what material they can get easily.

Checkpoint

1. How are the shelters of squirrels and beavers alike?
2. Why didn't all Native Americans use the same building materials?
3. **Take Action!** Make a thick paste with flour and water, and put it on waxed paper to dry. How would you describe the dried paste?

Activity

Building a Bird's Nest

Think about a bird's nest or pictures of nests you have seen. Then try to build a bird's nest.

Picture A

Picture B

Picture C

Gather These Materials

shirt-box lid
small twigs
straw
long, dry grass

string
mud
water

Follow This Procedure

1 Make a chart like the one on the next page. Record your results on your chart.

2 Use the box lid to build the nest in.

3 Take a few handfuls of twigs and straw and place them in the box lid. (Picture A) Count how many handfuls of each material you use. Record how much of each material you use.

4 Arrange the materials in a circle, and build up the edges of the circle—leaving a hollow in the center.

5 Use the grass and string to twist and weave around the twigs and straw to hold them together. (Picture B)

6 Cover the circle of dry materials with mud. Pat and pinch the muddy materials into a bowllike shape. (Picture C)

7 Add drops of water to the mud if needed to keep the mud damp while you shape the nest.

> **Predict: What will happen to the nest when the mud dries?**

8 Keep on shaping the nest as the mud begins to dry so the nest will keep its bowllike shape and be large enough to hold three or four small bird's eggs.

State Your Conclusions

1. What was difficult about building the bird's nest?

2. Think about what you know about building materials. What other materials might also be used to make a nest?

Let's Experiment

Now that you have built a bird's nest, how do you think birds get their nests to stay where they build them? Without climbing a tree, use what you know about scientific methods to find out.

Record Your Results

Material	How much used

Chapter Review

Reviewing Words and Concepts

Write the letter of the word or phrase that best completes each sentence.

1. Animals build ____ for protection from weather and danger.
2. A material that comes from the earth and can be used by living things is a ____.
3. Sand is heated with lime and soda to make ____.
4. Clay and a rock called shale are mixed to make ____.
5. To make ____, iron ore is heated with carbon.
6. Squirrels often build their nests high up in a ____.
7. Many animals find shelter in hollow trees or under ____.
8. The ____ cuts down trees to build a lodge for shelter.
9. Native Americans built shelters with the resources that were ____.
10. In parts of the Southwest, Native Americans made houses of ____, a mixture of sandy clay, water, and straw.

a. bricks
b. steel
c. logs
d. shelters
e. beaver
f. adobe
g. glass
h. tree
i. nearby
j. natural resource

Connecting Ideas

1. Copy the concept map. Use the terms at the right to complete the map about resources for building.

shelters   bricks
              lumber
iron ore   limestone

Natural Resources   **Building Materials**

A. trees — E. ____

B. clay — F. ____

C. ____ — G. steel

D. ____ — H. cement

I. ____

2. Write a sentence or two about the ideas in the concept map.

Interpreting What You Learned

1. How are nails made?
2. How are animal shelters like those that people build?
3. Explain how the shelters of squirrels and beavers are alike and how they differ.
4. What materials did Native Americans and early European settlers in America use for shelters? Why?
5. What natural resources are used to build a brick wall?

  ## Performance Assessment

What can you build with natural resources?

Materials • craft sticks or twigs • pebbles • clay • metric ruler • plastic wrap (about 15 cm x 15 cm) • paper • pencil

Collecting Data

1. Draw a rectangle 10 centimeters high and 15 centimeters wide.
2. Arrange the pebbles and the craft sticks or twigs inside the rectangle. Make them look like a wall that you will build.
3. Leave a space in the middle of the rectangle between the materials. The space will be for a window on your wall.
4. When the materials in your wall are arranged, use pieces of clay to hold the materials together.
5. Use scissors to cut a piece of plastic wrap to make a window for your wall. Connect the plastic to the wall with clay. The plastic represents a glass window.
6. Make three more walls like this. Stand the walls up and connect them to form a model house. Place craft sticks, twigs, or other materials over the opening on top to form a roof.
7. When you are finished, look at your house. What natural resources are used in your house? Record your observations.

Analyzing Data

Compare your house to houses made in early America. What other natural resources might you have used?

2

Heat on the Move

Oh wow, that's weird!

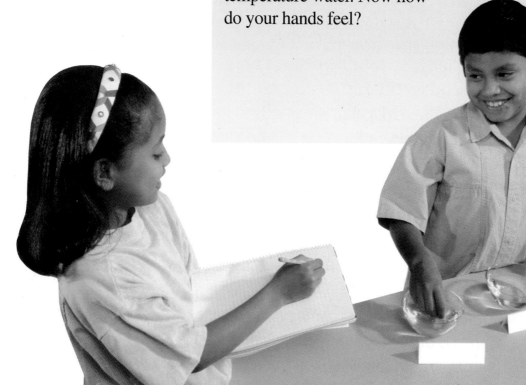

What makes things feel warm?

Put ice water in one bowl, room-temperature water in a second bowl, and warm water in a third. Place one hand in the ice water and one in the warm water for 1 minute. Describe how each hand feels. Then put both hands in the room-temperature water. Now how do your hands feel?

For Discussion

1. *Why did your hands feel differently?*
2. *How do you explain your observations?*

2.1 *Heat in Shelters*

> ### *How do shelters help animals?*

Outside, an icy wind howls and the temperature drops below zero, but Snoopy doesn't care! Notice in the picture that Snoopy has space heaters to keep him warm. In real life, however, animals don't have heaters! People who have pets usually keep them inside, but what about other animals? How do animals in the wild keep warm? How do unheated shelters help animals stay warm?

Heating Up

You might remember the lizard absorbs energy from the sun to warm its body. The bodies of lizards don't produce their own heat. The bodies of lizards and many other animals in the world have the same temperature as their surroundings. But the bodies of other animals, such as dogs, deer, birds, and you, produce their own heat. These animals get heat from the energy in the food they eat. These animals don't have to depend on the sun to heat their bodies. The bodies of these animals are always warm and give off heat to their surroundings.

In the Discover Activity, you learned that heat always flows from warm places and objects to cooler ones. Let's see how this fact affects shelters.

PEANUTS reprinted by permission of UFS, Inc.

▲ *Of course, dogs don't really have space heaters, but some dogs might wish they did.*

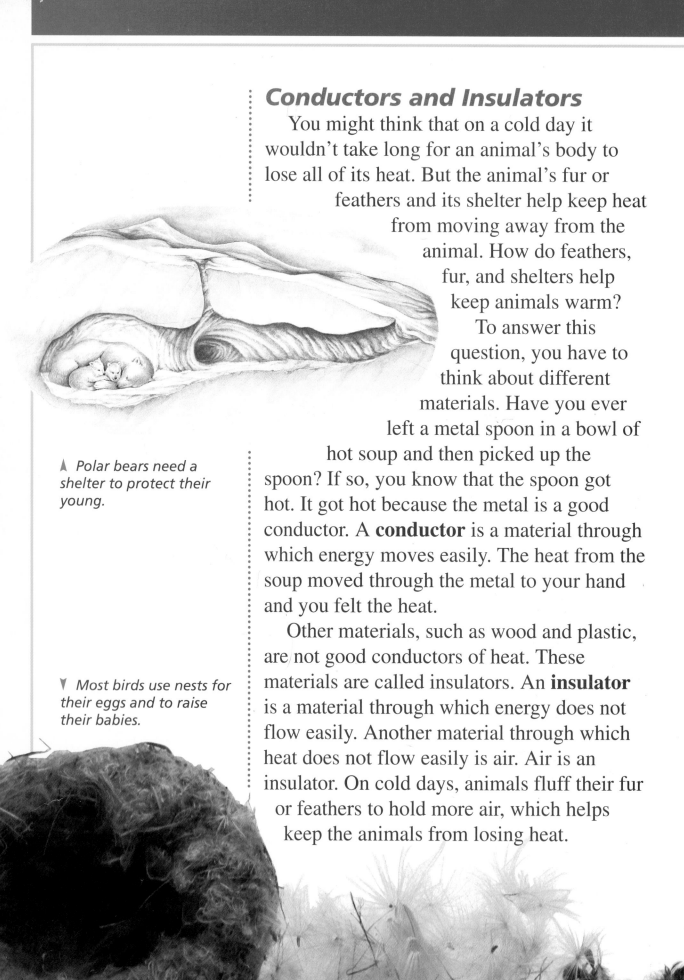

Conductors and Insulators

You might think that on a cold day it wouldn't take long for an animal's body to lose all of its heat. But the animal's fur or feathers and its shelter help keep heat from moving away from the animal. How do feathers, fur, and shelters help keep animals warm?

To answer this question, you have to think about different materials. Have you ever left a metal spoon in a bowl of hot soup and then picked up the spoon? If so, you know that the spoon got hot. It got hot because the metal is a good conductor. A **conductor** is a material through which energy moves easily. The heat from the soup moved through the metal to your hand and you felt the heat.

Other materials, such as wood and plastic, are not good conductors of heat. These materials are called insulators. An **insulator** is a material through which energy does not flow easily. Another material through which heat does not flow easily is air. Air is an insulator. On cold days, animals fluff their fur or feathers to hold more air, which helps keep the animals from losing heat.

▲ Polar bears need a shelter to protect their young.

▼ Most birds use nests for their eggs and to raise their babies.

When building their shelters, these animals use natural resources. These natural resources are often good insulators. Squirrels, for example, line their nests with moss, dried grasses, leaves, and bark. Birds, too, line their nests with materials that are good insulators. The bird's nest in the picture is lined with feathers and milkweed seeds such as those shown in the picture.

Even snow is an insulator because the snow has a lot of air trapped in it! The polar bear in the picture digs a tunnel in the snow. Then the bear packs down the snow at the end of the tunnel to make a den. The snow helps to keep the cold air out and the bear's body heat in.

Notice the picture of the hornet's nest. The nest is made of a thin paper that the hornet makes from wood. The paper and the air in the spaces between the layers of paper are insulators. However, a hornet's nest keeps heat out—not in. Insulators help keep heat from moving—either out of or into a shelter.

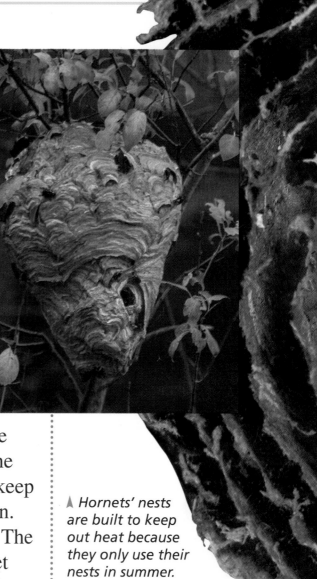

⋀ Hornets' nests are built to keep out heat because they only use their nests in summer.

Checkpoint

1. How do some animals produce heat in their bodies?
2. What does an insulator do?
3. **Take Action!** Make a diagram to show how conductors move heat from one object to another.

Activity

Using Insulators

What kinds of materials make good insulators? Try this activity to find out how some materials compare.

Picture A

Gather These Materials

cover goggles
3 plastic containers
3 small plastic bags
sand

shredded paper
3 small rubber bands
3 equal-sized ice cubes

Follow This Procedure

Picture B

Picture C

1. Make a chart like the one on the next page. Record your results in your chart.

2. Put on your cover goggles.

3. Fill the bottom of a plastic container about one-third full of sand. (Picture A)

4. Repeat step 3 with a second container using shredded paper. The paper should be packed down.

5. Do not put any insulating materials into a third container.

6. Place an ice cube in each of three plastic bags. Squeeze the air out of each bag and then seal it with a rubber band. (Picture B)

7. Set one of the bags in the empty container. This container with no insulation is your control.

Record Your Results

Container with	Description of ice cube
No insulation	Completely melted
Sand	
Shredded paper	

8 Place a bag on the insulating material in the middle of each of the other two containers. Surround each plastic bag with the same insulating material that is in the bottom of the container. Add material on top to fill the container and pack it down. (Picture C)

Predict: *In which container do you think the ice will melt the slowest?*

9 Observe the ice in the control container until it is completely melted. Then remove the plastic bag from the other two containers and observe the ice cubes. Record your results.

State Your Conclusions

1. In which container did the ice melt slowest?
2. Use what you know about insulators to explain your results.

Let's Experiment

How do you think the amount of insulation will affect how well the material insulates? Use what you know about scientific methods to find out.

2.2 *Using Fuel*

▶ *How do people heat their homes?*

On a cold, winter day, could you warm your home with body heat the way animals do? You could if your home were the size of a fox's burrow. You might also crowd large numbers of friends and relatives into your home. But over the years, people have found ways other than body heat to warm their homes.

History of Fuel

Thousands of years ago, people discovered how to start and use a fire. Fire gave people heat, light, and a way to cook. Early people used wood to start a fire. Wood is a **fuel**—a material that can be burned to produce useful heat. Remember that wood is a natural resource that comes from trees.

▼ *Over the years, people have used different fuels to heat their shelters.*

In 1776, people burned wood for cooking and heating their homes.

Keeping the furnace filled with coal was hard work.

Wood has been used as a fuel for a longer period of time than any other fuel. In fact, it is still used as a fuel in some countries. But by the 1800s in the United States, people started looking for another source of fuel.

People began to burn coal instead of wood. Look at the pictures showing the use of different fuels in the United States. Between 1885 and 1950, coal was in wide use. But coal is dirty! And as the picture shows, people had to put the coal into the furnace or have a machine to do it for them. Also, as some of the coal supplies began to be used up, coal became more costly. People began looking for other fuels.

By the 1950s, oil and natural gas began taking the place of coal. These fuels were cleaner and were easier for people to use. Oil and gas are still the most popular fuels for heating homes today. But some people heat their homes with electricity—which, of course, is often produced by using coal.

Oil is brought to homes by trucks and stored in a large tank.

This man is reading the meter that measures how much gas is used.

Energy Sources

People use many different sources of energy to heat their homes and cook their food. They also use energy sources to run their refrigerators, toasters, and other appliances. The graph below compares the different energy sources used in the United States. On a circle, or pie graph, such as this, the larger the section, or piece of the pie, the more that energy source is used. Use the graph to answer the questions.

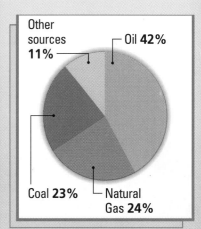

Other sources 11%
Oil 42%
Coal 23%
Natural Gas 24%

What Did You Find Out?
1. *Which energy source is used most?*
2. *Which energy source is used the least?*
3. *Which two energy sources are used about the same?*

Heat It Up!

Keeping warm air on the move

The rooms of a building get warm because the fire in the furnace heats the air in the furnace. Then the warm air is pushed through the ducts in the wall and into the rooms through open heat vents. The heated air moves through a room by convection. **Convection** is the flow of energy that occurs when warm air rises and cool air falls. The cold air vents on the walls allow cool air to return to the furnace. In the furnace, the cool air is warmed again and sent back through the house. In this way, the room and the rest of the house stay warm and cozy.

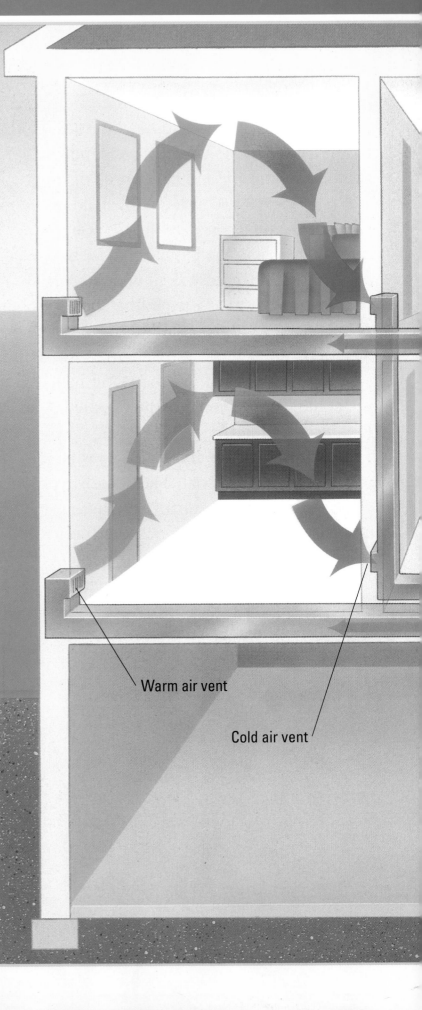

Warm air vent

Cold air vent

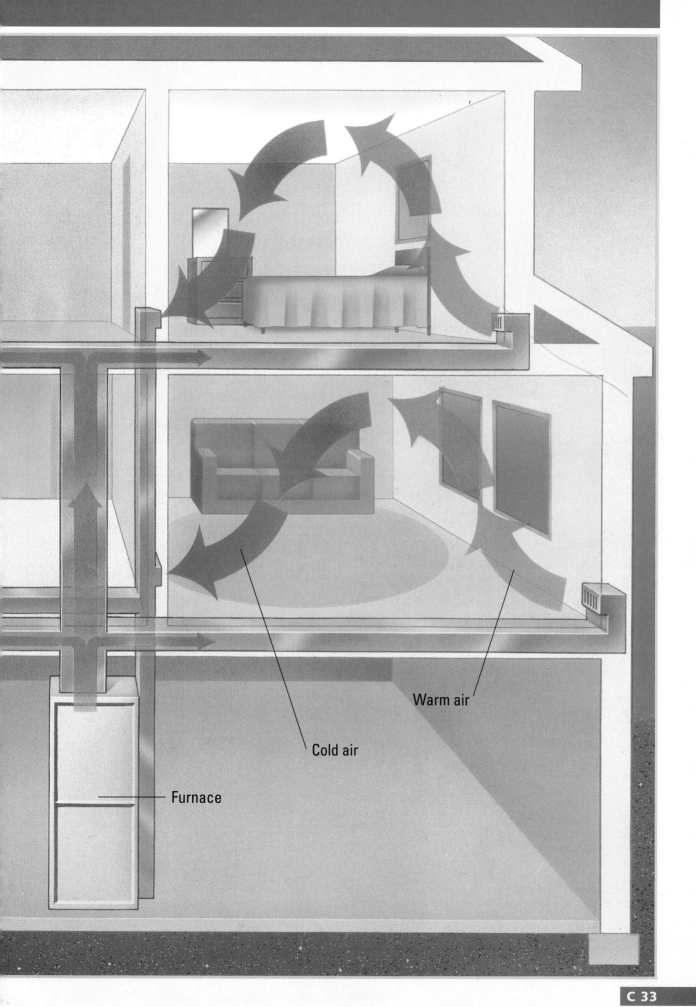

Warm air

Cold air

Furnace

Keeping Heat In or Out

People line their homes with insulators. Animals line their shelters with such natural resources as feathers and grass which are also good insulators. People and other animals have the same heating problem—how to keep the heat from escaping.

Since warm air rises, a lot of heat in a home escapes through the attic. To stop this heat loss, the man in the picture is putting insulation on the attic floor. He is using a fiberglass blanket that comes in rolls, as shown in the picture. Sometimes people pour or blow in pieces of fiberglass or other material between the floors and the ceilings or walls.

Heat can also be lost through and around the windows of a building. By covering windows with heavy drapes or shutters, heat loss can be cut down. Using storm windows also helps. Let's see how storm windows help to stop heat from escaping from a building.

▲ Insulation may also be put between the roof and the ceilings of rooms in a house.

➤ These windows also help keep heat from entering buildings in the summer.

▲ *Insulation in the walls and air between the window panes help keep the cold air out and warm air in.*

Putting a storm window outside of a window leaves an air space between the two windows. Air, as a good insulator, helps keep heat from escaping. Look at the windows in the pictures. These windows help keep heat in without storm windows. The windows will have two or three panes of glass with air between the panes.

Buildings also can lose a lot of heat through holes or cracks around windows and doors. To seal these cracks, you can use felt, plastic, rubber, or other insulating materials. In a well-insulated home, you'll be as snug and warm in winter as the girl in the picture. Insulation keeps heat from escaping from a building. And it also keeps cold air from getting in. Insulation also keeps heat from entering a shelter, as in the hornet's nest. Therefore, in hot weather, insulation will help your shelter stay cool! By using insulation, less energy is needed to heat or cool homes.

Into The Field

Can you find doors and windows that leak air?

Find a way to locate air leaks. Record what you discover.

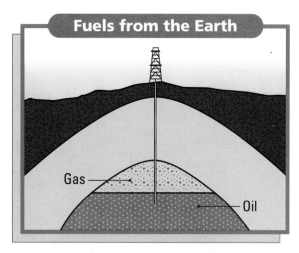

Fuels from the Earth

Gas

Oil

Fuel for Tomorrow

You're probably wondering why it's so important to insulate. It's important because the fuels used to heat and cool your home are limited natural resources.

Electricity is not a natural resource, but many power plants burn fossil fuels to produce electricity. Coal, oil, and gas are natural resources called fossil fuels. That's because they come from plants and animals that died millions of years ago. Look at the diagram showing where gas and oil are buried deep beneath the earth's surface. It takes millions of years for these resources to form.

No one knows how much oil, gas, and coal the earth contains. What is certain is the fact that at the rate people are using these fuels they will be gone soon. Most scientists predict that oil and gas will be used up in about fifty years. Coal supplies may last two hundred years more.

▼ *Coal can be mined from deep under the ground or from a strip mine.*

In time, new sources of fuel must be found as the world population grows. But for now, it is important to conserve fuel. To **conserve** fuel means to use resources carefully.

One way to conserve fuel is to use other sources of energy. Some people have built homes that are heated by energy from the sun—solar energy. Solar energy heats the house in this picture. Other houses make use of solar energy in another way. They have windows that face toward the south so a lot of sun shines into the house and warms it.

The best way people can conserve fuel is by insulating their homes. If a building is well-insulated, you burn less fuel to heat it. You also use less electricity to cool the building during hot weather. By using our resources wisely today, there will be more left for tomorrow.

▲ The black collectors on this solar house absorb energy from sunlight to heat the house.

Checkpoint

1. What are fossil fuels?
2. How does convection help heat move through a building?
3. How can people slow down heat loss from their homes?
4. Why is it important to conserve fuels?
5. **Take Action!** Find out from a family member what kind of fuel is used to heat your home.

Activity

Conserving Energy

Can windows with two panes help conserve energy? Try this activity using plastic bags to see what happens.

Picture A

Picture B

Picture C

Gather These Materials

cover goggles
small plastic bag
large plastic bag

2 ice cubes
2 small rubber bands
small dish

Follow This Procedure

1 Make a chart like the one on the next page. Record your results on your chart.

2 Put on your cover goggles.

3 Place an ice cube in the small plastic bag. (Picture A)

4 Seal the bag with a rubber band. (Picture B) *CAUTION: Be careful with the rubber band.*

5 Put the small plastic bag inside the large plastic bag. (Picture C)

6 Blow some air into the large plastic bag. Be careful not to burst the bag. Seal the bag.

7 Put the other ice cube in a small dish. Place the dish and the bag with the ice cube on a desk.

Predict: *What will happen to each ice cube?*

Record Your Results

	After 3 minutes	After 10 minutes
Ice cube in dish		
Ice cube in double plastic bags		

8 Watch what happens to each ice cube.

9 Describe what has happened to each ice cube after 3 minutes. Record what you see.

10 Record what the ice cubes look like after 10 minutes.

State Your Conclusions

1. What was the difference in the size of the ice cubes after 3 minutes? after 10 minutes?

2. Using what you know about heat and insulators, how do you explain the difference? Do you think windows with two panes of glass help conserve energy? Why or why not?

Let's Experiment

Do window curtains help conserve energy? Which kinds of curtains work best? Use what you know about scientific methods to find out.

Chapter Review

Reviewing Words and Concepts

Write the letter of the word or phrase that best completes each sentence.

1. A lizard has the same _____ as its surroundings.
2. The bodies of animals such as dogs and birds produce their own _____ from the energy in the food they eat.
3. An animal's _____ helps keep it from losing heat.
4. Materials through which energy moves easily are _____.
5. A material that can be burned to produce useful heat is a _____.
6. Oil and _____ are cleaner and easier to use than coal.
7. Materials through which energy does not flow easily are _____.
8. The flow of energy that occurs when warm air rises and cool air falls is called _____.
9. Using _____ energy in homes helps to conserve fuel.
10. To _____ means to use resources carefully.

a. insulators
b. convection
c. heat
d. fur
e. conductors
f. natural gas
g. fuel
h. conserve
i. solar
j. temperature

Connecting Ideas

1. Copy the concept map. Use the terms at the right to complete the map to show how heat moves.

conductor   air
metal   convection

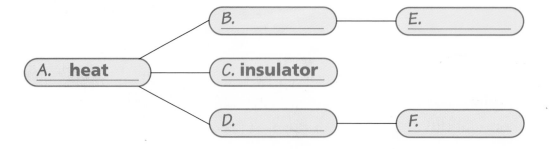

2. Write a sentence or two about the ideas shown in the concept map.

Interpreting What You Learned

1. Explain how feathers or fur can help keep an animal warm.
2. Why are coal, oil, and gas called fossil fuels?
3. How can the use of solar energy help conserve fuel?
4. Explain how heat gets from a furnace to the rest of the house.
5. How does insulating houses help conserve fuel?
6. How do storm windows help conserve energy?

Performance Assessment

How does a furnace move warm air?

Materials • cardboard tube • thermometer • straw • masking tape

Collecting Data

1. Read the temperature on the thermometer. Record your reading.
2. Hold the thermometer over one end of the cardboard tube. Tape the thermometer to the end of the tube. Make sure the bulb of the thermometer is over the opening in the tube.
3. Stand the cardboard tube on a table so the end with the thermometer is facing up.
4. Lift the edge of the tube and slide one end of the straw so it is under the tube.
5. Blow into the other end of the straw for one minute. Breathe in through your nose. Breathe out into the straw so your breath goes into the tube.
6. After one minute, read the temperature on the thermometer. Record your reading.
7. Draw a diagram of your mouth, the straw, the tube, and the thermometer. Add arrows to show how warm air moved.

Analyzing Data

Explain why the air temperature at the top of the tube changed.

3

Machines in Building

Wear cover goggles for this activity.

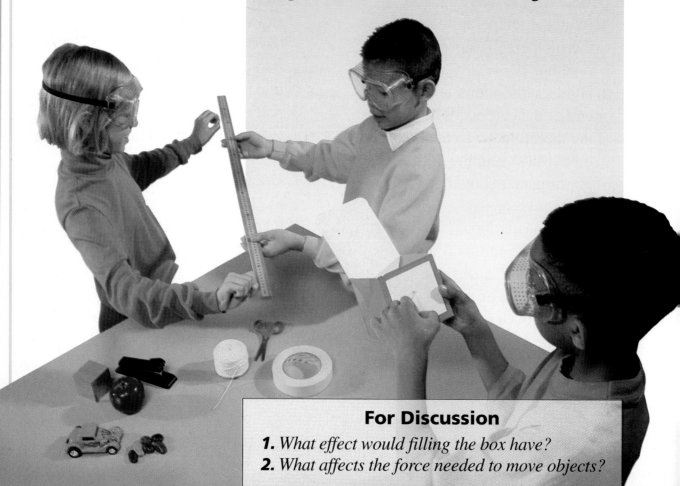

Discover Activity

How can you measure forces?

Cut a rubber band and pull on each end. Pull a little harder. What happens? Use a rubber band to measure force. Tie a piece of string to each end. Connect one end to a small box. Pull on the other end. Use the stretch of the rubber band to compare the force needed to move things.

For Discussion

1. *What effect would filling the box have?*
2. *What affects the force needed to move objects?*

3.1 Simple Machines and Work

▶ *How do simple machines help people to build shelters?*

You, too, can be a builder! Maybe you can't build a bird's nest or a beaver's lodge, but you can build a skyscraper. Does this idea sound impossible? With plastic blocks, you can build almost anything. These building blocks are light and snap together easily. You can join them in many different ways. Like the girl in the picture, all you need is time and imagination.

Building a real house is more difficult. Building materials are heavy and don't just snap together. You may need some tools to help you. Let's find out more about these tools and how they are used to help build shelters.

▼ *What is the girl building with the plastic blocks?*

Simple Machines

How are simple machines helpful in building a house?

Many tools are used to build a house. The six tools being used in the picture all use energy to do work. These tools are **simple machines**— machines with few or no moving parts. The wheelbarrow makes pushing heavy loads easy because its wheels are fastened together by an axle. Notice that the ramp is slanted so that the wheelbarrow moves up it easily. Nails are used to hold parts of the house together; sometimes screws are used instead. Why might a screw hold some things together better than a nail?

Nails are **wedges.**

The ramp is an **inclined plane.**

A **pulley** is used to lift large, heavy loads.

A **screw** is used to fasten things together.

The hammer is a **lever.**

The wheelbarrow has a **wheel and axle.**

⊿ *What kind of a simple machine is the ladder that the roofer in the pictures is using?*

Into The Field

When do you do work?

List ten activities that you might do today. Circle the activities in which you are doing work.

Push, Pull, and Lift

No matter how helpful simple machines are, the builder still has to do work. Work is something we all do. When you sweep a floor, pick up a book, or throw a ball you are doing work.

What, then, is work? To find the answer, look at the pictures of the roofer. In each picture, something is moving. First the man picks up the shingles. Then he moves the shingles from the ladder to the roof and nails them in place. The shingles move because something makes them move. What makes them move? Remember from the Discover Activity that the something that makes objects move is force.

A **force** is a push or a pull. For example, the man pulls to pick up the shingles. The force makes the shingles move. The work is the lifting of the shingles. **Work** is something done whenever a force makes an object move through a distance. Simple machines make work easier because the work takes less force.

Work or No Work

You're doing work when you throw a ball. But suppose you try to lift a heavy bundle of shingles. You try, but no matter how much force—or energy—you use, you can't lift the shingles. Have you done any work? The answer is no! No matter how much force you use, you are doing no work unless the object moves. So if you don't move the shingles, you are doing no work. However, if you throw a ball, you're doing work because the ball moves.

> ## Checkpoint
>
> 1. How do simple machines help in building shelters?
> 2. Where does the force come from when you pick up a book?
> 3. How do you know if you are doing work?
> 4. Take Action! Try to remove a nail from a piece of wood without and with a hammer. Explain the results.

Activity

Measuring Work

You know that it takes energy to do work. How much work can a marble do? Try this activity to find out.

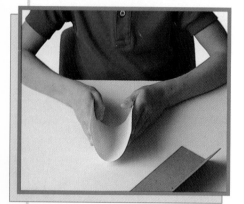

Picture A

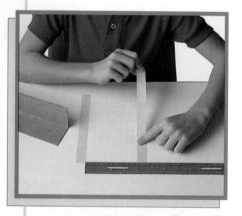

Picture B

Picture C

Gather These Materials

piece of cardboard, 10 cm X 30 cm
file card

masking tape
metric ruler
marble

Follow This Procedure

1. Make a chart like the one on the next page. Record your results on your chart.

2. Fold the cardboard in half lengthwise. Fold the file card in half widthwise. (Picture A)

3. Stick two pieces of masking tape on a table top about 10 cm apart. Each piece of tape should be about 10–15 cm long. (Picture B)

4. Place the file card next to the tape on your left, so that one of the surfaces of the card lies flat on the table. Lay the folded edge of the card along the left edge of the tape.

5. Place one end of the folded cardboard next to the edge of the other piece of tape. Raise the opposite end of the cardboard 1 cm above the table top. (Picture C)

Predict: **What will happen when the rolling marble hits the file card?**

6 Place the marble at the top of the raised cardboard track. Then, let the marble roll down the track to hit the folded file card.

7 Measure how far the marble moved the file card. Record your results.

8 Repeat steps 4–7 three more times, with the end of the cardboard raised to 3 cm, 6 cm, and 9 cm above the tabletop. Measure how far the file card moves each time.

Record Your Results

Height	Distance card moved
1 cm	
3 cm	
6 cm	
9 cm	

State Your Conclusions

1. How high was the end of the track when the file card moved the farthest?

2. How did raising the cardboard track affect the results?

3. Using what you know about work and force, explain how the marble was able to do work.

Let's Experiment

Now that you have seen how a marble can do work, what would happen if you use a marble that is twice as big as the one you used? Use what you know about scientific methods to find out.

▲ One beaver may cut down more than two hundred trees in a year!

▼ Notice the sharp edge of the beaver's front teeth.

3.2 *Animals' Simple Machines*

▶ *What body parts of animals are used as simple machines?*

Have you ever seen a bird swing an ax or a rabbit use a shovel to dig a hole? Of course you haven't! Animals don't have the simple machines that people use. But animals do have body parts that they use in much the same way that people use simple machines.

Wedges and Levers

Remember how well the beaver in the picture can cut down trees. To see how, notice the beaver's front teeth in the picture. They are shaped like the chisel shown in the picture. The beaver uses its teeth in the same way that a carpenter uses a chisel or a lumberjack uses an ax. These workers use wedges to split wood apart, and to cut or make holes in an object. The beaver does the same with its front teeth.

Though they have a different shape than beavers' teeth, the beaks of some birds are also wedges. Look at the picture of the woodpecker's beak. The woodpecker has a beak that is shaped like a thin chisel such as the one in the picture. Using its beak, the woodpecker in the picture is chipping away at the wood to make a hole in the tree. Then the woodpecker will use the hole for a nest.

Most birds can also use their beaks like a pair of tongs that you might find in the kitchen. Tongs are really two levers fastened together at one end. Birds use their beaks in this way to pick up and carry materials they use to build their nests.

Think for a minute about the size of a carpenter ant or a termite. These tiny animals do not have teeth, but they have strong jaws. Their jaws are shaped somewhat like the beak of a woodpecker. They can chisel their way through a rotten tree or the wooden frame of a house with no problem. Carpenter ants make their nests in dead trees and old lumber. Many termites also carve out their tunnels in dead wood, and they often move into the wooden parts of a person's house.

▲ The woodpecker is throwing chips of wood out of the hole it is chiseling.

▼ The woodpecker's beak and the chisel are tools that make work easier.

Claws as Machines

Many animals use their claws as wedges and levers to build shelters. Rabbits, for example, have claws that are perfect for digging burrows in the ground. Look at the close-up of the rabbit's paw. Notice that each toe ends in a claw that is curved and pointed. Each claw is like a small wedge that the rabbit uses to loosen the soil. The claws are also like "built-in shovels." A shovel is a lever. To lift out the dirt, the rabbit uses its claws and hind feet like people use the shovel in the picture.

▼ *The rabbit scoops out a hole to build a nest.*

Gophers also use their claws as wedges and levers to dig tunnels for shelters. One gopher can make a 90-meter tunnel in a single night.

Bears have sharp, powerful claws and paws that they use as shovels or crowbars. Using its claws and paws as shovels, a bear can dig a shelter out of snow or soil. Some bears use caves as shelters. If a rock is blocking the opening to a cave, the bear can easily move the rock. To move a rock, a bear uses its paw, claws, and leg as a crowbar. Because their front paws do the work, the claws on the front paws are longer than the claws on the back paws.

Besides using its beak as a wedge, the woodpecker can also use its claws as wedges. Woodpeckers have two toes pointed forward and two toes pointed backward. Each toe ends in a long, sharp, curved claw. Each claw is like a tiny pick, or wedge, that can dig into tree bark and hang on. The claws help keep a woodpecker from falling off the tree while the bird pecks out a hole.

Checkpoint

1. How are the beaks and teeth of some animals like wedges?
2. How are a rabbit's claws like a wedge and a lever?
3. **Take Action!** Bite into an apple. Draw a picture of the teeth marks. What simple machine do they look like?

Size of Birds' Nests

Birds use their beaks, feet, and claws as wedges and levers to build nests. Birds build nests of all sizes and shapes. The graphs below show how the size of a bird's nest compares with the size of the bird. Use the graphs to answer the questions:

Bird	Height of Nest (cm)
Hummingbird	3
Osprey	183
Eagle	45

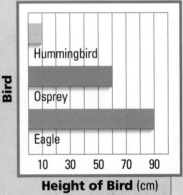

Height of Bird (cm)

What Did You Find Out?
1. How tall is an eagle? the eagle's nest?
2. How much taller is a hummingbird than the height of its nest?
3. Which of the three birds is tallest? Which nest is tallest?
4. How much taller is an eagle's nest than a hummingbird's nest?

Activity

Beaks as Tools

Why do you think different birds have different kinds of beaks? Try this activity to find out how different kinds of beaks work.

Picture A

Gather These Materials

cover goggles
pinch-type clothespin
glue
2 craft sticks, spoon,
   scissors, toothpick

10-12 pieces of each:
   uncooked macaroni,
   raisins, marbles,
   dry puffed cereal
small cup

Follow This Procedure

1 Make a chart like the one on the next page. Record your results on your chart.

2 Put on your cover goggles.

3 Holding the clothespin open, glue the sticks inside the clothespin. (Picture A) When the glue dries, the clothespin works like a long beak. The clothespin, scissors, toothpick, and spoon will be used as "beaks" to pick up food.

Picture B

4 Pretend these materials are different kinds of bird food: macaroni (worms), raisins (grubs), marbles (snails), and cereal (insects).

5 Scatter the "food" on a large table.

Predict: *How well will each "beak" work as a food gathering tool?*

Picture C

Record Your Results

	Macaroni	Raisins	Marbles	Cereal
Clothespin beak				
Scissors beak				
Toothpick beak				
Spoon beak				

6 Holding the clothespin at the pincer end, try to pick up and place in the cup as many pieces of "food" as you can in 2 minutes. (Picture B) Count how many pieces of each "food" you were able to pick up. Record your results. Empty the cup back onto the table.

7 Using the scissors like pincers, repeat step 6. Be careful with the scissors; keep them pointed down. (Picture C)

8 Repeat step 6 using the toothpick as a spear and then the spoon as a scoop. Use only one hand to get food with each "beak."

State Your Conclusions

1. Which "beak" worked best for getting different "food"?
2. Which "beak" would work better at crushing large seeds?

Let's Experiment

Now that you have seen how the "beaks" worked with these "foods," try picking up small bits of plastic foam floating in water.

Chapter Review

Reviewing Words and Concepts

Write the letter of the word or phrase that best completes each sentence.

1. Tools with few or no moving parts are _____.
2. Nails are _____ and are easy to pound into wood.
3. A ramp is an _____ that makes it easier to push heavy loads from one level to another.
4. To lift large, heavy loads, a person can pull on a rope attached to a _____.
5. Many animals use their _____ as wedges and levers to build shelters.
6. A wheelbarrow is a simple machine that has a _____.
7. Most birds can use their _____ in the way people use the two levers in a pair of tongs.
8. A push or a pull is a _____.
9. When a force makes an object move through a distance, _____ is done.
10. Simple machines make work _____ because the work takes less force.

a. claws
b. inclined plane
c. force
d. simple machines
e. pulley
f. easier
g. beaks
h. work
i. wedges
j. wheel and axle

Connecting Ideas

1. Copy the concept map. Use the terms at the right to complete the map to show how work is done.

work   **force**   **movement**

(A. _____) + (B. _____) = (C. _____)

2. Write a sentence or two about the ideas shown in the concept map.

Interpreting What You Learned

1. How are simple machines used to build a house?
2. Describe how a force can do work.
3. Explain why pushing hard on an object may not be work.
4. How does a beaver use its front teeth like a wedge?
5. How does a bear use its claws and legs as a lever?

  ## Performance Assessment

How much force can a bridge withstand?

Materials
- cover goggles
- 50 toothpicks
- 6 thick books
- paper cup
- metric ruler
- 50 1-cm balls of clay *(not modeling clay)*
- masses *(marbles or pennies)*

Collecting Data
Part A

1. Put on your cover goggles. Push one end of a toothpick into a ball of clay. Push the other end into another ball of clay.
2. Connect these with other toothpicks and other balls of clay. Build a bridge at least 15 centimeters long. You may use 50 toothpicks and 50 balls of clay.
3. Store your bridge overnight in a warm place so the clay hardens.

Part B

4. Put on your cover goggles. Make two stacks of books at least 15 centimeters high and 10 centimeters apart. Be sure the stacks are the same height.

5. Bend a paper clip to make an "S" shape. Poke the bottom of the "S" through the rim of a paper cup.
6. Place your bridge so it connects the stacks of books. Hang the paper clip and paper cup from the bottom of the bridge.
7. Add marbles or pennies one at a time to the paper cup. Add them until the bridge sags and finally breaks. Record the amount of force needed to break the bridge.

Analyzing Data
How could you strengthen your bridge so more force would be needed to break it?

Kid Inventor Beats the Cold

Chester Greenwood's ears made him famous. The only thing unusual about his ears was that they hurt when they got cold. This was a big problem for Chester because he grew up in Farmington, Maine. The winters there are very cold. But Chester found a way to beat the cold.

In 1873, Chester got ice skates for his fifteenth birthday. He rushed outside to try the skates on a frozen pond near his house. At first Chester had fun racing around on the ice. But before long his ears began to ache and he had to go back indoors.

The next time Chester wanted to go skating, he tied a wool scarf around his head. The scarf kept him warm,

Winters in Farmington, Maine, got very cold.

but it was so itchy that Chester didn't even get to the pond. What Chester needed was a way to keep only his ears warm. But what could he do?

Then Chester had an idea—ear flaps! He bent pieces of wire into loops and had his grandmother sew fur on one side of the loop for warmth. She sewed velvet on the other side of the loop for softness. Then his grandmother used a wire to fasten the loops to Chester's cap. On his next trip to the pond, Chester found that his fur-covered ear flaps worked. His ears were warm at last.

Other people saw Chester's ear flaps and wanted some for themselves. Chester's grandmother and mother were soon busy making

lots of ear flaps for neighbors and friends.

At 19, Chester patented his invention. This means that he was on record as the inventor of earmuffs. Anyone who made and sold earmuffs would have to pay Chester a certain amount of money. As you may guess, Chester went into the earmuff business. He set up a factory in town and designed earmuff-making machines. He was on his way to making Farmington the earmuff capital of the world. Chester's inventing didn't stop at earmuffs.

The fur-covered ear flaps worked. His ears were warm at last!

He went on to make more than 100 other inventions. What is special about inventors like Chester? They do not have to go to college. And inventors don't even have to be adults! But whatever their age, inventors are curious. They want to know how things work. They are good at noticing problems, and they want to think of a way to solve them. You might be an inventor too.

On Your Own

Do you think that other things people use everyday were invented because someone had a problem? Try to find out who invented some other things that people use everyday–such as a light bulb, the telephone, or the radio. How were these things invented?

Outside with the Animals

Celina Gonzales

Occupation: Zoo Keeper
Hobbies: Horseback riding and playing with her dogs

When Celina was young, her parents were always telling her to come inside. If she had her way, she would stay outside all day long with her cats and dogs. Now Celina has her way. She stays outside all day with the animals at the San Antonio Zoo. Celina Gonzales is a zoo keeper.

What does a zoo keeper do?

"Mainly we feed and clean up after the animals. We also keep an eye on them in case they are sick or hurt."

Can you play with the animals?

"No, you always have to remember that the animals at the zoo are not tame. Zoo animals are wild. You never know when one of them might attack you. Some of the animals, like the squirrel monkeys, will jump on my back, and I feed them peanuts from my hand. But I would never pick them up or play with them—they might bite."

What do the animals eat?

"Most of them eat a prepared food called chow along with vegetables and fish. When I feed the animals, I move slowly and quietly so they don't get scared."

What's the best part of working at the zoo?

"I guess the best part is just getting to be outside, working with all of the animals. However, it is hard work. Cleaning up after the animals isn't that much fun. But cleaning is important—it helps keep the animals from getting sick. I really like taking care of the animals. And as I work with them, I am also learning more about them."

Solar Heating: Building Shelters

What happens to a sidewalk on a sunny day? It absorbs energy from the sun and gets warm. The sun's energy can be captured to use for warming homes. This process is called solar heating.

1 A flat metal plate called a solar collector, or solar panel, can be mounted on the roof to collect the sun's energy and become warm.

2 Many solar heating systems use water to heat the home; warm water moves through pipes inside the house.

3 The water is carried into a heat exchanger inside a water tank; this process warms a separate water supply used for bathing and washing.

4 The water circulates up through pipes into the collector; in the collector, heat from the panel warms the water.

Find Out On Your Own

Place a can covered with black paper and a can covered with white paper in the sun. Fill both with water and find out which will become warmer. Record the results.

Module Performance Assessment

Conservation Fair

Using what you learned in this module, help prepare a Conservation Fair for your school. Complete one or more of the following activities. You may work by yourself or with others in a group.

Photography

Prepare a videotape or photo exhibit to illustrate your thoughts about conserving natural resources. Be sure to include spoken comments for the videotape or written comments for the photo exhibit.

Music

Write words to a song about conserving natural resources. You may use music from a song you already know or compose your own. Teach the song to a group of classmates and perform it for the fair.

Art

Make a drawing of a house. Show where to insulate the house to prevent heat loss.

Investigation

Talk to members of your family, your neighbors, and friends. Find out what actions they are taking to conserve natural resources. Make a chart or poster to show good ideas for conserving natural resources.

Writing

What if you were a candidate to be a member of your community's school board? What would you do to improve your school building? What would you do to conserve energy and other natural resources? Write a campaign slogan telling why you should be elected.

Module Review

Reviewing Words and Concepts

Write the letter of the word or phrase that best completes each sentence.

1. Work is made easier to do by using ____.
2. Even today, the kind of ____ that people build depends on where they live.
3. Trees, stones, and iron ores are kinds of ____ that people use to build shelters.
4. Squirrels line their nests with ____, such as moss, leaves, and bark.
5. Coal, oil, and natural gas are fossil ____.
6. Heated air from a furnace moves through a room by ____.
7. One way to ____ fuel is to use other sources of energy.
8. When you move an object, you have done ____.
9. Nails and ____ are simple machines used to hold parts of a house together.
10. When simple machines are used, the work takes less ____.

a. insulators
b. convection
c. force
d. shelters
e. simple machines
f. conserve
g. fuels
h. work
i. screws
j. natural resources

Interpreting What You Learned

1. How do conductors and insulators affect the flow, or movement, of energy?
2. Why do we need to conserve fossil fuels and not solar energy?
3. Explain how animals are able to build shelters without tools and machines. Give an example.
4. What different kinds of natural resources do people use to build shelters?

Applying What You Learned

1. Compare the building of a beaver's lodge to the building of a person's house. How are they the same? How are they different?
2. Suppose you built a snow house and sat in it for a half hour. Would you be warm or cold? Explain why.
3. Compare solar energy to a fossil fuel. How are they the same? How are they different?

Moving

Moving

Could an animal live without moving a muscle? Not for long! Animals need to keep moving in order to survive. In this module, you'll find out why animals are always on the move. You'll also see how plants and objects are able to get around. And you'll learn how people's ways of traveling have changed.

CHAPTER

1 Ways of Moving

How can seeds move without legs? Like many living things, seeds can move in amazing ways, even without legs!

CHAPTER

2 Moving to Survive

Let's get out of here! When hot days turn cold, some animals head for warmer lands.

CHAPTER 3 People on the Move

It's time to check your oil.
Modern cars go fast, but they also pollute the air. The future may belong to other types of vehicles.

Ways of Moving

Hey, look how far it went!

How can you move a cotton ball?

Pretend that a cotton ball is a small seed. Place it on your desk. Think of different ways you can move the cotton ball. Then try out your ideas. Which ways work best?

For Discussion

1. How can you move it without touching it?
2. How can water be used to move it?

How Seeds Are Scattered

▶ **How can seeds be moved?**

You hop over each crack as you walk along the sidewalk. Here's something you didn't see before. A small plant, like the one in the picture, is growing in a crack in the sidewalk. You remember that most plants grow from seeds. How did a seed get here?

Scattering Seeds

Suppose you planted seeds in a garden. You probably would spread out the seeds in soil. When seeds are scattered, each seed gets more space. If conditions are right, the seeds can germinate. When new plants are spread apart, they are better able to get enough water and sunlight to live and grow.

◀ *This plant grew from a seed.*

In the Discover Activity, you moved a cotton ball in different ways. Seeds can be moved in different ways, too. For example, you can use your own energy to move seeds around. Energy from wind, moving water, and animals also helps scatter seeds.

Wind, Water, and Seeds

Think about the seeds in such fruits as tomatoes and oranges. Fruits develop from a plant's flowers. The fruits cover and protect a plant's seeds.

Energy from wind scatters the fruits of many plants. Dandelions, like those in the picture, produce fruits with tiny hairs. Maybe you've seen these fruits floating in the wind like tiny kites. A gentle breeze can carry dandelion fruits long distances.

Coconuts, like the one in the picture on the left, are fruits of a palm tree. Do you think they can float in the air? No, they're too heavy. But they can float in ocean waters to faraway places.

▼ A palm tree and coconut with a seed

➤ Dandelion fruits and seeds

How Animals Scatter Seeds

You hike along a wooded path. Later, you find small, sticky objects clinging to your clothes. These objects can be fruits. The fruits of some plants are burs. They have small hooks that help them stick to your clothes!

Burs also catch on a mammal's fur or a bird's feathers. Animals can carry burs a long distance before the seeds inside the burs fall to the ground.

That's not the only way animals help scatter seeds. Animals may eat fruits and drop the seeds to the ground. Birds and other animals also eat fruits, such as the rose fruits in the picture. Later, the seeds of these fruits pass through the animals' bodies and drop to the ground. Then what might happen to the seeds?

Into The Field

How do animals scatter seeds?

Observe several different kinds of animals. Tell how you think each one might scatter seeds.

▼ Birds eat fruits with seeds.

Checkpoint

1. How can scattering seeds help plants?
2. Name some fruits that can be scattered by wind and water.
3. How can animals scatter seeds?
4. **Take Action!** Design and draw a fruit that can be carried by wind, water, or animals.

Activity

Seeds Get Around

Fruits and seeds don't have legs. Yet, they move away from the parent plant. How do they do this?

Picture A

Picture B

Picture C

Gather These Materials

cover goggles
different kinds of seeds
  and fruits with seeds

bowl
water
fake "fur"

Follow This Procedure

1 Make a chart like the one on the next page. Record your observations in your chart.

2 Put on your cover goggles.

3 Your teacher will tell you the names of the different seeds being used. Draw one seed of each kind in your chart.

Predict: Which of the seeds that you have will float in water?

4 Fill a small bowl with water. See if the seeds will float. (Picture A) Record your results.

Predict: Which of your seeds will stick to the "fur"?

5 Hold a piece of "fur" up with one hand. Toss one of each kind of seed against the fur. Which of the seeds stick? (Picture B) Record your results.

Record Your Results

Seed name	Seed diagram	Floats in water	Sticks to animals	Twirls in air	Floats in air

Predict: Do some seeds twirl in the air or float in the air?

6 Some seeds are carried by wind. Hold one of each kind of seed. Drop them. Which seeds twirl in the air instead of dropping straight down? (Picture C) Record your results.

7 Some seeds can float in the air. Try blowing one of each kind of the seeds in the air. Which seeds float? Record your results.

State Your Conclusions

1. What are some special features of seeds that float in water?
2. What are some special features of seeds that stick to animal fur?
3. What are some special features of seeds that float in air?

Let's Experiment

Imagine that a cotton ball is a seed. How would you change it so that it could be spread by water, wind, or animal fur? Use what you know about scientific methods to find out.

1.2 Using Energy to Move

▶ **How do people and animals move?**

It's not easy moving your body through a strong wind! The gusts of air push against you as you walk. In the last lesson, you learned how the energy from wind, from moving water, and from animals can move seeds to distant places.

Do you use energy when you move? You probably know the answer to that question. Whenever you move your body, you use energy. But you don't get your energy from wind. You get it from the food you eat.

How People Move

Notice how the boy in the picture moves his body. Now raise your arm into the air. Wiggle your toes. How can you move your body in so many different ways? Your bones and muscles work together to help you move.

You have more than 200 bones in your body. All your bones together make up your **skeleton** (skel′ ə tən). Your skeleton helps hold your body up and give it shape. Your bones also protect parts of your body, such as your brain, heart, and lungs.

▲ Using bones and muscles to move

Find where the arm bones meet at the elbow in this picture of the skeleton. A **joint** is a place in the skeleton where bones fit together. Different kinds of joints help you move in different ways. Your elbow joint allows you to move your lower arm back and forth. Your shoulder joint allows you to move your whole arm around in a big circle.

The picture shows how muscles and bones work together. Muscles work in pairs. When you bend your knee, one muscle relaxes. The other muscle **contracts** (kən trakts′), or becomes shorter. **Tendons** (ten′ dəns) are parts of your body that look like thin ropes. They attach your muscles to your bones. When your muscle contracts, tendons pull the bones. The pulling makes the bones move. The next time you bend your leg, think about how your muscles and bones are working.

▼ *The human skeleton*

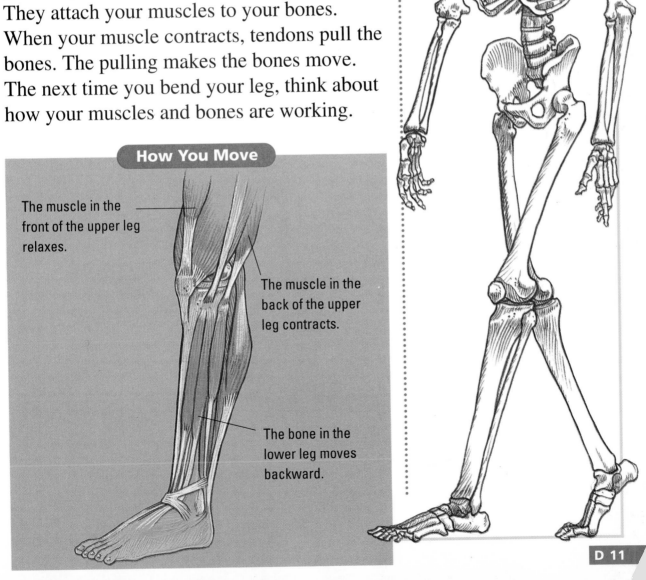

How You Move

The muscle in the front of the upper leg relaxes.

The muscle in the back of the upper leg contracts.

The bone in the lower leg moves backward.

Animals in Motion

Animals move in different ways.

The perch moves through water by contracting muscles on one side of its body, while the muscles on the other side relax. Then it repeats this action with the muscles on the opposite side.

The sidewinder moves across sand by looping a section of its body sideways. Then it lifts this section in front of its head. As it lifts its head and moves it forward, the snake's body moves forward.

This mallard can flap its wings and take off from water or land. The bullfrog leaps forward by using its muscles to suddenly straighten its strong back legs.

Perch

Sidewinder

Mallard duck

Bullfrog

How Other Animals Move

Suppose you are in a submarine deep under the sea. You wonder if the amazing animals move their bodies the same way you do. Whoosh! An octopus, like the one below, swims by the window. It stretches its eight arms through the water. An octopus uses its arms for catching food. On each arm, an octopus has round muscles that act like suction cups. They can hold on to anything the octopus catches.

An octopus has no bones. Most octopuses have no shells either. How can they move? An octopus uses its muscles to draw water into its body. As the octopus contracts its muscles to force the water out again, the octopus moves backward.

The clam below has no bones. Hard top and bottom shells protect its soft body. A clam pushes its foot out from between its shells and grabs the mud on the ocean floor. Then, the strong foot muscles contract, pulling the clam's body toward the foot. Clams work hard to move!

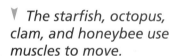
▼ The starfish, octopus, clam, and honeybee use muscles to move.

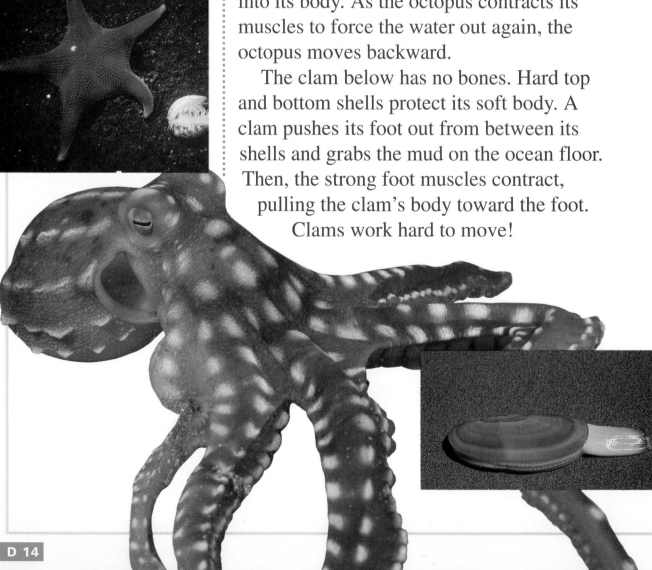

A starfish, like the one on the left page, has a hard shell under a thin layer of skin. A starfish stretches its arms to move. Each arm has little feet, which can grab an object and pull the starfish along. Strong muscles help a starfish twist and turn its body.

Crabs are animals with **exoskeletons** (ek′ sō skel′ ə təns), hard coverings that support the body. Each leg is connected to its exoskeleton by muscles. These muscles move the legs. Insects also have exoskeletons. This honeybee has muscles under its exoskeleton that move its legs and wings.

An earthworm is another interesting animal that has no bones. An earthworm wiggles through the soil by contracting and relaxing sets of muscles.

You can see that you do have something in common with most other animals. You contract and relax your muscles to move.

Checkpoint

1. How do muscles work in pairs?
2. How does a frog move?
3. What animals have exoskeletons?
4. **Take Action!** Learn an exercise to stretch your muscles. Teach it to your classmates.

INVESTIGATE

Stick-on Starfish

How can you use a medicine dropper to discover how a starfish moves? Let's investigate and find out.

What To Do
A. Cut out a square of paper 4 by 4 centimeters.
B. Hold the paper on the palm of your hand and try to pick it up using a dropper. Record the results in a chart like the one below.
C. Wet the paper again and try to pick it up using the dropper. Record the results in your chart.

Record Your Results

	Dry Paper	Wet Paper
Picked up with dropper		

What Did You Find Out?
1. *The many feet of a starfish are somewhat like the dropper. The feet have suction disks on their ends. Explain how the feet of a starfish might work as the starfish moves about.*
2. *Would it be easier for a starfish to move over a dry surface or a wet surface? How do you know?*

Activity

Watching Those Moves

Every animal has a different way of moving. But, what if an animal has no legs? How does it move?

Picture A

Picture B

Picture C

Gather These Materials

plastic jar	cornmeal
large spoon	apple peels
potting soil	leaves
black paper	water
scissors	earthworms
tape	paper towel
aluminum foil	metric ruler

Follow This Procedure

1 Make a chart like the one on the next page. Record your observations in your chart.

2 Make a habitat for the earthworms. Use the spoon to fill a large plastic jar with potting soil. Don't pack down the soil. (Picture A)

3 Use black paper to make a sleeve that fits around your jar. Tape the sleeve in place. (Picture B) Cover the jar with aluminum foil. Use a pencil to poke holes in the foil.

4 Mix some cornmeal, apple peels, and leaves into the soil. (Picture C) Moisten the soil with water. Then, put some earthworms on the soil.

Predict: *Without legs, how does an earthworm move?*

Record Your Results

	Body diagram	Body length
Stretched		
Shortened		

5 After a few minutes, remove the black sleeve and observe how the earthworms move into the soil.

6 Place one worm onto a moist paper towel. Keep the worm and paper towel moist as you make your observations.

7 Wait for the worm to stretch itself out. Then, measure its length in cm. Record your results. Make a drawing of your stretched worm.

8 Watch what happens to the length of the worm's body as it moves. Measure its length in cm as it shortens. Record your results.

9 Make a drawing of your worm as it shortens. Return the worm to the jar when finished.

State Your Conclusions

1. Describe how an earthworm moves. Remember, it does have body muscles.
2. Explain why an earthworm could not move if it had no muscles.

Let's Experiment

Will an earthworm move faster or slower on moist wax paper or on moist sandpaper? Use what you know about scientific methods to find out.

Chapter Review

Reviewing Words and Concepts

Write the letter of the word or phrase that best completes each sentence.

1. Energy from wind, moving water, and animals helps to _____ seeds.
2. The places where the bones of a skeleton fit together are _____.
3. When seeds are scattered, the new plants are better able to get enough water and _____ to live and grow.
4. When one muscle of a pair relaxes, the other muscle _____, or becomes shorter.
5. A ropelike part of the body that attaches muscles to bones is a _____.
6. The fruits of a plant cover and protect the _____.
7. All the bones of the body make up the _____.
8. A bullfrog leaps forward by using its _____ to suddenly straighten its back legs.
9. Crabs and insects are animals with _____, hard coverings that support the body.
10. Animals such as the octopus and earthworm have no bones to _____ their bodies.

a. tendon
b. seeds
c. contracts
d. scatter
e. skeleton
f. joints
g. sunlight
h. muscles
i. support
j. exoskeletons

Connecting Ideas

1. Copy the concept map. Use the terms at the right to complete the map about seeds and animals moving.

   bones   wind
   water   animals
   muscles

   A. seeds

   B. _____
   C. _____

2. Write a sentence or two about the ideas shown in the concept map.

   D. _____

   E. _____
   F. _____

Interpreting What You Learned

1. Why is your skeleton important?
2. How do joints help your body move in different ways?
3. How do tendons help your muscles and bones work together?
4. Describe how a perch swims.
5. Explain what happens when a muscle contracts.
6. How are animals without skeletons able to move?
7. How is an exoskeleton different from your skeleton?

Performance Assessment

How does a clam move?

Materials • cutout clam *(for tracing)* • construction paper • straw • stapler • scissors • metric ruler • pencil • masking tape

Collecting Data

1. Using the cutout clam your teacher gives you, trace two clams on the piece of construction paper.
2. Cut out the clams you traced. Place one cutout clam on top of the other. Staple the sides together.
3. Starting at the back of your clam, push the straw between the sheets of paper toward the front of the clam. Push until the straw sticks out of the front of the clam. The straw represents the clam's foot.
4. Model the movement of a clam. Push the straw forward as far as it will go. Then slide the clam forward toward the front of the straw. Repeat this movement several times.
5. Use the metric ruler to measure a distance of 1 meter on a table. Use two pieces of tape to mark the distance.
6. Starting at one piece of tape, hold the clam still and push the straw toward the other piece of tape. Then hold the straw still and move the clam to the end of the straw.
7. Do this until you reach the other piece of tape. Count how many times your clam moves its foot to go 1 meter. Record your results.

Analyzing Data

How would the length of a clam's foot affect how many times it would have to move to go 1 meter?

2

Moving to Survive

I didn't know there were so many kinds of birds in my yard.

Discover Activity

Why do birds move?

You can learn a lot about birds just by observing them. To attract birds, make a simple bird feeder like the one shown below. Fill the bottom of the feeder with bird seed. Hang your feeder outside in a tree. Observe the birds that visit your feeder.

For Discussion

1. Why did the birds move?
2. How did the birds move?

2.1 *Meeting Needs*

> **What are some reasons animals move?**

Suppose you are going on a camping trip. What things will you need? You might first think about food and water. And don't forget the tent. It will provide a safe shelter. Don't forget sleeping bags to keep you warm. You move quickly, reaching and bending and turning, to collect all the things you need.

Why Animals Move

Like you, other animals move in different ways to get the things they need. What are some things animals need? They need food and water. How do the monkeys in the picture move to get food? Animals move to find shelter and space to live, too. As you read, you'll also learn about interesting ways animals move to protect themselves.

▼ *Monkeys move to find and get food.*

Motion for Survival

Animals move for food and protection.

The hermit crab carries its home on its back. This crab wears an empty shell for protection as it moves. As the hermit crab grows larger, its shell home stays the same size. So the crab must find a larger shell to move into for protection.

Flamingos eat saltwater plants or small shellfish. These colorful birds will fly hundreds of kilometers to find this food. Flamingos protect themselves by staying in large flocks or flying away. If an enemy comes near, the flock might all rush toward the enemy at once to scare it.

Hermit crab

Flamingo

Gazelle

Sea lion

The Thomson's gazelle is one of the fastest animals on the open plains and grasslands of East Africa. Gazelles can run as fast as 80 kilometers per hour. When one gazelle spots an enemy, such as a pack of wild dogs, it will bounce with stiff legs to warn the other gazelles. Then all the gazelles will bounce to warn one another and run in all directions.

With its strong front flippers, the sea lion can swim underwater much better than it can move on land. It often dives into the water for safety. The search for food takes sea lions wherever fish and shrimp are easy to catch. Sea lions keep their young safe in hard-to-reach places.

▲ *A hummingbird*

Moving to Find Food and Water

It's surprising how many different ways animals move to find and catch food! Here's one clever way a chimpanzee gets food. It makes a tool by tearing the leaves off a small tree branch. Then the chimpanzee uses this tool to poke deep inside an ant's nest. After a short time, the chimpanzee pulls out a stick covered with ants for eating!

Picture a giraffe stretching its long neck to nibble at leaves in a tall tree. But to get water, a giraffe must spread its front legs apart. Then it bends its long neck down to drink water. From that position, it's not easy keeping track of nearby enemies! To protect themselves, giraffes take turns drinking. While some giraffes drink, others watch for lions or other enemies.

In the Discover Activity, you observed birds moving. Birds move in many unusual ways to gather food. A tiny hummingbird, like the one pictured, flaps its wings so quickly that all you can see is a blur. This bird hovers in the air, getting food from flowers through its long, thin beak.

Into The Field

How do animals move when they seek food or protection?
Observe several animals. Explain why you think they move the way they do.

An elephant uses its trunk to pick up an object as small as a peanut or an object as large as a tree. How do the elephants in the picture put food in their mouths? They put food in their mouths with their trunks. Elephants also take up water with their trunks. Then they drink by spraying the water into their mouths.

Hawks are large and powerful birds. They soar in circles over fields and streams searching for food. When they see a small animal they can eat, such as a rabbit or fish, the hawks swoop down to catch it with their sharp talons. Some hawks even knock other birds out of the air and eat them.

Cattle egrets (ē′ grets) are birds that move in flocks and work together to eat. Some of these birds flap their wings in tall grass to disturb the insects hidden there. Other egrets snap up these insects for food. Then, the egrets trade places so that each of them has a chance to eat.

▲ *African elephants*

Checkpoint

1. Why do animals move?
2. How does a gazelle move for protection?
3. Explain how three animals move to get food and water.
4. **Take Action!** Draw a picture of an imaginary animal. Show how the animal moves to get food.

Activity

Let's Get Out Of Here

Earthworms can tell if something is dangerous. What do they do when danger is present?

Picture A

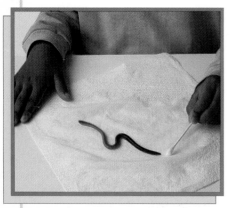
Picture B

Picture C

Gather These Materials

habitat with
  earthworms
paper towel

water
cotton swab

Follow This Procedure

1 Make a chart like the one on the next page. Record your observations in your chart.

2 Remove an earthworm from its habitat. Place the earthworm onto a moist paper towel. Be sure to keep the worm and towel moist throughout this activity. (Picture A)

> **Predict: Can an earthworm sense a sound? What will it do if it does?**

3 Slap your desk top near the worm. Observe the worm. Record what you see.

> **Predict: What will an earthworm on a moist paper towel do if it is touched?**

4 Gently touch a cotton swab to the front, middle, and tail end of your worm. (Picture B) Observe the worm. Record what you see.

Record Your Results

Your action	What worm does
Slap on desk	
Touched while on paper towel	
Touched while on soil	

Predict: *What will an earthworm do if it is touched while on top of soil?*

5 Place your worm back into its habitat. Touch it gently with the cotton swab. (Picture C) Record what the worm does.

State Your Conclusions

1. Can earthworms sense sound and know when they are being touched? How do you know?

2. Based on your observations, how might an earthworm protect itself from danger? Why is this important to the worm?

Let's Experiment

Place vinegar on a cotton swab. How does an earthworm react if it is touched with the vinegar? Does the front, middle, or tail of the earthworm sense the vinegar? Use what you know about scientific methods to find out.

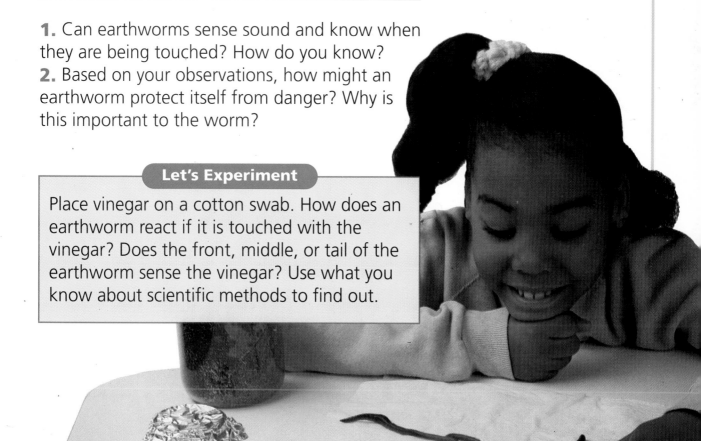

Moving From Place to Place

▶ *Why do animals travel long distances?*

Suppose you and your family take a trip. You might take a vacation or visit a relative. Many animals travel, too. Let's find out why.

Traveling Over Land

Many animals **migrate** (mī′ grāt), or move from one place to another. Animals often migrate in search of food and shelter when seasons change. Zebras, such as those in the picture, migrate in large groups. During the dry season in Tanzania, Africa, grasses and other plants do not grow well in the southern part of the Serengeti National Park. The zebras migrate toward the west and north where more rain falls and grass grows. The map on the next page shows the migration routes of the zebras.

▼ *A herd of zebras*

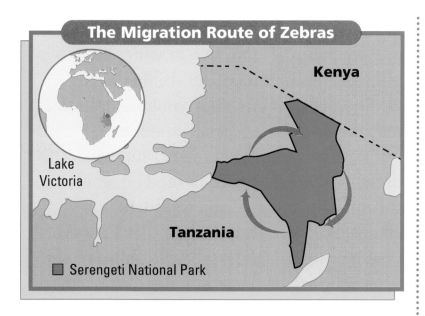

The Migration Route of Zebras

Lake
Victoria

Kenya

Tanzania

☐ Serengeti National Park

Every year, the caribou (kar′ ə bü) of northern Canada travel hundreds of kilometers. When winter snow and ice cover their feeding grounds, these large, brown deer can no longer find plants to eat. They travel south in search of food and shelter. When spring arrives, the caribou return to their northern habitat. The snow is melting, and the caribou can again find food. Each time the caribou migrate, they follow the same route.

Some animals, such as deer, bears, and monkeys, often wander short distances for food. During a year, these short trips may add up to a lot of travel!

Another type of animal traveler, the male polar bear, wanders alone over the cold, icy land near the North Pole. It searches for seals, otters, and fish to satisfy its hunger.

Traveling In Water

Some animals that live in water also migrate. Finding food, surviving cold weather, and having their young are three reasons why these animals migrate.

During the summer, many blue whales live in the Arctic Ocean. They feed on small, shrimp-like animals called krill. When winter comes, the krill move deeper into the ocean to avoid the cold. The whales cannot feed in such deep water. They migrate to warmer seas near Mexico to find food. You can see their path by looking at the map below. Blue whales follow the same route every year.

Salmon, like those on the next page, live part of their lives in freshwater streams and part in the ocean. They begin their lives in freshwater streams. They live in these streams for three or four years. Then, schools of salmon follow the streams to rivers, and the rivers to the open seas.

▼ *Blue whale*

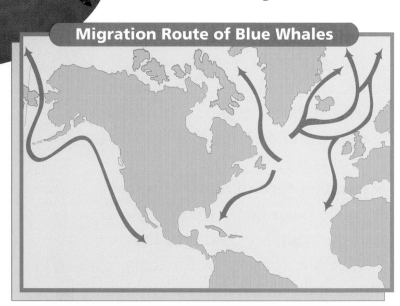

Migration Route of Blue Whales

Salmon live in the ocean for several years. Then, the salmon find the same river they swam down before! How do salmon find their way? The answer might have something to do with the salmon's sense of smell.

Night and day, salmon keep swimming up the river. Even waterfalls don't stop them. They flip and twist to swim up and over waterfalls in great leaps. Finally, they reach the streams in which they hatched. The map shows the migration route that some Atlantic salmon follow.

When a salmon reaches the freshwater stream, the female digs a hole in the bottom of the stream. There, it lays many tiny eggs and then dies. When the eggs hatch, the young salmon live and grow in the fresh water. Then the young salmon begin their long journey to the sea.

▲ *Atlantic salmon*

Migration Route of Atlantic Salmon

Traveling Through Air

It's a cool day in late autumn. Suddenly, you hear loud honking noises. In the distance, you see a flock of geese like the flock in the picture on the left. The birds are flying south. You might notice that the geese fly in the shape of the letter *V.*

Like many other kinds of birds, these geese are flying to warmer places. That way, they can find plenty to eat all winter. They can also find water to drink that isn't frozen.

The picture below shows a Canada goose. Canada geese spend the spring and summer months in Canada. There they hatch and raise their young. Then these geese fly to the southern part of the United States for the fall and winter. Canada geese follow the same migration routes every year. The map shows the routes some of these geese follow.

Geese flying in a V-formation

Migration Route of Canada Geese

Swallows are birds that migrate to warmer places for the winter. In fact, the people of San Juan Capistrano, California, await the arrival of flocks of swallows every year. When they migrate, these birds always make a stop in this city right on schedule!

Birds aren't the only animals that migrate through the air. Some bats migrate to find insects to eat. A few kinds of bats migrate to find places to hibernate. When an animal **hibernates** (hī′ bər nāts), it goes into a deep sleep during the cold winter. It uses very little energy and does not move or eat. The animal uses stored body fat for food.

Some animals hibernate in large groups. One kind of ladybird beetle spends the summer eating insects along the coast of California. When winter comes, thousands of these beetles travel together to the dark, wooded hills away from the ocean. There, they hibernate for the winter. In the spring, the beetles return to the California coast. You can see that animals survive by traveling in a lot of interesting ways!

Checkpoint

1. Why do land animals migrate?
2. Name three reasons that animals migrate in water.
3. What are two animals that migrate through air?
4. **Take Action!** Work in small groups. Make up a play about an animal that migrates.

Animals in Action

Some animals migrate daily. Other animals migrate over a few years. Many animals migrate according to the seasons. But no matter how often animals migrate, they can travel thousands of kilometers within a year.

The graph below shows the number of kilometers that some animals migrate in a year.

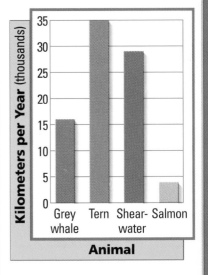

What Did You Find Out?
1. *Which animal migrates the farthest?*
2. *Does the whale or the salmon migrate farther? By how many kilometers?*
3. *The shearwater and the tern are both birds. How many kilometers more does a tern migrate each year than a shearwater?*

Activity

Moving On

You can't actually follow a bird or whale as it migrates. But, you can watch a mealworm as it moves for food.

Picture A

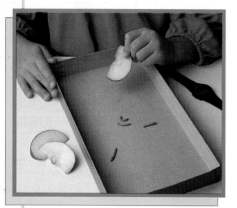

Picture B

Picture C

Gather These Materials

shoe-box lid

mealworms

apple slices

watch or timer

cereal flakes

plastic spoon

Follow This Procedure

1 Make a chart like the one on the next page. Record your observations in your chart.

2 Place three or four mealworms in the center of the shoe-box lid. (Picture A)

3 Place a few apple slices in one corner of the lid. (Picture B) *CAUTION: Do not put any of the apple slices in your mouth.*

Predict: How long will it take a mealworm to move to the apple?

4 Use a timer or watch to find out how long it takes for the first mealworm to reach the apple. Record the time.

5 Remove the apple slices and return all the mealworms to the center of the lid.

6 Put a spoonful of cereal flakes in one corner of the lid. (Picture C) *CAUTION: Do not put any of the cereal in your mouth.*

Predict: *How long will it take a mealworm to move to the cereal?*

7 Use a timer or watch to find out how long it takes for the first mealworm to reach the cereal. Record the time.

8 Return the mealworms to their original container.

State Your Conclusions

1. Explain why mealworms would move to the cereal or apple.

2. What evidence do you have that mealworms move at different speeds toward different foods?

Let's Experiment

Will mealworms move toward light or dark? Design and carry out an experiment to find out. Use what you know about scientific methods to find out.

Record Your Results

	Time for first mealworm to reach food
Apple	
Cereal	

Chapter Review

Reviewing Words and Concepts

Write the letter of the word or phrase that best completes each sentence.

1. Many birds and other animals move to find water and _____.
2. Gazelles will bounce to warn other gazelles of _____.
3. An elephant uses its _____ to put food and water into its mouth.
4. Animals often _____, or move from one place to another, when the seasons change.
5. Salmon return to the same _____ streams in which they were hatched to lay eggs.
6. Each time caribou migrate, they follow the same _____.
7. Animals such as bats _____, or go into a deep sleep during the cold winter.
8. Many birds spend spring and summer in northern places and fly _____ for the fall and winter.
9. Sea lions can swim _____ better than they can move on land.
10. The male polar bear wanders _____ in search of seals, otters, and fish.

a. route
b. trunk
c. alone
d. south
e. freshwater
f. underwater
g. danger
h. migrate
i. food
j. hibernate

Connecting Ideas

1. Copy the concept map. Use the terms at the right to complete the map about migrating animals.

mammals   water
land   fish   birds

A. migration
B. air
C.
D.
E.
F.
G.

2. Write a sentence or two about the ideas shown in the concept map.

Interpreting What You Learned

1. How is the way an elephant gets its food different from that of a monkey?
2. Describe the migration patterns of the zebra and caribou.
3. How do egrets work together to get food?
4. Explain why whales migrate in the winter.
5. How does an animal that hibernates survive during a cold winter?
6. Describe how salmon return to the stream where they were hatched.

Performance Assessment

How does an elephant move water?

Materials • small measuring cup • plastic bowl • water • dropper

Collecting Data

1. Measure 20 milliliters of water into a small measuring cup. Pour the water from the cup into a plastic bowl.
2. Place a dropper into the water in the bowl. Push in the dropper's bulb, then release it to fill the dropper with water. The dropper represents an elephant's trunk.
3. Lift the dropper out of the water and place the tip of the dropper in the small measuring cup. Squeeze the dropper's bulb so the water in the dropper goes into the cup.
4. Fill the elephant's "trunk" with water again. Then move the water to the measuring cup and release it again.
5. Do this until you move 20 milliliters of water. Count how many times you fill the dropper to reach 20 milliliters. Record your results.

Analyzing Data

How would the size of an elephant's trunk affect how much water it can move?

People on the Move

Hey, look how far it went!

Discover Activity

Whose sailboat is fastest?

Build a sailboat like the one shown using a piece of foam board, a straw, a piece of plastic, and a piece of aluminum. Try out your boat in a large pan of water. How can you change your boat to make it move faster? Try out your ideas.

For Discussion

1. What is the best shape for the boat?

2. What is the best size and shape for a sail?

3.1 *Travel Long Ago*

How did people travel long ago?

Imagine what your life might have been like if you lived years and years ago. Cars and trains and buses weren't even invented. People only dreamed that one day airplanes would fly through the air. How would you get from one place to another? Would you have to walk everywhere?

If you lived in the mid 1800s, maybe you would have ridden a bicycle like the ones in the picture. But walking and riding bicycles weren't the only ways people moved around. In this lesson, you'll learn about a few more.

▼ *An 1800s bicycle race*

Canoes used energy from people.

Horse-drawn carriages and oxen-drawn wagons were early ways of getting around.

Using Energy From Living Things

Clippity clop! Clippity clop! Many years ago, this was a familiar sound as people traveled by horseback. People also rode other animals, such as mules and camels. These animals need a lot of energy to carry people. How do animals get energy?

Through the years, people also have used machines to help them move from place to place. Long ago, people used their own energy to move carts and wagons with wheels. That must have been hard work!

People learned that animals and machines could work together. Animals could use their energy to make the machines move. What simple machine do you see in the carriage in the picture? What animal pulls the carriage?

Notice the canoes in the picture. They are wedges that cut through the water. The energy for moving canoes comes from people paddling. Keep reading to learn more about how canoes and other boats move in water.

Using Water and Wind Energy

Remember how energy from moving water helps scatter seeds. Years ago, people realized that energy from moving water could help move boats, too. But water was not always moving in the direction people wanted to go. And if water was not moving fast, it could not move boats quickly. How could people move more quickly across the water? They used their own energy to paddle and row.

People realized that they could use energy from the wind, too. They put sails on rafts and boats. Remember how you tried to make your sailboat move faster in the Discover Activity. Gradually, people learned to build bigger and better sailboats. They learned to use many different sizes and shapes of sails to catch and direct the energy from the wind. Energy from wind made water travel easier.

▲ Sails helped boats move faster.

Checkpoint

1. How does energy from animals move machines?
2. How do people use energy from wind and water to move?
3. Take Action! Design and make an object that uses wind or water energy to move.

Activity

Don't Get Lost With This

A bicycle may be your favorite way of getting around, but what are some other ways? How does each way differ and how are they alike?

Picture A

Picture B

Picture C

old magazines   glue

scissors   cardboard

ruler

Follow This Procedure

1 Make a chart like the one on the next page. Record your observations in your chart.

2 Gather some old magazines.

3 Find pictures that show many different ways in which people move about, for example: boat, roller blades, airplane, bicycle, skateboard, and walking.

4 Use your scissors to cut the pictures out. (Picture A)

5 Glue each picture onto a piece of cardboard that measures 15 cm by 15 cm. (Picture B)

6 Put at least 15 pictures into a pile. (Picture C)

Predict: How many ways can you sort the pictures to show how people move?

7 Sort your pictures into two piles. Pile 1 will have ways of moving that do pollute the air. Pile 2 will have ways of moving that do not pollute the air.

8 Record your observations.

9 Repeat the sorting of your pictures. This time think of other ways to sort them. For example, you could sort your pictures by: type of fuel used, speed, cost of fuel, and safety. Record your way of sorting.

Record Your Results

Ways of getting around	
Pollute	Do not pollute

State Your Conclusions

1. How many pictures were in your piles for moving about with and without polluting the air?
2. What does this tell you about the role of humans and the problem of air pollution?
3. Do your picture piles give you some ideas for ways of reducing the use of fossil fuels? Explain.

Let's Experiment

Figure out how much time you spend moving from place to place during a week. How much of that time spent uses up fuel and how much time does not? Suggest how you can do the same moving about but use less fuel.

3.2 Modern Transportation

> *How do people travel in modern times?*

Imagine standing on a city sidewalk. Maybe you hear engines rumbling and horns honking and brakes squealing. These sounds may even be interrupted by the noise of a jet engine overhead. Since the first carts and wagons, transportation has changed a lot.

Transportation Through Time

The invention of the engine changed the way people moved from place to place. The time lines below show how different kinds of transportation have changed over the years. Notice the kinds of vehicles that use steam, electricity, and petroleum products.

Transportation: Past, Present, and Future

steam

electricity

petroleum products

1850   1900

In the 1700s, people began using energy from steam. By burning coal, wood, or oil, they could produce enough steam to make machines move. In the 1800s, steam engines were first used to power trains and ships.

In the early nineteenth century, steam automobiles were seen in large towns in the United States, Britain, and France. These early engines were dirty and heavy. Early steam automobiles were not very successful.

During the 1880s, electric motors were first used to power trolley cars. By 1900, electric automobiles were being used. The electricity was provided by batteries, but they ran down very quickly.

The engines in most modern vehicles use fuels made from **petroleum** (pə trō′ lē əm), a dark, oily liquid found deep inside the earth. Gasoline and other fuels are made from petroleum. On the next two pages, you will learn more about modern engines.

1950

2000

Motion from Heat

Heat engines burn fuel and release energy.

An engine that burns fuel is called a heat engine. As the heat engine burns fuel, energy is released from the fuel. This energy is then used to make things move.

When you ride in airplanes, cars, or buses, a heat engine is burning fuel to move you along. Heat engines provide the energy used by trains to carry heavy loads. Heat engines also run bulldozers, cranes, tugboats, and many other machines that help us do work. What machines can you think of that get energy to run from heat engines?

Fuel pipe Gasoline is carried to the engine through the fuel pipe.

Engine The fuel is burned in the engine to release energy.

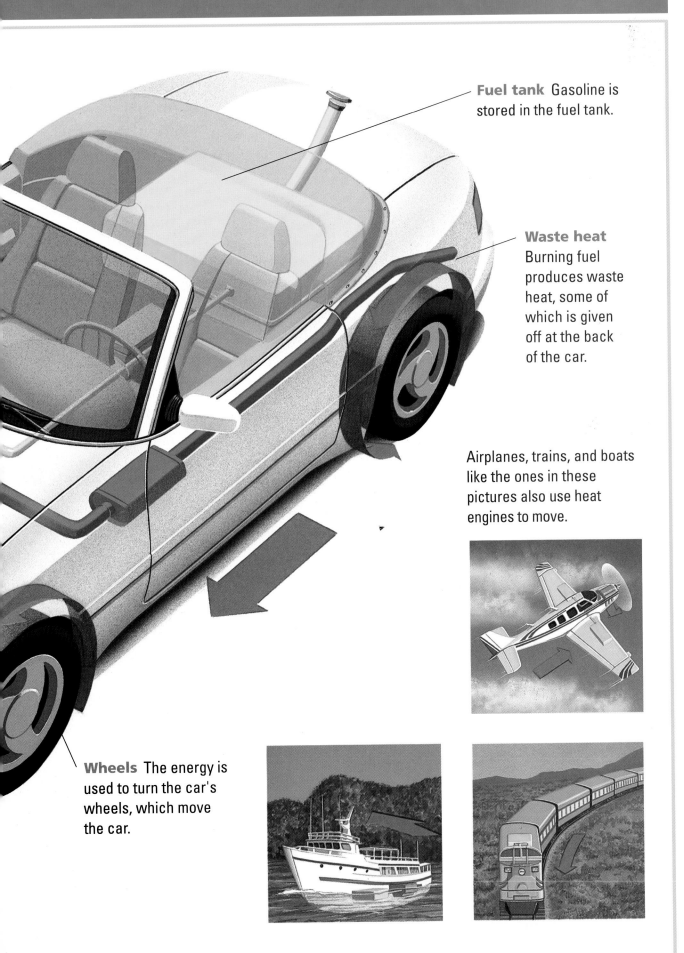

Fuel tank Gasoline is stored in the fuel tank.

Waste heat Burning fuel produces waste heat, some of which is given off at the back of the car.

Airplanes, trains, and boats like the ones in these pictures also use heat engines to move.

Wheels The energy is used to turn the car's wheels, which move the car.

Energy Use for Transportation

You might wonder how people get petroleum out of the ground. People pump the petroleum, or crude oil, from the ground. It is pumped through oil wells that are dug deep into the earth. Find the oil well in the diagram below.

After the petroleum is out of the ground, materials such as water, natural gas, and impurities are removed. Then the crude oil is transported through pipelines to refineries. In these refineries, the crude oil is made into several different petroleum products. One of these products is the gasoline that provides energy for heat engines.

▼ Study this diagram to see how people get gasoline for their cars.

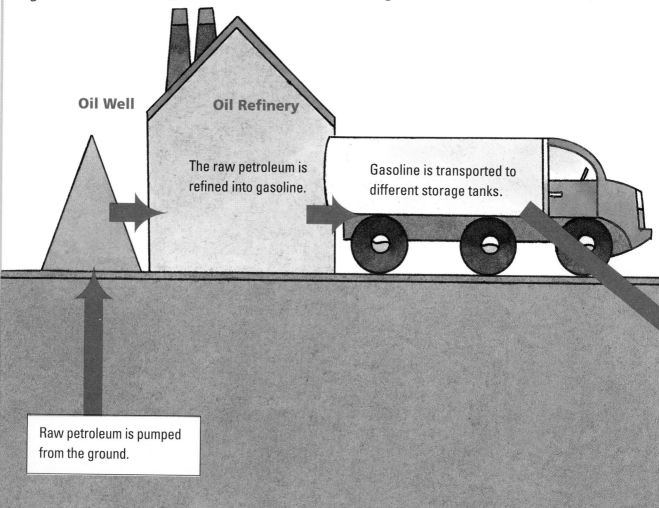

Oil Well

Oil Refinery

The raw petroleum is refined into gasoline.

Gasoline is transported to different storage tanks.

Raw petroleum is pumped from the ground.

Gasoline is transported to many different locations by tanker ships, railroad cars, and trucks. The gasoline is stored in large storage tanks. Then, trucks usually deliver the gasoline to smaller storage tanks at gas stations, such as the one shown here.

Gasoline and other petroleum products are used to power the engines in automobiles, trucks, buses, farm vehicles, motor boats, and airplanes. The diagram below shows that automobiles using gasoline give off harmful materials into the air. As you read, you will learn more about this problem. You also will read about how people are working to help control the problem.

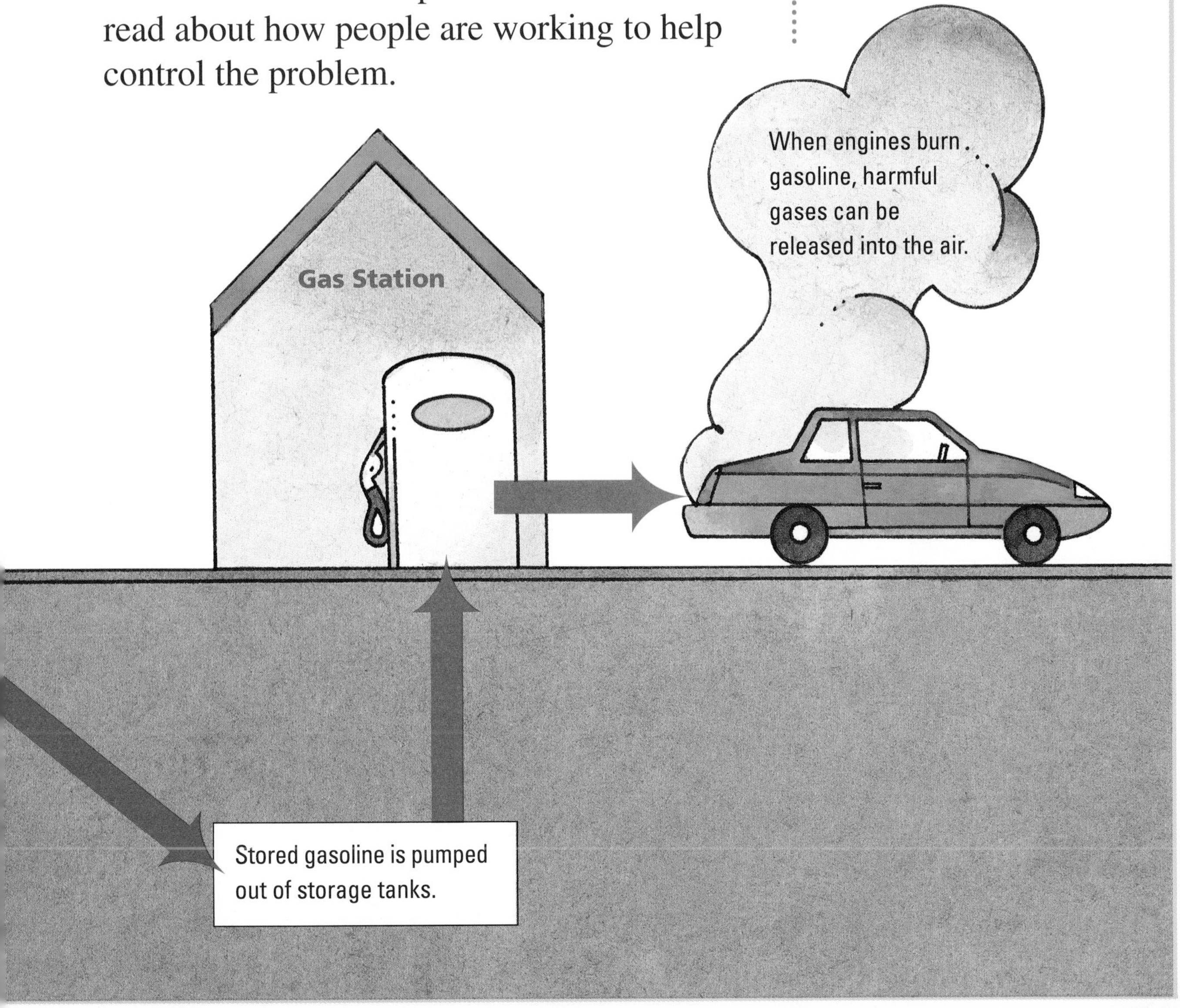

Gas Station

When engines burn gasoline, harmful gases can be released into the air.

Stored gasoline is pumped out of storage tanks.

Transportation and Its Effects

More people are now traveling than ever before. Many people drive many miles each day getting to work and back home again. As you can see in the picture, many cars fill the roads. But this increase in travel causes some problems. Cars, trucks, and other vehicles give off harmful materials into the air. **Pollution** (pə lü′ shən) is anything harmful added to the air, water, or land.

Air pollution can be harmful to people's health. Air pollution also can harm crops, other plants, and even buildings. As people become more aware of the problem of air pollution, they are working together to try to reduce it.

▼ Imagine the amount of pollution these cars add to the air each day.

You know that petroleum is a very important natural resource. People have pumped petroleum from the earth for many years. Petroleum is a **nonrenewable resource** (non ri nü′ ə bəl rē′ sôrs), one that cannot be replaced. Because people are using so much petroleum, the world's supply is getting lower.

You might wonder what can be done about this problem. More and more, people are working to save the world's natural resources. Many people are cooperating to control the use of petroleum. They are trying to find ways to make the supply of petroleum last for a long time. Even you can help. Read the next two pages to find out what people are doing.

Getting Around

People travel from place to place in many ways. Some travel by bus or train. Others travel by car or plane.

The graph below shows how people in this country travel around cities. Each bar on the graph shows the number of miles the vehicle travels per gallon of fuel. Study the graph and then answer the questions.

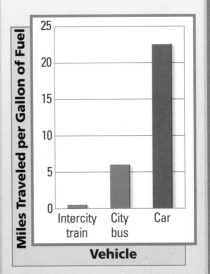

What Did You Find Out?
1. *How many miles does a bus travel per gallon of fuel?*
2. *How many miles does a car travel on a gallon of fuel?*
3. *Which travels further on a gallon of fuel, a bus or a train?*
4. *Why might using a train still save fuel?*

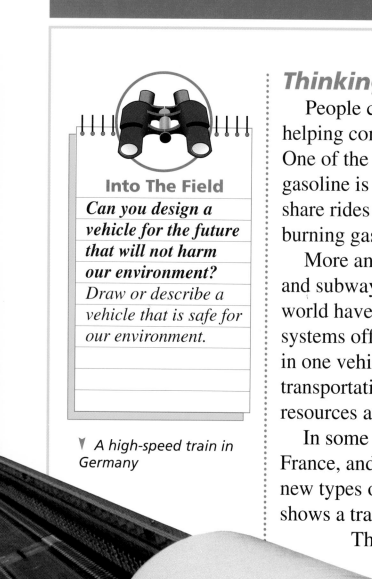

Into The Field

Can you design a vehicle for the future that will not harm our environment?

Draw or describe a vehicle that is safe for our environment.

▼ *A high-speed train in Germany*

Thinking About the Future

People can help conserve petroleum, while helping control air pollution at the same time. One of the simplest ways of using less gasoline is through car-pooling. If people share rides with others, fewer cars will be burning gasoline and polluting the air.

More and more people are taking trains and subways. Many cities throughout the world have mass-transit systems. These systems offer ways to transport many people in one vehicle. Using this kind of transportation helps conserve natural resources and control pollution.

In some parts of the world, such as Japan, France, and Germany, people are developing new types of high-speed trains. The picture shows a train now being used in Germany. This train causes less pollution than many other kinds of trains being used today.

But people still need to drive automobiles. When drivers keep their automobiles in good condition, their cars use less gasoline and give off fewer harmful materials into the air.

Many modern cars are built in a way that limits the air pollution they cause. In many parts of the United States, laws limit the amount of pollution an automobile can cause.

You've read about what some people are doing to make transportation safer for the environment. But what can you do? The picture might give you a good idea. A bicycle doesn't pollute the air at all. Where does a bicycle get energy to move? The energy comes from the person riding the bicycle. But there's even more good news about riding a bicycle. The exercise can help keep you healthy. Not only that, but bicycling is fun!

▲ *Riding a bicycle helps the environment and you.*

Checkpoint

1. What kinds of energy powered early engines?
2. How does a heat engine use energy?
3. How do people get gasoline?
4. How can traveling change the environment?
5. How can people help control air pollution?
6. **Take Action!** Design a car of the future. Show how it uses energy.

Activity

Dirt That Sticks

You can't see it, but it's there. What? The dirt in the air that you breathe. If you can't see it, how do you know it's there?

Picture A

Picture B

Picture C

Gather These Materials

cover goggles   clear plastic sheet
poster board   tape
scissors   petroleum jelly
metric ruler   hand lens
pencil   string

Follow This Procedure

1 Make a chart like the one on the following page. Record your observations in your chart.

2 Put on your cover goggles.

3 Cut out a piece of poster board measuring 20 cm by 20 cm.

4 Draw lines 2 cm in from each side. Make a frame by cutting out the inside part of your poster board. (Picture A)

5 Cut a sheet of clear plastic that measures 20 cm by 20 cm.

6 Tape the plastic sheet onto your frame. (Picture B)

7 Use your pencil to punch a hole through the frame. Tie a long piece of string through the hole so that your frame can be hung up.

8 Stand the frame up and smear petroleum jelly over both sides of the plastic. (Picture C)

9 Use a hand lens to check the sticky surfaces for dirt. Record what you see.

Predict: *What might you see after the frame has hung for several days?*

10 Use the string to hang your frame in your classroom.

11 Several days later use a hand lens to check the sticky surfaces. Record what you see now.

Record Your Results

	Observations
Sticky surfaces before	
Sticky surfaces days later	

State Your Conclusions

1. Are there dirt particles in the air you breathe? Why don't you usually see them?

2. Why did you use the petroleum jelly on the plastic?

Let's Experiment

How could you find out where the dirtiest air in your school building is? Use what you know about scientific methods to find out.

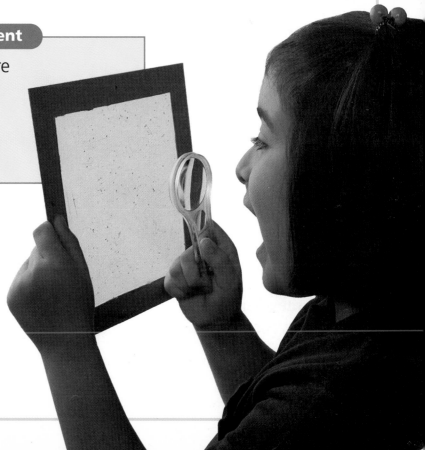

Chapter Review

Reviewing Words and Concepts

Write the letter of the word or phrase that best completes each sentence.

1. Animals can use their _____ to move machines.
2. Gasoline is made from _____, a dark, oily liquid found deep inside the earth.
3. Steam engines were first used to power trains and _____.
4. Canoes are moved by energy from _____.
5. Sailboats are moved by energy from _____.
6. Electric motors were first used to power _____ cars.
7. An engine that burns fuel is called a _____ engine.
8. Electric automobiles get electricity from _____.
9. Petroleum is a _____ resource, one that cannot be replaced.
10. Cars and trucks give off _____, anything harmful added to the air, water, or land.

a. petroleum
b. people
c. ships
d. trolley
e. pollution
f. batteries
g. energy
h. heat
i. wind
j. nonrenewable

Connecting Ideas

1. Copy the concept map. Use the terms at the right to complete the map about how people get gasoline.

   refineries   gasoline
   storage tanks   oil well
   heat engine

   A. **crude oil** — B. _____
   C. _____ — D. _____
   E. _____ — F. _____

2. Write a sentence or two about the ideas shown in the concept map.

Interpreting What You Learned

1. What are some ways that people used to travel many years ago?
2. Why is petroleum important to modern types of engines?
3. How do people get petroleum out of the ground?
4. How have cars, trucks, and other vehicles caused some of the pollution problems in our environment?
5. How can people help conserve petroleum?

Performance Assessment

How can you make a toy car move?

Materials • cover goggles • piece of cardboard • 2 pieces of paper • 3 straws • 4 plastic lids with holes • tape • balloon • metric ruler • sharpened pencil

Collecting Data

1. Put on your cover goggles. Roll each of the pieces of paper tightly around a straw. When each piece of paper is rolled up, tape it to form a tube. Make sure the straw can turn inside the tube.
2. Tape the tubes across the bottom of the piece of cardboard to make axles for your car.
3. Use the sharpened pencil to carefully poke holes in the middle of each of the four plastic lids. Then push the ends of the straws through the holes in the lids to make four wheels for your car.
4. Turn your car over and push it to make it move. Make sure the wheels are turning smoothly.

5. Push one end of the remaining straw into the balloon. Tape the mouth of the balloon to the straw.
6. Tape the straw to the top of the cardboard. At least 5 centimeters of the straw should stick over the back end of your car.
7. Put a piece of tape next to one of your car's front wheels. This is the starting line for your car.
8. Blow into the straw to inflate the balloon. Hold your finger over the end of the straw, then release your finger. Wait until your car stops moving, then measure the distance that it traveled.

Analyzing Data

How could you change the distance your car travels?

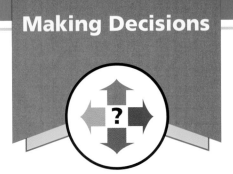

Traveling Along

Traveling uses energy. If you walk or ride a bike, you use energy in your muscles. Cars, buses, trains, boats, and planes use energy from fuel.

Needs and Goals

Today, we try to conserve fuel so we will not run out in the future. Also, using less fuel causes less pollution and saves money.

In order to plan how you and your family can save fuel, you can ask yourself questions like these:

- How can we travel less?
- How can we use less fuel to travel?
- How can we use no fuel to travel?

Walking, roller skating, and riding a bike use no fuel at all.

Gathering Information

In order to see how to save fuel, you have to think about your family's travel patterns.

- Where do we need to go?
- Where do we want to go?
- How do we usually get there?

Then you can find answers to the questions you asked.

- Traveling less might mean combining errands. A shopping trip could include a stop at the library.
- Trains and buses use less fuel to carry each person than cars do. Car pooling is another way to save fuel. Suppose one person rides 48 kilometers in a car. Such a ride uses about 4 liters of gas.
- Walking, roller skating, and riding a bike use no fuel at all.

Possible Alternatives

To plan ways of saving fuel, think about your own community. For example, many areas have buses or trains. Other places do not have any kinds of public transportation at all.

You also need to think about the needs of your family. For example, if your school is not very far away, you can save fuel by walking to school.

Evaluating Alternatives
Copy the chart below. In the first column, fill in places to which you and your family travel. For example, maybe you go to dance practice each week.

Making the Best Choice
Then fill in the second column of the chart. Remember that ways to save fuel might include combining trips.

The Best Way to Travel

Place	Transportation
School	
Store	
Visit friend	

For example, one of your parents might drive you to the barber shop and then to the grocery store on the same trip.

Now You Do It

1. What are some ways your family could travel that would save gasoline?

2. What changes in your community would help your family save gasoline?

3. *On Your Own* Measure or estimate how far you can walk without getting tired. Find out or guess what places are that distance from your home. (Remember to allow for a round trip!)

4. *Critical Thinking* Suppose you are within walking distance from your home. Imagine that it is rainy, or it has gotten dark. How would you travel home? Why?

Helping People Help Themselves

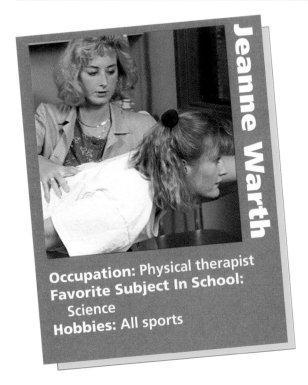

Jeanne Warth

Occupation: Physical therapist
Favorite Subject In School: Science
Hobbies: All sports

Jeanne thought about being a doctor or a nurse when she grew up. Then a friend of hers broke his leg and needed physical therapy. And Jeanne got an idea. Today Jeanne Warth is a physical therapist.

What does a physical therapist do?

"Lots of different things. We work with babies. We help kids with learning disabilities. And we work with people of all ages who are disabled or have been hurt."

What do you do for these people?

"Sometimes it's a matter of teaching the person how to move different parts of the body. It might be retraining the person to get out of bed, to walk, or to climb stairs."

What do you like best about your job?

"I get real satisfaction from helping people help themselves. The smiles and thank you's when people overcome an injury or do something they thought they would never be able to do again—they are really rewarding. And the excitement is always there. You find a new challenge in each patient you meet."

What kinds of challenges?

"The first challenge is to figure out what kind of treatment is needed. Then you have to make that treatment fit the patient. And sometimes you have to explain things a few different ways—some people learn things one way, others need to learn it a different way. It's like a teacher helping students. You have to be creative and meet the patients' needs."

Trains That Seem to Fly

The train in this picture doesn't really fly, but it does stay about 10 centimeters above the ground! It's all done with magnets.

4 One of these trains in Japan traveled at a speed of over **500 kilometers** per hour.

3 The train levitates, or floats on air.

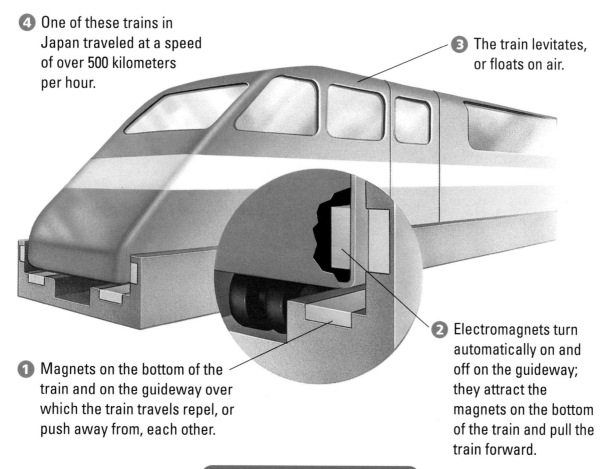

2 Electromagnets turn automatically on and off on the guideway; they attract the magnets on the bottom of the train and pull the train forward.

1 Magnets on the bottom of the train and on the guideway over which the train travels repel, or push away from, each other.

Find Out On Your Own

Draw a train on cardboard and tape a magnet to the bottom. Make the train move forward by holding a magnet in front of it. Now make the train move backward.

Module Performance Assessment

Energy Exhibit

Using what you learned in this module, help prepare an energy exhibit for your classroom. Provide information about energy for moving from place to place and ways to conserve energy. Complete one or more of the following activities. You may work by yourself or with others in a group.

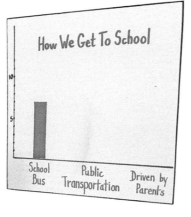

Conservation

Take a survey of how many students take the school bus, are driven by parents, or use public transportation to get to school. Make a graph to show the results of your survey. Also, show a plan to help reduce the consumption of gas by car-pooling or taking public transportation.

Art

Make a drawing to show the different ways in which animals move. Show at least one animal with a skeleton, one with an exoskeleton, and one with no skeleton. Label how each animal moves. Tell from where the animals get energy to move.

Drama

Prepare a skit that shows how transportation has changed through the years. Explain what type of energy powered each form of transportation.

Biology

Make a bulletin board showing the different migratory routes of some animals. You may want to show the routes of just one group, or of several different types of animals. Where do these animals get the energy to migrate?

Transportation

Imagine that gasoline-powered vehicles were not allowed in your town for one day. How would people get from place to place? Make a plan to provide people with transportation. List what problems you see.

Module Review

Reviewing Words and Concepts

Write the letter of the word or phrase that best completes each sentence.

1. When muscles ____, tendons pull the bones and make them move.
2. Your ____ helps hold your body up and gives it shape.
3. Your elbow ____ helps you move your lower arm back and forth.
4. Your muscles are attached to your bones by ____.
5. Each leg of a crab is attached to its ____ by muscles.
6. Animals use stored body ____ for food when they hibernate.
7. Caribou follow the same route each time they ____.
8. The engines of most modern vehicles use fuels made from ____.
9. The ____ given off by vehicles can be harmful to people's health.
10. People are looking for ways to use less petroleum because it is a ____ resource.

a. tendons
b. petroleum
c. joint
d. fat
e. exoskeleton
f. nonrenewable
g. skeleton
h. pollution
i. migrate
j. contract

Interpreting What You Learned

1. How does the scattering of seeds help plants?
2. How did the invention of the engine change the ways in which people travel?
3. How do some animals work together to get food?
4. How do your bones, tendons, and muscles work together to enable you to move?

Applying What You Learned

1. How are seeds that are scattered by wind different from seeds that catch on fur or feathers?
2. How are the migration patterns of zebras, caribou, and whales alike?
3. How has the invention of the engine caused an increase in the pollution of the environment?
4. How do flamingos and gazelles protect themselves?

Sounds All Around

Sounds All Around

Think about it. Just about everything can make a sound. We live in a world of sounds. Birds chirp, leaves rustle, car horns honk, school bells ring, and people talk. In this module, you'll find out how sounds are made, heard, and changed.

CHAPTER

1 Sound Waves

Why do sounds sound? Sounds are vibrations that spread out in waves and vary in volume and pitch.

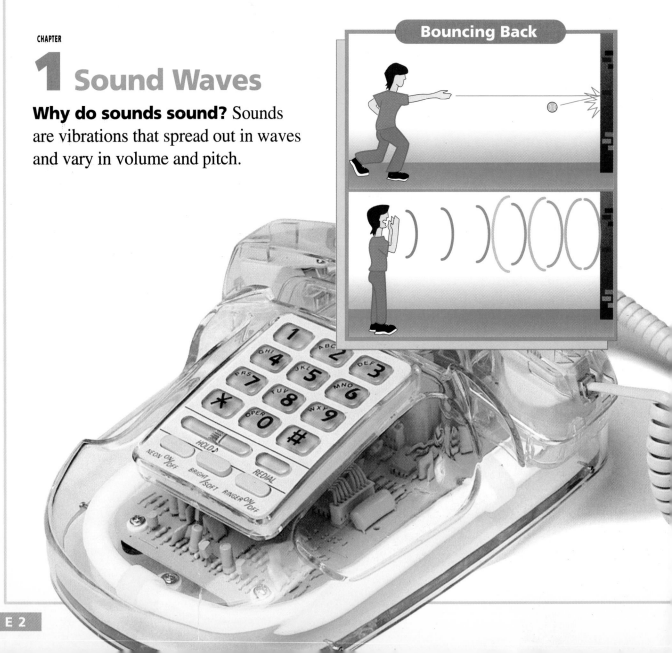

Bouncing Back

CHAPTER

2 Using Sound

Now hear this! Animals make and hear sounds in many different ways and for different reasons.

CHAPTER

3 Louder Sounds

Could you speak a little louder? People have discovered how to make soft sounds loud enough to hear.

Sound Waves

Can you tell what song this is?

How can you describe sounds?

Place four glass jars of the same kind and size on your desk. Fill the jars with different amounts of water. Gently tap the middle of the first jar with a spoon. *Be careful not to hit the jar too hard.* Describe the sound that you hear. Repeat with each jar.

For Discussion

1. How are the sounds alike? different?
2. How did you change the sounds?

1.1 *Making Sound*

What is sound?

The world is full of sounds—loud sounds and soft sounds, high sounds and low sounds. Many sounds keep us safe by warning us of danger. The loud buzz of a smoke alarm wakes us if a fire starts while we are asleep. Notice the fire department ambulance in the picture. The screech of its siren warns cars to get out of the way.

Sounds also help wild animals stay alive. They use sounds to warn one another of danger and to find food.

You have been hearing sounds for as long as you can remember. But did you ever wonder what sound is?

▼ *The sound of the siren comes from the speakers near the headlights.*

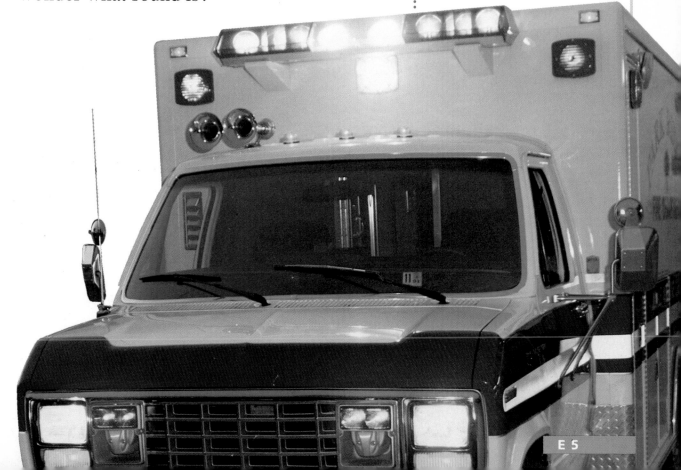

*Can you tell what
makes each sound?
Go outside and listen
for sounds. Take a
tablet and pencil with
you. Write down all
the different sounds
you hear. Tell what
made each sound.*

▼ *School bells help
students know when to
enter and leave the
building.*

How Sound Is Made

Remember that everything you can see and touch is matter. Some things you cannot see, such as air, are also matter. Air is a gas that you cannot see, but you can feel air as it touches your skin.

You also learned that light is a kind of energy. Sound is another kind of energy. All the sounds around you are made when matter vibrates. **Vibrate** (vī′brāt) means to quickly move back and forth. The sounds may seem different, but they are all alike in one way. All the sounds are made by something that causes matter to vibrate.

Look at the school bell in the picture. When the clapper hits the bell, energy from the clapper causes the bell to vibrate. Energy from the vibrating bell causes the air around the bell to vibrate also. The sound energy moves out from the bell in all directions, producing waves of sound energy in the air.

The school bell also causes the wall to which it is attached to vibrate. If you placed your hand against the wall under the bell, you could feel the vibrations. You have probably felt objects vibrating at other times, too. For example, if you were to put your hand on a radio that is playing, you would feel vibrations.

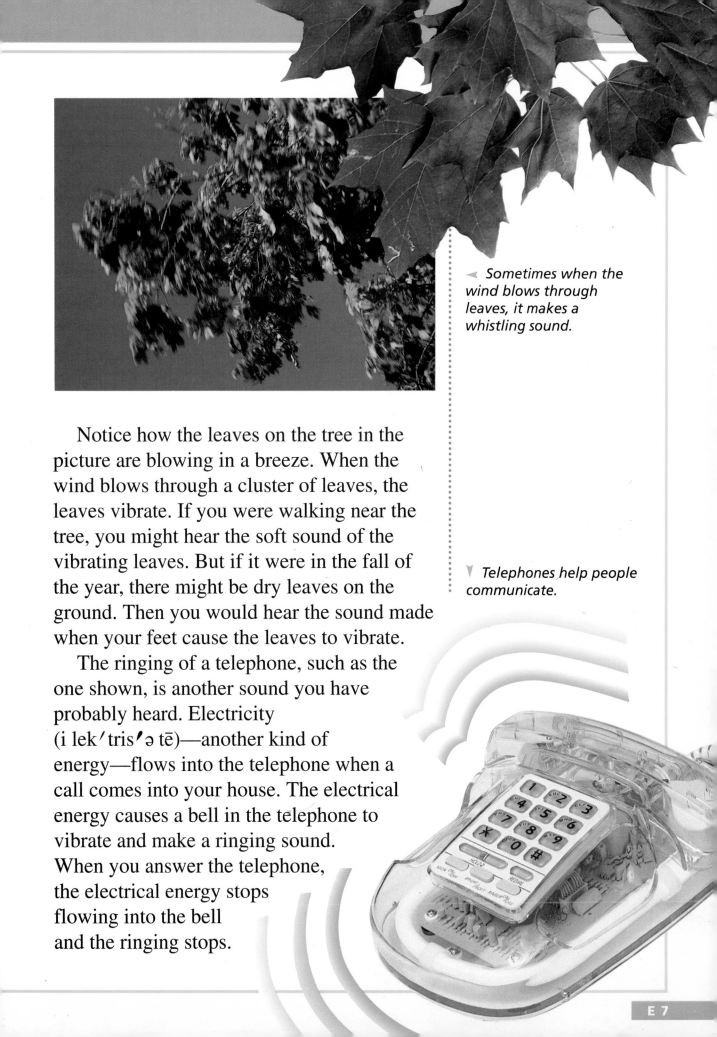

◀ *Sometimes when the wind blows through leaves, it makes a whistling sound.*

▼ *Telephones help people communicate.*

Notice how the leaves on the tree in the picture are blowing in a breeze. When the wind blows through a cluster of leaves, the leaves vibrate. If you were walking near the tree, you might hear the soft sound of the vibrating leaves. But if it were in the fall of the year, there might be dry leaves on the ground. Then you would hear the sound made when your feet cause the leaves to vibrate.

The ringing of a telephone, such as the one shown, is another sound you have probably heard. Electricity (i lek′tris′ə tē)—another kind of energy—flows into the telephone when a call comes into your house. The electrical energy causes a bell in the telephone to vibrate and make a ringing sound. When you answer the telephone, the electrical energy stops flowing into the bell and the ringing stops.

Sound All Around

What things around you can make sounds?

There's a lot to look at in this scene. And if you could put yourself anywhere in the scene you would hear lots of sounds.

Look at the picture and, on a sheet of paper, make a list of all the things that you think can make a sound. After each object on the list, write what part of the object might vibrate to make sound. Compare your list with your classmates' lists.

Sounds can also be grouped according to whether or not the sounds are helpful. Make another list of objects in the picture that make sounds that are helpful.

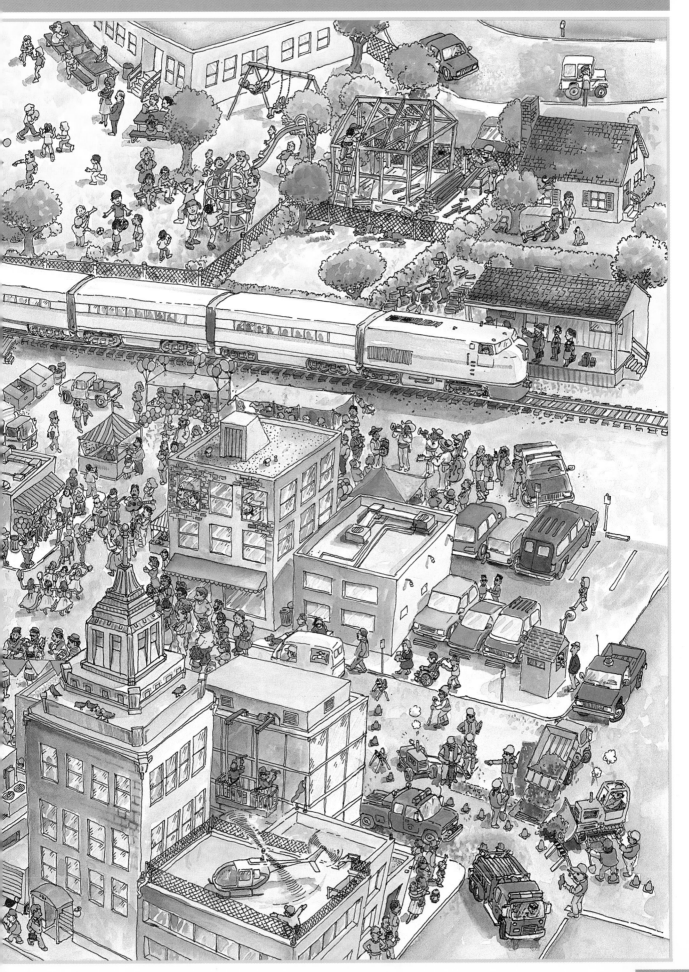

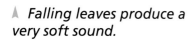
▲ *Falling leaves produce a very soft sound.*

▲ *The volume of a person's voice can be soft or loud.*

Different Volume

Have you ever been listening to music and had someone say, "Could you please turn that down?" The person really means for you to turn down the volume of the music.

The **volume** of sound is the loudness or softness of the sound. Your whisper in a movie theater has a low volume, while your shout at a baseball game has a high volume.

The diagram compares the volume of some common sounds. The volume of the sound made by falling leaves is very soft. How would you describe the volume of sound made by the people talking in the picture to the left? The sound of engines of a jet plane, such as the one taking off in the picture, is much louder than people talking. That's why airport crew members use flags to signal one another. They cannot talk loud enough to be heard above those jet engines!

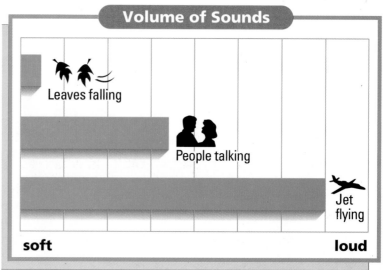
Volume of Sounds

Leaves falling

People talking

Jet flying

soft   loud

But what makes some sounds louder than others? The volume of sound that an object makes when it is hit depends on how hard the object is hit. For example, try tapping your desk lightly. The sound you make is a soft sound. Now tap the desk harder. Notice what happens to the sound. It takes more energy for you to tap the desk hard, so the sound waves you make have more energy, and sound is louder.

Look at the bells in the picture. The larger the bell, the larger the clapper in the bell. A large clapper strikes a bell with more energy than a small clapper does. So the large clapper makes sound waves that have more energy than the waves made by the small clapper. Which bell will ring the loudest?

At times, loud sounds help keep you safe. For example, the siren on the fire department ambulance has to be loud to be heard above the other sounds around you. But loud sounds can also be harmful. Listening to loud music or other loud sounds for a long period of time can be harmful to your ears.

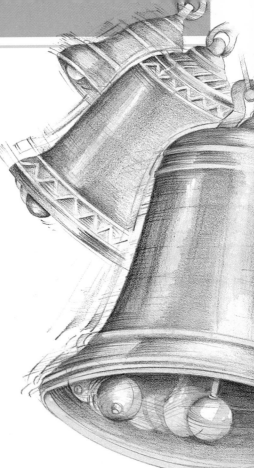

▲ *You probably like the sound of ringing bells better than the sound of a jet plane.*

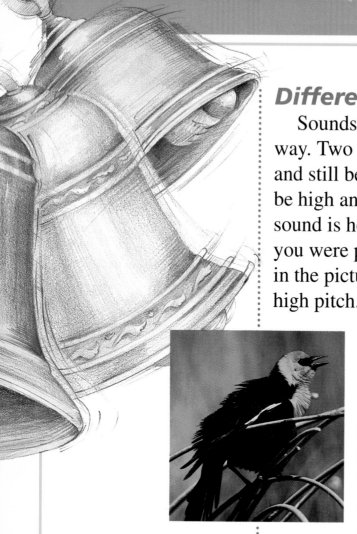

Different Pitch

Sounds can also be different in another way. Two sounds can have the same volume and still be different. One of the sounds can be high and one can be low. The **pitch** of a sound is how high or how low the sound is. If you were pretending to meow like the kitten in the picture, you might make a sound with a high pitch. However, if you were trying to sound like the roaring lion in the picture, you might make a sound with a low pitch.

What do you suppose makes the pitch of sounds different? If you said, "vibration," you're right. If an object vibrates slowly, it will make a low sound. If an object vibrates quickly, it will make a high sound.

To see how this works, let's look at the bells in the picture again. Large bells usually vibrate more slowly than small bells. So the sound waves moving out from a large bell will be farther apart and the sound will have a low pitch. But a small bell will vibrate faster. The sound waves will be closer together. What will the pitch of the sound of a small bell be?

▼ The sounds that these animals make have different pitches.

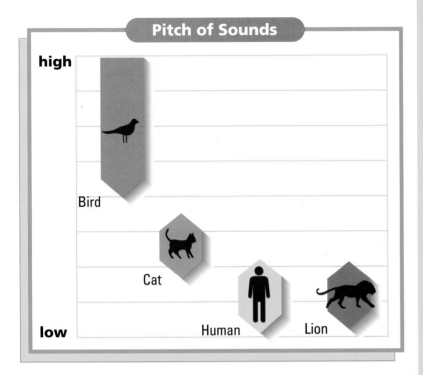

Pitch of Sounds

high

Bird

Cat

Human   Lion

low

The diagram compares the pitch of the sounds of animals shown in the pictures with the pitch of a man's voice. The bird makes the highest pitched sound. Which animal makes the lowest pitched sound? Is the pitch of the sound made by the cat higher or lower than the pitch of the sound made by the lion?

Checkpoint

1. How is sound made?
2. What kinds of objects can make sound?
3. How can you cause an object to make a loud sound?
4. Why does a small bell make a higher pitched sound than a large bell makes?
5. Take Action! Make a diagram of a xylophone. Label the end of the xylophone that makes the highest sounds.

What Is the Pitch?

How does the length of a straw affect the pitch of the sound it makes? Let's investigate.

What To Do
A. Predict the pitch of the sound you can make with a long and a short straw.
B. Cut a long straw and a short straw as shown.

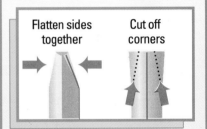

Flatten sides together   Cut off corners

C. Blow through the pointed end of each straw. *CAUTION: Be careful not to inhale and pull the straw into your throat.* Record your results on a chart such as the one shown below.

Record Your Results

Length of Straw	Pitch
Long	
Short	

What Did You Find Out?
1. *Did you predict the correct result?*
2. *How does the length of a straw affect the pitch of the sound made?*

Making Sounds

How is sound made? Try this activity to find out.

Picture A

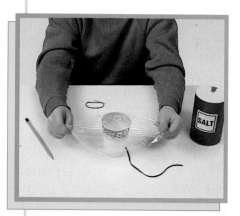

Picture B

Picture C

Gather These Materials

cover goggles
large paper cup
pencil
2 rubber bands

plastic food wrap
salt
scissors

Follow This Procedure

1 Make a chart like the one on the next page. Record your observations in your chart.

2 Put on your cover goggles.

3 Use the point of the pencil to carefully punch a tiny hole in the bottom of the paper cup. Cut 1 rubber band and push an end of it through the hole in the cup. Tie a knot so the rubber band cannot be pulled out. (Picture A)

4 Stretch a piece of plastic wrap over the top of the cup. Use the other rubber band to hold the plastic wrap tightly in place. (Picture B)

5 Sprinkle a few grains of salt on top of the plastic wrap. (Picture C) Hold the cup firmly while your partner slowly stretches the rubber band that is dangling from the cup.

Predict: What will happen to the salt if you pluck the stretched rubber band?

6 Gently pluck the stretched rubber band. Observe what happens to the salt. Record what you see.

7 Hold the cup near your ear while your partner slowly stretches the rubber band. *CAUTION: Do not hold the cup too close to your ear or stretch the rubber band so much that it breaks or pulls through the cup.*

8 Have your partner gently pluck the stretched rubber band with one finger. Record your observations.

Record Your Results

	Observations
Salt grains	
Cup placed near ear	

State Your Conclusions

1. Explain what happened to the salt on the cup when you plucked the rubber band.

2. What happened when you held the cup to your ear and your partner plucked the rubber band?

3. Based on your observations, how can you explain what makes sound?

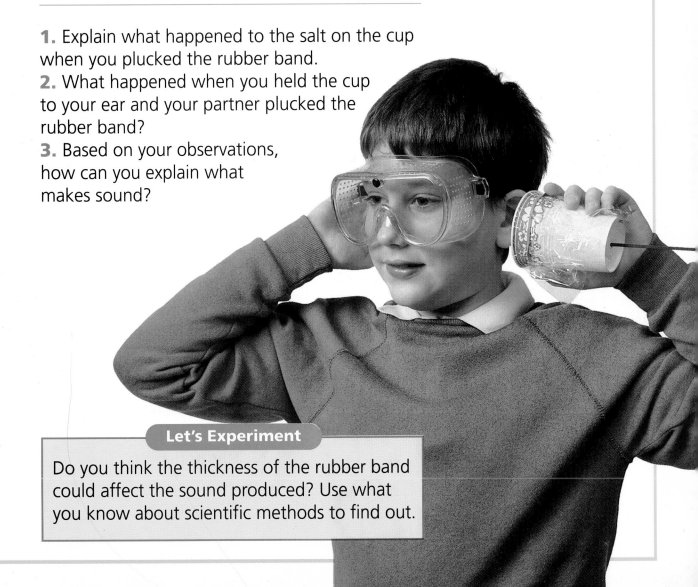

Let's Experiment

Do you think the thickness of the rubber band could affect the sound produced? Use what you know about scientific methods to find out.

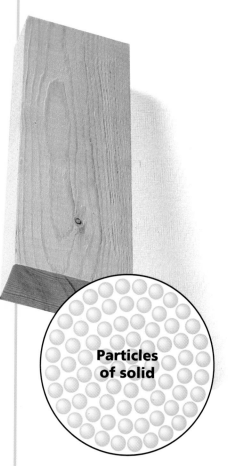

Particles of solid

▲ *Sound travels slower in a liquid than in a solid because the particles of the liquid are farther apart.*

1.2 *How Sound Travels*

▶ **How does sound reach my ears?**

You wake up in the middle of the night because you hear a loud sound. The sound that woke you up was a siren blaring several blocks away. How can you hear a sound being made so far away?

Sound Moving Through Matter

You know that sound waves move out in all directions from a ringing school bell. You also know that sound waves move through walls, so sound must travel through matter. To find out how, let's think about what matter is made of.

Remember that matter may be a solid, a liquid, or a gas. Let's look at how solids, liquids, and gases are different. Look at the pictures and diagrams of wood, water, and a balloon filled with air. All of these materials are matter. Wood is a solid, water is a liquid, and air is a gas. The diagrams show that all of these different kinds of matter are made up of particles. But notice that the particles in the wood are close together.

Particles of liquid

The particles in the water are farther apart than the particles in wood and move more freely. The particles in air are the farthest apart of all.

Sound waves travel through matter by causing the particles in matter to vibrate. When a particle begins to vibrate, it bumps into another particle. Then that particle bumps into another—and so on. The closer together the particles are, the faster they bump into one another. The energy of the sound waves moves from one particle to another as the particles bump into one another. So sound waves travel fastest in matter in which the particles are closest together.

The diagram compares the speeds at which sound waves travel through wood, water, and air. Through which state of matter does sound travel the fastest? Through which state of matter does sound travel the slowest?

Particles of gas

▲ Sound travels slowly through air because the particles are so far apart.

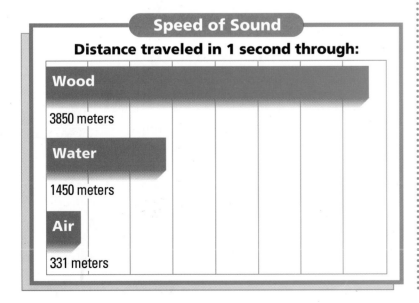

Speed of Sound

Distance traveled in 1 second through:

Wood	
3850 meters	
Water	
1450 meters	
Air	
331 meters	

Echoes

Look at the diagram showing a ball being thrown against a wall. When the ball hits the wall, it bounces back to the person who threw it.

Your voice can also bounce off a wall. Have you ever been in a large empty room and shouted or spoken loudly? If so, you probably heard your voice bouncing off the walls of the room. The sound you heard was an echo. An **echo** is a sound bouncing back from an object, as shown in the diagram. You might also hear an echo if you are in a place surrounded by hills or cliffs. Why might you hear an echo in a place like that? In what other kinds of places have you heard echoes?

▼ Dolphins also find their way around objects in the water by using echoes.

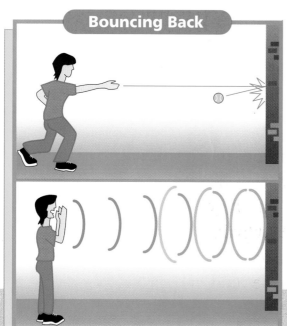

Bouncing Back

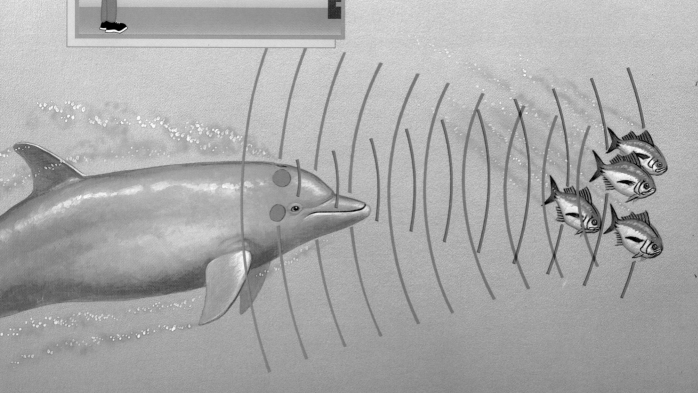

◄ The echoes of sounds that bats make as they fly help keep the bats from flying into things.

A few animals, such as the dolphin (dol′fən) and the bat in the pictures, use echoes to find food. As a dolphin swims through the water, it makes sounds. When the sound waves hit an object, such as a fish, they bounce back to the dolphin. Then the dolphin knows where the fish is. Remember that bats hunt for food at night, and bats do not see well. So as bats fly through the air, they are always making high-pitched sounds. The sounds bounce off of insects and the bat knows where the insects are. Also, sounds bouncing off trees help keep the bats from flying into the trees at night.

Checkpoint

1. Why does sound travel faster through wood than through air?
2. Where are you likely to hear an echo?
3. **Take Action!** Drop a bean into a large bowl of water. Compare what you see to sound waves.

Activity

Sound Travels Through Matter

How well does sound travel through different states of matter? Try this activity to find out.

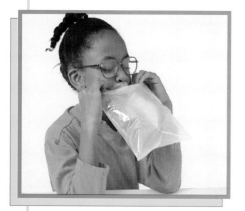
Picture A

Picture B

Picture C

Gather These Materials

sealable plastic bags
pencil with an eraser
cup

water
block of wood

Follow This Procedure

1 Make a chart like the one on the next page. Record your observations in your chart.

2 Fill one bag with air by blowing into it. Seal the bag tightly. (Picture A)

3 Use the cup to fill the other bag with water. Seal this bag tightly. (Picture B)

Predict: **Will sound travel best through air, water, or wood?**

4 Hold the bag of air next to your ear. Cover your other ear with your hand.

5 Listen while your partner taps the bag lightly with the pencil eraser. Record the sound as loud or soft.

6 Hold the bag of water next to your ear. Repeat the process in step 5. Record whether the sounds are louder or softer than with air.

Record Your Results

Sound through	Observations
Water	
Air	
Wood	

7 Hold the block of wood next to your ear. (Picture C) Listen while your partner taps the wood with the eraser. Record whether the sounds are louder or softer than with air and water.

State Your Conclusions

1. Through which material did you hear the loudest sound?
2. Through which material did you hear the softest sound?
3. Explain your observations based on what you know about how sound travels.

Let's Experiment

Now that you have tested these 3 materials, which materials do you think would make good sound insulators? Use what you know about scientific methods to find out.

Chapter Review

Reviewing Words and Concepts

Write the letter of the word or phrase that best completes each sentence.

1. Sound is a kind of _____.
2. Sound is made when matter _____, or quickly moves back and forth.
3. The loudness or softness of sound is the _____ of the sound.
4. The _____ of a sound is how high or how low the sound is.
5. Sound waves can _____ through matter.
6. The volume of the sound of a jet engine is _____.
7. Sound travels fastest in matter in which the _____ are closest together.
8. The pitch of the sound a bird makes is _____ than that of a man's voice.
9. Sound travels faster through a solid than through a _____.
10. Sounds bouncing back from an object are _____.

a. liquid
b. echoes
c. travel
d. higher
e. volume
f. particles
g. energy
h. vibrates
i. loud
j. pitch

Connecting Ideas

1. Copy the concept map. Use the terms at the right to complete the map about sound.

vibrations   echo
          volume

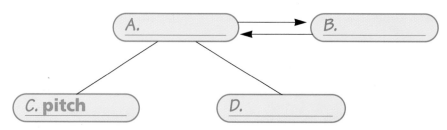

2. Write a sentence or two about the ideas shown in the concept map.

Interpreting What You Learned

1. Explain how an object makes sound.

2. How can the same object make sounds having different volumes?

3. How can you change the pitch of the sound an object makes?

4. Will dolphin sounds travel faster under or above water? Why?

5. In what ways is an echo like a ball thrown against a wall?

Performance Assessment

How can you make sound change pitch?

Materials • piece of cardboard • 6 straws • tape • scissors • meter stick

Collecting Data

1. Cut a piece of cardboard so it measures 5 centimeters in height and 10 centimeters in width. Lay the cardboard on a table.

2. Place a straw on the far left side of the piece of cardboard. Make the top of the straw line up with the top of the cardboard. Tape the straw in place.

3. Cut the other five straws to different lengths. Your shortest straw should be at least 5 centimeters long.

4. Arrange the straws you cut in order from longest to shortest. Place the longest cut straw just to the right of the straw already taped on the cardboard. Tape the cut straw in place.

5. Tape the other straws to the piece of cardboard in order of length. Make sure the tops of the straws all line up with the top of the cardboard.

6. Hold the piece of cardboard next to your mouth with the straws pointing down. Starting at one end of the piece of cardboard, blow over the top of the straw to make a sound. Move the cardboard while you blow so you hear sounds in all the straws.

Analyzing Data

How does the pitch of the longest straw differ from the pitch of the shortest straw?

2

Using Sound

Wear cover goggles
for this activity.

How can a balloon make sound?

Put on your cover goggles. Blow up a large balloon. *Be careful not to blow it up so much that it breaks.* Hold the neck of the balloon between the thumbs and forefingers of your hands. Pinch the neck and stretch it slightly. Let some air flow out of the balloon. Describe what you hear.

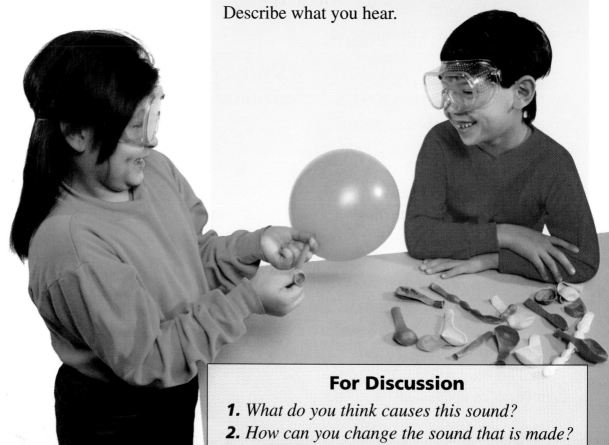

For Discussion

1. What do you think causes this sound?

2. How can you change the sound that is made?

2.1 Living Things Communicating

How do people and other animals use sound?

Both people and other animals use sounds to help them survive. When you were a tiny baby like the one in the picture, what did you do when you were hungry? You cried, right? Then someone probably fed you. People and many other animals begin at very early ages to use sound for communication. But, as you become an adult, you learn different ways to use sounds. For example, you talk, sing, shout, and so on. Let's find out how you make sounds.

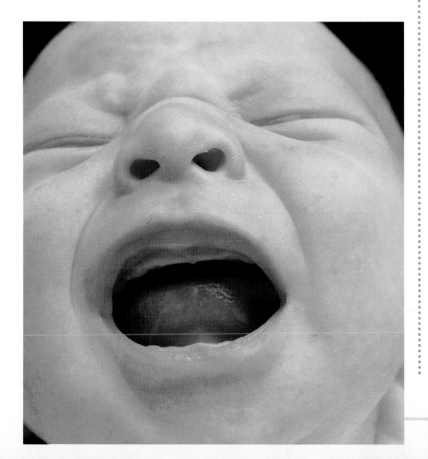

◄ *Crying is a baby's way of communicating its needs.*

Using Vocal Cords

Remember the Discover Activity. The stretched neck of the balloon vibrated when you let air out of the balloon. Your vocal cords are somewhat like the stretched neck of the balloon. **Vocal cords** are thin flaps at the top of your windpipe. When you speak, you direct air upward from your lungs past the vocal cords. The flow of air vibrates the flaps and this vibration produces sound. You can change the sounds to form words by using your mouth, teeth, and tongue.

Your voice is important in helping you to survive. Think about the times you have used your voice to call for help or to warn someone of danger. You also use your voice to ask for things you need. What other ways do you use your voice that help you get what you need to live?

If you touch your throat as you talk, you can feel the vibrations.

Location of Vocal Cords

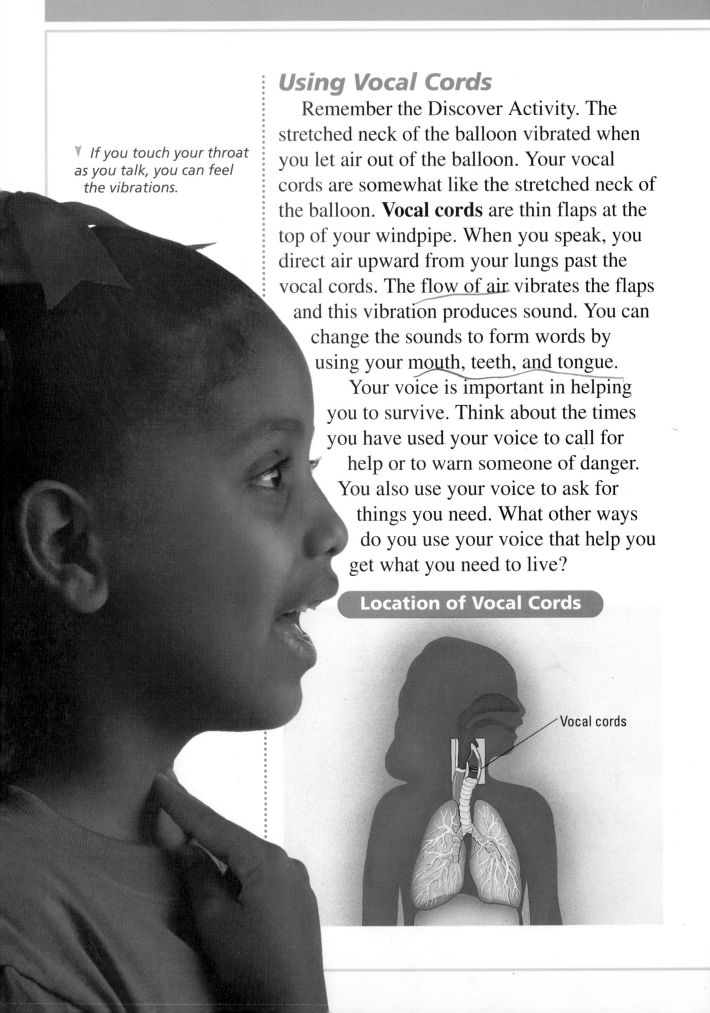

Vocal cords

Other animals also use sounds. You may think that most animals' sounds are just noise. But that's not true. Most animal sounds have a meaning. The animal may be making sounds that help it communicate with other animals. Animal sounds may mean things such as, "Hey, I'm over here," or "Stay away from me!" The sounds might also be warnings of danger. Animals use sounds to help them survive in many of the same ways that people use sound.

Animals, such as dogs and apes, make sounds with vocal cords very much like yours. However, these animals aren't able to make as many different sounds as you can make. The squirrel in the picture seems to be chattering—maybe to chase another animal away from its nest or from its food. The frog below croaks to attract other frogs, but may stop croaking if danger nears.

▲ *Squirrels use their vocal cords to communicate with other animals.*

◄ *The large air sac helps the frog make loud sounds.*

Other Ways to Make Sounds

Many animals don't have vocal cords, but they can make sounds in other ways. Let's find out about the ways that animals use other parts of their bodies to make sounds.

Notice the pictures of the rabbit and its foot. If you happen to scare a rabbit, it might make a thumping sound on the ground with a hind foot. This noise warns other rabbits that they might be near danger.

Many animals use sounds to warn one another, but sometimes they are warning you! For example, if you surprised a rattlesnake, the snake would try to scare you by shaking its tail of rattles. Most likely you would run, and perhaps too quickly to notice if the snake really was a rattlesnake. Many harmless snakes shake their tails among dry leaves, making a sound like a rattlesnake.

You may have noticed that crickets make a lot of sound, especially at night. Crickets make these sounds by rubbing their wings together.

▼ The sound the rabbit makes with its foot travels through the ground.

Grasshoppers, such as the one shown, use their wings to make sounds, too. Notice in the picture that the grasshopper has teethlike ridges on the inside of its back legs. The grasshopper rubs these ridges over hard veins in its wings to make sound.

Crawfish rub their feelers against their shells to frighten other animals away. This sound is like rubbing your fingers over the teeth of a comb. But the hard shell of a crawfish makes the sound a lot louder! A large shrimp uses its huge claw to make a loud snapping sound against hard objects. Whatever the sound, many animals use sounds to help them survive.

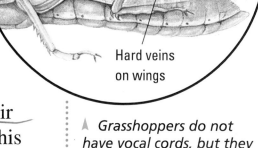

Teeth on legs

Hard veins on wings

▲ *Grasshoppers do not have vocal cords, but they can still make sounds.*

Checkpoint

1. How do vocal cords make sounds?
2. How do animals that don't have vocal cords make sounds?
3. **Take Action!** If you could not speak, how might you "talk" to a person who could not read? Design a way of making sounds that have meanings to help you.

Activity

Investigating Sounds

What can you learn about the sounds around you? Try this activity to find out.

Picture A

Picture B

Picture C

Gather These Materials

paper   pencil

Follow This Procedure

1 Make a chart like the one on the next page. Record your observations in your chart.

2 Plan a walk through your school building.

3 On your chart, list the locations you plan to stop and listen.

> **Predict: What different sounds do you think you will hear?**

4 Walk through the school building with a partner. Stop outside each door on your list. Do not go inside.

5 Listen to the sounds you hear coming from each room. (Picture A) Take notes about the sounds you hear. Record what you think might be making the sounds.

6 Repeat step 5 with the other locations on your list. (Pictures B and C)

Record Your Results

Location	Sounds heard	Possible activity

State Your Conclusions

1. What were some of the sounds you heard?

2. At which locations were the sounds similar? different?

3. How were the sounds you heard different from one another?

4. Based on your observations, what activities do you think were going on in each room?

Let's Experiment

Now that you have made lists of the sounds you heard, how could you group the sounds? List each sound in one of the groups you chose.

2.2 *Hearing Sounds*

▶ *How do living things hear sounds?*

Many sounds surround you everywhere you go. Some of the sounds may give you information that you need. Or the sounds may warn you of danger. A weather report may be coming from a radio. Someone may be yelling to warn you to move out of the way of a car. But if you can't hear these sounds, they can't help you survive. People and many other animals have ears for hearing these sounds. Let's find out how ears work.

The Ear

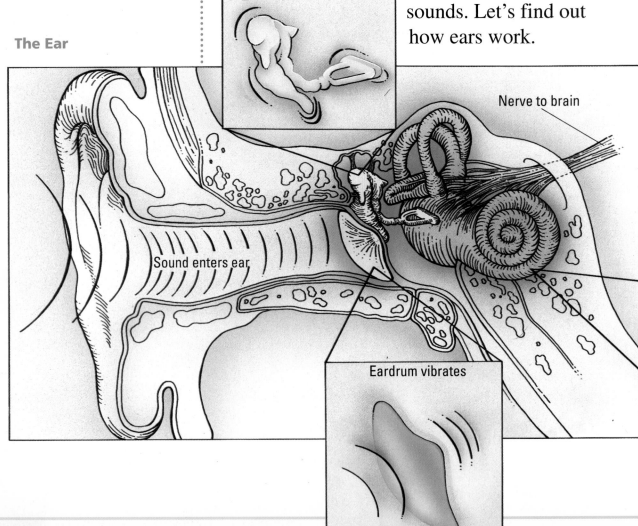

Tiny bones vibrate

Nerve to brain

Sound enters ear

Eardrum vibrates

Hearing With Ears

At all times, both of your ears are receiving sounds. Because of the direction the sounds are coming from, your left ear and right ear may hear the sound differently. This difference helps you know where sounds are coming from. When might it be helpful to know the direction sound is coming from?

The outer ear catches, or collects, sound waves. Then the outer ear directs the sound to the part of the ear inside your head. The sound waves hit a thin skin called the **eardrum**. Notice in the picture that the eardrum vibrates as the sound waves hit it. The vibrating eardrum causes the three tiny bones shown in the picture to vibrate. Find the part of the ear that is shaped like a snail's shell. A liquid fills this part of the ear and the vibrating bones cause the liquid to vibrate. The liquid carries the sound waves to a **nerve**—a part of the body that carries messages to the brain. Then your brain helps you understand the sound it received.

Many animals have ears similar to your ears. But, a dog's ears can hear high pitched sounds and soft sounds that even people can't hear! Many other animals can also hear high pitched sounds or soft sounds that people can't hear. Why do some animals have better hearing than people do?

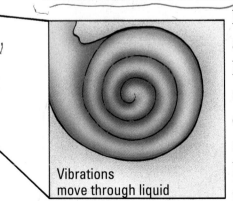

Vibrations move through liquid

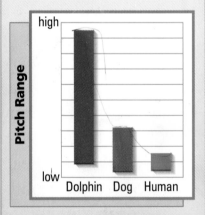

Animal Ears

Ears help animals survive in many ways.

Animals have many different kinds of ears. Each animal has ears that help it survive.

The jackrabbit often hides in low places in the earth or in tall grass. Its long ears help it to hear danger without lifting its head. A jackrabbit can hear its enemies from far away, so it has plenty of time to escape.

A jackrabbit's ears also help the rabbit to cool off in hot weather. When it is hot, the jackrabbit puts its ears up to give off extra heat and to catch a cool breeze.

German shepherds, like most dogs, have excellent hearing.

Jackrabbit

German shepherd

White-tailed deer

Their ears always stand up ready to catch the softest sound. The excellent hearing of German shepherds helps make these dogs good guides for blind people. German shepherds are also used to help people who are hearing impaired.

The white-tailed deer also has very sharp hearing. Its ears have joints at the places where the ears meet the head. So the deer can turn their ears and catch sounds from many directions.

Elephant

Elephants have the biggest ears of all, but their hearing is only average. The elephant flaps its huge ears like giant fans. In this way, the elephant's ears help the elephant to cool off and to blow away insects.

Unusual "Ears"

Not all animals have ears like yours. However, most animals have some way of receiving sound vibrations. Being aware of different sounds around them helps these animals to stay alive.

Probably the most unusual "ears" you might find are on some insects. Many insects, such as the butterfly in the picture, receive sound waves through antennas. **Antennas** are the long feelers on the heads of some animals. Some other insects have hairs on different parts of their body that pick up vibrations. The katydid in the picture has openings on its forelegs through which it receives sound vibrations.

Birds hear through little flaps of skin that are usually covered with feathers. These flaps catch sound and direct it toward the bird's inner ear. Birds have excellent hearing. This is especially important to owls and other night hunters that use hearing to find food in the dark.

▼ *Find the openings on the forelegs of this katydid.*

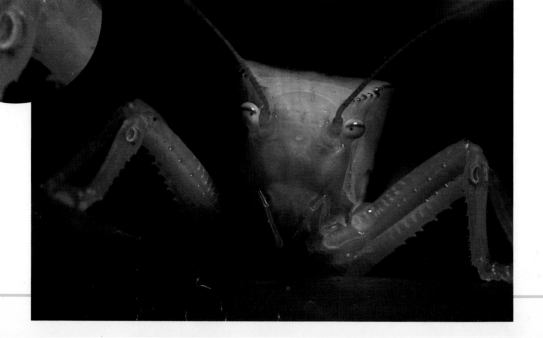

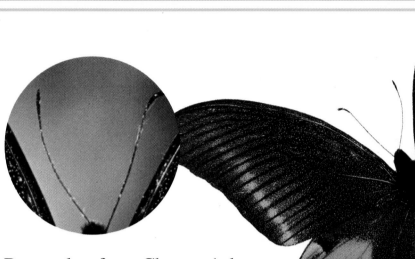

Remember from Chapter 1 that bats use echoes when they are hunting for food or flying. They have large cone-shaped outer ears that catch sound waves. The shape of their ears also helps bats know where sounds are coming from.

Notice the large spot on the side of the frog's body. This spot is a **membrane,** a very thin layer of skin. It covers the frog's inner ear and vibrates when sound waves hit it. Frogs can also feel vibrations through the ground.

Fish also have very unusual "ears." They have a line of grooves running down the sides of their head and body. These lines pick up vibrations from the water.

▲ The papilio butterfly from India has large antennas.

▲ If a frog feels the vibrations of someone walking nearby, it quickly jumps away.

Checkpoint

1. What happens to sound waves after they enter the outer ear?
2. How do the outer ears of some animals help them to hear well?
3. How do some insects hear?
4. **Take Action!** Make a model of a person's ear. Label the parts.

Activity

How Well Do You Hear?

Do you hear equally well with both ears? Try this activity to find out.

Picture A

Picture B

Picture C

Gather These Materials

chair

meter stick

masking tape

ticking clock

Follow This Procedure

1 Make a chart like the one on the next page. Record your observations on your chart.

2 Make a mark on the floor with masking tape. Measure 7 m from the mark. (Picture A) Mark each meter with a piece of tape.

3 Place a chair at the first mark. Ask a partner to sit in the chair, facing away from the marks, and cover his or her right ear.

Predict: *From how far away will your partner be able to hear the ticking?*

4 Stand behind your partner at the second mark. Hold the clock. Slowly walk backwards away from the chair. (Pictures B and C)

5 Ask your partner to say "Stop" when he or she can no longer hear the clock ticking. Place the clock on the floor at that point.

6 Measure the distance from the clock to your partner's ear. Record your results.

Record Your Results

	Distance between ear and clock	
	Left ear	Right ear
Your partner		
You		

7 Repeat steps 3–6 with the other ear. Record your results.

8 Change places with your partner and repeat steps 3–7. Record your results.

State Your Conclusions

1. Could you hear better with your right ear or your left ear?

2. Could your partner hear better with one ear than the other? Which one?

3. Which of you can hear better in the left ear? in the right ear?

Let's Experiment

Now that you have tested how well you hear with each ear, do you think you would hear better with both ears? Use what you know about scientific methods to find out.

Chapter Review

Reviewing Words and Concepts

Write the letter of the word or phrase that best completes each sentence.

1. Your ____ are thin flaps at the top of your windpipe.
2. Crickets make sounds by rubbing their ____ together.
3. Many animals use sound to help them ____.
4. When you speak, your vocal cords ____ to make sound.
5. Sound waves enter your ear and cause a thin skin called the ____ to vibrate.
6. The ____ is the part of the ear that carries messages to the brain.
7. A jackrabbit's long ____ help it to hear danger without lifting its head.
8. The white-tailed deer can turn its ears and catch sounds from many ____.
9. Many insects receive sound waves through ____, or long feelers on their heads.
10. A thin layer of skin, or ____, covers the inner ear of a frog.

a. antennas
b. eardrum
c. wings
d. ears
e. directions
f. nerve
g. vibrate
h. membrane
i. survive
j. vocal cords

Connecting Ideas

1. Copy the concept map. Use the terms at the right to complete the map about sounds being made and heard.

nerve   eardrum
    vocal cords

A. air from lungs   F. brain

B. ____ — C. sound — D. ____ — E. ____

2. Write a sentence or two about the ideas shown in the concept map.

Interpreting What You Learned

1. How does making sounds help animals?
2. How can animals without vocal cords make sounds?
3. Describe how an eardrum helps a person hear sounds.
4. Describe how two different outer ears affect hearing.
5. Compare a membrane on a frog's body to an eardrum.
6. How do antennas help an animal hear sounds?

  ## Performance Assessment

How well can you identify what makes sound?

Materials • 3 boxes with objects • paper • pencil

Collecting Data

1. Look at the three boxes your teacher has prepared for this activity. Do not open any of the boxes.
2. Pick up the box labeled *1* and shake the box. Listen to the sound it makes. Write a description of what you hear. Draw pictures of the objects you think might be in the box.
3. Pick up the box labeled *2* and shake the box. Listen to the sound it makes. Write a description of what you hear. Draw pictures of the objects you think might be in the box.
4. Pick up the box labeled *3* and shake the box. Listen to the sound it makes. Write a description of what you hear. Draw pictures of the objects you think might be in the box.
5. Open each of the boxes in order to identify the contents of the box.

Analyzing Data

Were you able to identify the objects in each box? What clues did you use to help you identify the objects?

3

Louder Sounds

It's coming in loud and clear over here.

How far away can you hear a ticking clock?

Stand near the clock and slowly walk away from it. Stop when you can't hear the ticking. Measure the distance from the clock to where you stopped. Tape cardboard tubes end to end to cover this same distance. Put one end near the clock and the other end near your ear. Does the ticking sound louder through the tubes?

For Discussion

1. *Why is the ticking louder through the tubes?*
2. *How far can you hear through the tubes?*

3.1 Megaphones

How far do sound waves travel?

The people in the picture are trying to yell something to a player on a football or baseball field. When they yell, their voices carry farther than the sound of their speaking voices. But, they may still be too far from the field to be heard. As sound waves move away from their source, they become weaker. If these people aren't heard, it probably won't make much difference. But sometimes when people are in danger, they need to hear directions from someone. How can you make your voice travel farther than it does when you yell? Why do you think one person in the picture is cupping her mouth?

▼ People often want to communicate with someone who is too far away to hear what is said.

> The megaphone the leader of the rowing team is using looks like those pictured below.

Uses of Megaphones

Police officers or firefighters often have to be heard over long distances. For example, the police may be warning people to move to safety during a flood or a storm. Or a firefighter may have to tell people trapped in a burning building what to do for safety.

Sometimes people can cup their hands around their mouth and then yell to be heard. Try cupping your hands around your mouth and then talking to someone a distance away. You can find out how much farther your voice can be heard.

Notice the picture of the rowing team at the top of the page. What is their leader using to talk to them? The leader is using a megaphone. A **megaphone** is a cone-shaped horn used to increase the loudness of the voice. A megaphone also increases the distance at which sound can be heard. One end of a megaphone is about the size of the human mouth, while the opposite end is much larger.

Directing Sound

As you learned earlier, when a sound is made, sound waves travel out in all directions. However, if you hold a megaphone up to your mouth, the megaphone directs the sound waves. The sound energy does not spread out as much as without the megaphone. So with more energy, the sound waves of your voice travel farther. And you can be heard farther away. Using a megaphone is like cupping your hands around your mouth isn't it?

When firefighters use a megaphone, what they say is directed toward where they point the megaphone. Then the people the firefighters are trying to help can hear what the firefighters say to them.

Helping Sound Travel

Without megaphone

With megaphone

▲ Sound waves travel out in all directions. A megaphone directs the sound waves.

Checkpoint

1. How might a megaphone be useful?
2. How does a megaphone help sound travel farther?
3. **Take Action!** Make megaphones using different materials. Compare how well they work.

Making Sounds Louder

How can you make sounds louder? Try this activity to find out.

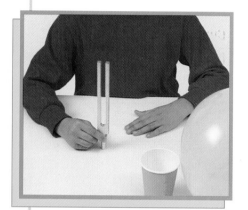

Picture A

Gather These Materials

cover goggles
tuning fork
table

inflated balloon
waste basket
paper cup

Follow This Procedure

1 Make a chart like the one on the next page. Record your observations in your chart.

2 Put on your cover goggles.

3 Tap the tuning fork on your hand to make it vibrate. Listen to the sound it produces.

Predict: How will the sound change when the tuning fork touches an object?

Picture B

4 Tap the tuning fork again. This time, place the handle of the tuning fork on a table. Write what happens to the sound. (Picture A)

5 Tap the tuning fork again. This time touch the handle of the fork to the inflated balloon. *CAUTION: Be careful not to break the balloon.* Record your observations. (Picture B)

6 Tap the tuning fork again and touch the handle to the bottom of a metal waste basket. Record your observations.

Picture C

7 Repeat step 6, touching the vibrating tuning fork to different places on a paper cup. Record your observations. (Picture C)

State Your Conclusions

1. What happened to the sound when you placed the vibrating tuning fork against the table? the balloon? the metal waste basket?

2. What happened to the sound of the vibrating tuning fork when you touched the fork to the cup? What part of the cup was most effective in making the sound louder?

3. Based on what you have observed, how can you explain the differences in sound?

Vibrating tuning fork against:	Observations
Table	
Balloon	
Waste basket	
Cup sides	
Cup top	
Cup bottom	

Let's Experiment

How could you use a ruler to make sounds higher or lower? Use what you know about scientific methods to find out.

Into The Field

Does the size of a paper cone affect how well it amplifies sound?

Use paper cones of different sizes to amplify sound. How well do they work? CAUTION: Do not listen to loud noises.

➤ Police officers may use bullhorns that are attached to the top of their cars.

3.2 *Making Sound Louder*

How can we make sound louder?

You have learned that police officers and firefighters may use megaphones to direct the sound of their voices. However, sometimes their voices still may not be heard because of the distance or other sounds. For example, dangerous fumes might accidentally escape in a place where a lot of people live. Police officers need to let the people who live in the area know that they should leave. If the police officers drive down the streets using a megaphone to warn people, the officers' voices probably won't be heard. How can the officers communicate with people who are farther away than their voices can be heard through a megaphone?

◀ *Firefighters often use bullhorns to talk to people in burning buildings.*

Bullhorns

One way that a person's voice can be made louder is by using a bullhorn, such as the one shown in the picture. A **bullhorn** is a megaphone with a built-in microphone. It can increase the energy of the sound waves made by the speaking voice up to 100 times. To use a bullhorn, you speak into its mouthpiece, which is a small microphone. The microphone changes the sound energy into electrical energy, or **electric signals**. These signals travel into another part of the bullhorn that amplifies them. **Amplify** means to make louder. The amplified signals then move into the speaker of the bullhorn. The speaker changes the signals back into sound waves having more energy than the sound waves that entered the mouthpiece. Since the sound waves have more energy, the volume of the sound is louder. The sound waves are also directed by the shape of the bullhorn. So the amplified sound can be heard up to ten times as far away as the unaided voice.

▼ *Bullhorns are often used to control crowds.*

Microphones

Microphones of today are smaller and work better.

Microphones are used to amplify the sound of people's voices, music, or any other sounds. Look at the diagram of the microphone. When sound waves hit a microphone, a part inside of the microphone begins to vibrate. The microphone changes the sound energy of the sound wave into electric energy. Then the electric energy travels through the wire to an amplifier. The amplifier strengthens the electric energy, which travels to a speaker. Because the electric energy is stronger, the volume of the sound it produces is louder.

Amplifying Sound

Sound energy

Microphone

Wire

Amplifier

Speaker

Sound energy

1876 First microphone was the large telephone transmitter invented by Alexander Graham Bell.

1920–1940 A rod of carbon was the vibrating part of carbon microphones. These large, heavy microphones were used in radio broadcasting.

1900

1920

1950s–1960s The vibrating part of dynamic microphones is a tiny, thin sheet of plastic. Dynamic microphones can be held easily in one hand.

1938–1940s A light metal ribbon was the vibrating part of ribbon microphones. Although they picked up more sound than carbon microphones, they were still heavy and hard to move.

1970 Electret microphones can be clipped to a collar and are so small they are hardly seen. These tiny microphones are also used in hearing aids.

1940	1960	1980

Hearing Aids

Hearing is important to the safety and survival of people. So people who have a loss of hearing try to find ways to improve their hearing. You may have a friend or a relative with a hearing problem. If so, the person may wear a hearing aid. As with the microphone, hearing aids have become smaller over the years and at the same time more helpful.

Notice the picture of the woman using a hearing aid. People had to sit close together to use this hearing aid. Another early hearing aid was the ear trumpet—a large metal horn. It looked somewhat like a megaphone—only used backwards. People with a hearing loss would hold the small end of the horn up to their ear. Then people who wanted to talk to them would speak into the large opening of the horn on the other end. Sound waves from the voices of the people speaking were directed by the horn to the ear of the hearing-impaired person.

Later, people began to wear hearing aids that had microphones in them. These were usually large and bulky and needed electricity to operate. So the person who wore them also had to wear a battery pack.

Early hearing aids were large and often hard to use.

▲ *Today, hearing aids are about the size of a penny.*

During the 1960s, a tiny battery was made that can be used in tiny hearing aids. As shown in the pictures, these hearing aids fit completely inside the ear. Some hearing aids fit behind the ear and send sound vibrations directly to the nerve leading to the brain. These hearing aids help people who have inner ear damage. But some people have problems because the hearing aids also amplify background noises. So scientists are still working to make better hearing aids to help keep people safe.

Checkpoint

1. How might bullhorns help people?
2. How have microphones been improved?
3. How do hearing aids help people to hear better?
4. Take Action! Use a megaphone you made in Lesson 1 as a hearing aid. Explain how it works.

Harmful Sounds

As you know, sounds can be soft or loud. Sounds that are painfully loud can cause hearing loss. Also, some other sounds can damage your ears if they are listened to for more than a half hour a day over a period of time. Use the graph to answer the questions:

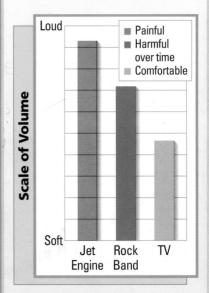

What Did You Find Out?
1. *Which sound is softer, a TV or a rock band?*
2. *Which sound is louder, a rock band or a jet engine?*
3. *Which sounds can harm your ears if you listen to them for long periods of time?*
4. *Which sound is most likely to cause hearing loss?*

Activity

Exploring Shapes of Speakers

How can you amplify the sound from a record? How does the shape of the "speaker" affect the volume of sound? Try this activity to find out.

Picture A

Picture B

Picture C

Gather These Materials

cover goggles
record player
old record
hand lens

straight pin
file card
small empty match box
paper cup

Follow This Procedure

1 Make a chart like the one on the next page. Record your observations in your chart.

2 Put on your cover goggles.

3 Use the hand lens to observe the grooves on the old record.

4 Put the record on the record player and turn on the record player. Use the hand lens to observe the grooves as the record moves. (Picture A)

5 Hold the straight pin over the moving record. Gently place the pin in one of the grooves of the record. Do not try this activity at home. The pin will damage the record. Record your observations. *CAUTION: Be careful when using the pin.*

Predict: *How can you change the sound when you touch the pin to the record?*

6 Push the pin through the corner of a file card. Then touch the pin to a groove of the moving record. (Picture B) Write your observations.

7 Repeat step 6 using a small match box instead of the file card. (Picture C)

8 Repeat step 6 using a paper cup.

State Your Conclusions

1. What did the grooves on the record look like when you looked through the hand lens?

2. How did the sound produced by the straight pin alone compare with the sound produced by the pin when you used the file card? the small box? the paper cup?

3. Based on what you have observed, what should the shape of a speaker be?

Record Your Results

	Observation: describe the sound
Pin in groove	
Pin through file card	
Pin through box	
Pin through paper cup	

Let's Experiment

What would happen if you used a larger or smaller cup? Use what you know about scientific methods to find out.

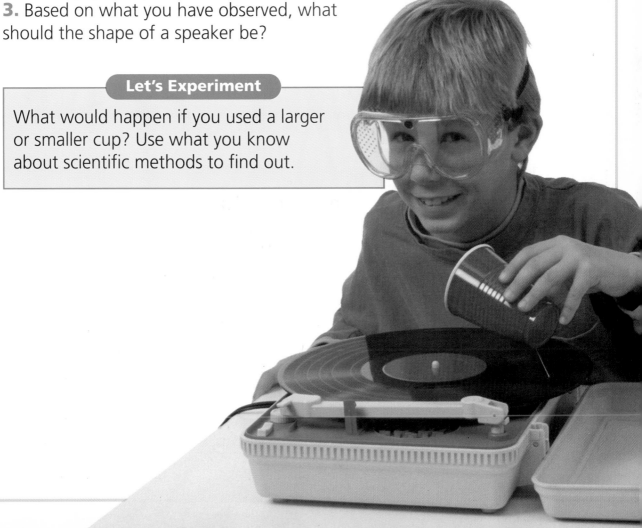

Chapter Review

Reviewing Words and Concepts

Write the letter of the word or phrase that best completes each sentence.

1. A cone-shaped horn without a microphone that is used to increase the loudness of the voice is a ____.
2. A microphone changes sound energy into ____.
3. A megaphone with a built-in microphone is a ____.
4. A megaphone increases the energy in sound waves by ____ the sound.
5. A bullhorn makes signals louder, or ____ them.
6. When sound waves hit a microphone, a part inside the microphone begins to ____.
7. The ear ____ was an early hearing aid.
8. In a bullhorn, electric signals are changed back into sound waves by the ____.
9. Police officers may use a megaphone to ____ people to move to safety.
10. Some tiny ____ fit completely inside the ear.

a. amplifies
b. trumpet
c. hearing aids
d. bullhorn
e. warn
f. directing
g. vibrate
h. megaphone
i. speaker
j. electric signals

Connecting Ideas

1. Copy the concept map. Use the terms at the right to complete the map about sound.

amplifies   bullhorn
directs   sound

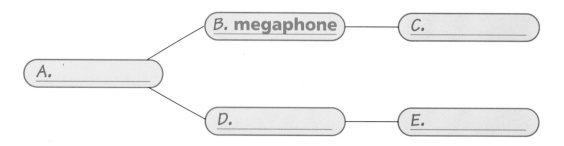

A. ____
B. megaphone
C. ____
D. ____
E. ____

2. Write a sentence or two about the ideas shown in the concept map.

Interpreting What You Learned

1. How is a bullhorn different from a megaphone?
2. How are the sound waves that leave a bullhorn different from the sound waves that enter it?
3. How have microphones changed over time?
4. Explain how hearing aids have been improved over time.

Performance Assessment

How can you change the pitch and volume of sound?

Materials • 2 straws • plastic or rubber tubing • funnel • scissors • masking tape

Collecting Data

1. Use the two straws and scissors to make pitch pipes. Flatten one end of each straw and cut off the corners to make a point. Set one pitch pipe aside to use later.
2. Using the other pitch pipe, push the end of the straw you did not cut into one end of the tubing. Tape around the tubing where the straw and tube come together so no air escapes.
3. Push the tip of the funnel into the other end of the tubing. If it does not fit, push the end of the tubing into the tip of the funnel. Tape around the tubing where the funnel and tube come together so no air escapes.

4. Pick up the pitch pipe without the tubing or funnel. Blow into the pitch pipe to make sound. Write about the pitch and the volume of the sound it makes.
5. Pick up the pitch pipe that is attached to the tubing and funnel. Hold the funnel so that the mouth of the funnel faces you. Blow into the pitch pipe to make sound. Write about the pitch and the volume of the sound it makes.

Analyzing Data

Compare the sounds made by the two pitch pipes. How are they the same? How are they different?

How Loud Is Too Loud?

You probably think of pollution as something that makes the water, land, or air dirty. Noise can be pollution, too. Noises that are too loud or high pitched, or go on too long can harm you. They can make you cranky and disturb your sleep. They can even cause hearing loss.

Needs and Goals

You can't control all the noises you hear around you. You can't make an ambulance not sound its siren. There are noises that you do have control over, though. Finding out which ones those are will help you cut down on noise pollution.

Noise can be a kind of pollution.

Gathering Information

Some sounds can cause hearing loss if you listen to them for a long time. The table shows some noises and how they can affect you.

Possible Alternatives

Make a list of loud sounds you hear around you. See where these sounds are on the chart. Could they bother you or even hurt your ears?

Evaluating Alternatives

Look at your list. Ask these questions:
- Can you turn the sound down on any of these machines: TVs, radios, and tape players?

Effects of Sound on Hearing

Sources	Effects
Jet plane takes off less than 30 meters	Possible eardrum damage
Aircraft carrier deck	Possible eardrum damage
Earphone at loud level	Painful (can be harmful)
Firecracker, loud thunder, siren nearby	Painful (can be harmful)
Radio held close to ear, car horn at 1 meter	Uncomfortable (can be harmful)
Subway train, power lawn mower, jack hammer	Possible hearing damage
Heavy city traffic, food blender	Possible hearing damage
Garbage disposal, freight train 20 meters	Possible hearing damage
Automobile on highway	Annoying
Typewriter, window air conditioner	Annoying
Singing birds, normal talking	Quiet
Refrigerator, soft background music	Quiet
Dripping faucet, countryside at night	Quiet
Light rainfall, blowing leaves, whisper	Very quiet
Breathing	Just able to hear

- Some sounds are louder when you stand closer to them. Can you stand farther away from machines like power mowers?

Making the Best Choice
What sounds can you make softer? What can you do to protect yourself from sounds you can't control?

Look down your list again. Have you done anything about any of the loud sounds?

Now You Do It

1. What things do you plan to do to make your life quieter?
2. How might you be able to measure the success of your plans?
3. *On Your Own* Some jobs are noisier than others. Make a list of jobs people do that make a lot of noise. Find out what people in these jobs do to protect their ears.
4. *Critical Thinking* Some communities pass laws that limit the amount of noise. What kinds of laws might they make?

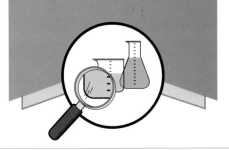

A Bridge Between People

Tyrone Nash

Occupation: Sign-language interpreter
Hobbies: Singing, dancing, playing volleyball

Have you ever given your friend a secret message? And only you and your friend knew its meaning? Tyrone and his friend did that in high school. They both knew the sign-language alphabet so they could give each other messages from one side of the classroom to the other. And they didn't make a sound! Tyrone got so interested in sign language that he went to school to learn more ways of signing. Now he is a sign-language interpreter.

What does a sign-language interpreter do?

"I'm a bridge between people who can hear and those who can't. Most of the time, deaf people can get along without an interpreter. But sometimes it's very important for them to understand exactly what is being said. For example, they might be talking to a lawyer or a doctor."

Do you spell everything out?

"Some things are spelled out. You may have seen the sign-language alphabet. But there is also a sign-language vocabulary. There's a sign for the word *walk*, a sign for the word *rain*, and so on. It would take much too long to spell out each word."

How do you learn all those signs?

"You learn by understanding the meanings and then practicing. It's very important to know all I can because there are many ways of saying the same thing in sign language. Do you say, 'I will see you later,' in formal English, or do you shorten that to 'See ya later'? Deaf people do the same thing."

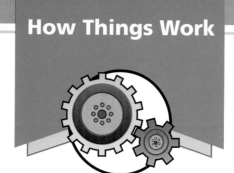

Changing Pitch by Sliding

A trombone is a brass instrument. You can play a trombone by vibrating your lips on its mouthpiece. Look at the picture to find out how a trombone changes the pitch of the notes.

1 A trombone has a long slide for changing the pitch of a note.

2 When you pull the slide out, you make the tube long; the air in a long tube vibrates slowly, producing a low sound.

3 You can make the pitch higher by making the tube short; air in a short tube vibrates quickly, producing a high sound.

5 Some trombones have three valves instead of a slide; as each valve is pressed down, the tube gets longer or shorter, changing the pitch.

4 As you pull the slide to different positions, you make different notes.

Find Out On Your Own

Fill each of four bottles with a different amount of water. Blow over the mouth of each bottle. Write a paragraph explaining what happens and why.

Module Performance Assessment

Sound Museum

Using what you learned in this module, help prepare exhibitions on sound and hearing to be used at a local museum. Complete one or more of the following activities. You may work by yourself or with others in a group.

Drama

Make up a story to act out as a puppet show. Think of as many sounds as you can to make the story lifelike. You can record your own sounds, like running water and crackling paper. You might also use sounds from a record or tape from the library.

Art

Draw a picture comparing how far sound travels when a person speaks, shouts, uses a megaphone, or uses a bullhorn.

Biology

Make a poster called "Unusual Ears." Draw or cut out pictures of animals with unusual ways of receiving sound vibrations. Write a sentence for each picture explaining how that animal hears. Make a second poster called "Unusual Voices," showing animals that use different parts of their bodies to make sounds.

Environment

Imagine that you are the safety officer in your community. Decide which sounds in your classroom or community could be considered harmful sounds. Write some new rules or laws that would help get rid of these noises.

Writing

Pretend you have ears that can move like cat or dog ears. Would you be able to hear better? Write an explanation of why or why not.

Module Review

Reviewing Words and Concepts

Write the letter of the word or phrase that best completes each sentence.

1. All sounds are made by something that causes matter to ____.
2. The sound made by falling leaves has a very soft ____.
3. Large bells usually vibrate slowly and have a low ____.
4. Sound waves travel fastest in ____ in which the particles are closest together.
5. People and some other animals use their ____ to make sound.
6. When sound waves enter your ear, they cause your ____ to vibrate.
7. Many insects have ____ that receive sound waves.
8. The sounds that leave the speaker of a ____ are louder than the sound waves that entered the mouthpiece.
9. Before sound is amplified in a microphone, sound energy is changed to ____.
10. You hear an ____ when sound waves hit an object and bounce back.

a. matter
b. antennas
c. pitch
d. electric signals
e. vocal cords
f. bullhorn
g. eardrum
h. volume
i. echo
j. vibrate

Interpreting What You Learned

1. How is sound produced?
2. Explain how the outer ear and the eardrum help people hear sounds.
3. Explain two ways that the volume of a person's voice can be increased.
4. How are a person's vocal cords and eardrums alike? How are they different?

Applying What You Learned

1. Explain why sound from a bullhorn is louder than from a megaphone.
2. Will a large drum or a small drum make a higher sound? Why?
3. Name at least two characteristics you can use to classify sound. Then list some sounds for each characteristic you name.

Protecting the Earth

Protecting the Earth

People share the earth with billions and billions of living things. Like us, they need clean water, clean air, and space in which to live. But sometimes people add harmful things to the earth's water, air, and living spaces. In this module, you'll find out how people change the earth and what they can do to help protect it.

CHAPTER

1 Clean Water

Is it safe to drink? Polluted water hurts everyone—fish, plants, and people. It's time to clean it up.

3 Making a Difference

Every little bit helps. By working to protect the earth, people can save plants, animals, and other living things.

CHAPTER

2 All About Trash

Pull out the papers from the trash! Papers and other products that can be recycled often end up in the trash and are not used again.

Clean Water

It keeps splitting!

Discover Activity

How can you clean up oil?

You might have heard about the many problems oil spills cause. How can you remove oil from water? Fill a flat pan with water. Pour enough cooking oil into the pan to make a thin film of oil on the water. Think of a way to remove the oil. Then try it. Compare your results with those of your classmates.

For Discussion
1. *How did you clean up the oil?*
2. *Would your method work on a large oil spill?*

1.1 *Rippling Waters*

▶ *What has happened to our water?*

Graceful birds take flight over the sparkling water in the picture. Under the water, fish dart from place to place. Clean water is important for all the plants and animals that live in this habitat.

Water Resources

More and more, people are joining forces to change our world for the better. Many people are working to clean and protect our waters. Water is our most important natural resource. In fact, all living things need water to live. On the next few pages, you'll learn more about how water is important to you and other living things.

▼ *Water is important to all living things.*

Water Everywhere

Water is the earth's most important natural resource.

Here's a riddle to solve. All plants and animals need this to stay alive. You use it every day. What is it? It's water!

Where do you get water? You probably just turn on a faucet to get all the water you use. The water from your faucet probably came from a river, or a lake, or a well. But no matter where your water comes from, there's an important fact to remember. You couldn't live without water. In which of the ways shown in the picture do you use water every day? In what ways that are not pictured do you use water?

Living Things in Water

You gaze at the calm water. No sign of life appears. But, under the water, the scene looks different. The water is filled with life and bustling with activity. Animals of many kinds thrive. Fish, like those in the picture, silently glide through the water in search of food.

Sunlight reaches below the water's surface. Algae and other producers use sunlight to make the sugars they need to survive. Food for animals is plentiful in the water. Living things have lots of space to live and grow. These living things get everything they need from their water habitat.

Many different things can change the water habitats of plants, algae, and animals. For example, rain and melting snow can wash dirt and other materials into water. Some of these materials can be harmful. Also, plants and animals that were once alive decay in water. Sometimes, harmful materials enter bodies of water as a result of people's activities. **Water pollution** (pə lü′ shən) is any harmful thing that might be added to water. Many bodies of water all over the world are polluted. But, you cannot always see pollution in the water. Sometimes, water that looks very clear can be polluted.

▼ *Living things in a water habitat*

► *Litter needs to be kept out of waterways.*

How can water pollution change the habitats of plants and animals? Harmful materials in water, such as certain wastes from cities, factories, and farms, can be poisonous. They might make animals ill. Some plants and animals might be unable to live in polluted waters.

Harmful materials in water can travel through a food chain. Producers in the water might take in these materials and store some of them. Then small fish might eat some of the producers. What happens to the harmful materials when larger fish or animals eat the small ones? Why would you choose not to eat food that had lived in polluted waters?

Litter, such as that shown here, sometimes clutters waterways. Some kinds of trash can even harm animals. For example, an animal might be cut by a sharp edge on a metal can. You can help prevent this kind of water pollution by throwing litter into trash cans.

In the Discover Activity, you learned about cleaning one kind of pollution from water. In the next lesson, you will read more about keeping water clean.

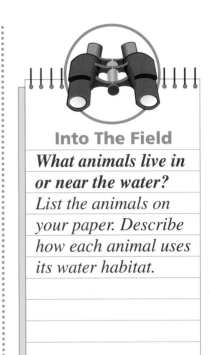

Into The Field

What animals live in or near the water?

List the animals on your paper. Describe how each animal uses its water habitat.

Checkpoint

1. Why is water our most important natural resource?
2. Name five ways people use water.
3. How can water pollution affect plants and animals?
4. **Take Action!** Make a poster showing why clean water is important.

Activity

Observing Plants in Polluted Water

Polluted water can harm both plants and animals. In this activity, you'll observe the effects of polluted water on the growth of a water plant.

Picture A

Gather These Materials

cover goggles   cooking oil
4 clear plastic cups   vinegar
4 sprigs of elodea   3 spoons
water   masking tape
soap   marker

Follow This Procedure

1 Make a chart like the one on the next page. Record your observations in your chart.

2 Put on your cover goggles.

3 Use masking tape and a marker to make four labels: *soap, cooking oil, vinegar,* and *clean water.* Attach each label to a cup. (Picture A)

Picture B

4 Fill each cup two-thirds full of water.

5 Add 2 spoonfuls of soap to the cup marked *soap.* Stir. (Picture B)

6 Add 2 spoonfuls of cooking oil to the cup marked *cooking oil.* Stir.

7 Add 2 spoonfuls of vinegar to the cup marked *vinegar* and stir.

8 Do not add anything to the cup marked *clean water.*

Picture C

Record Your Results

	Clean water	Water with soap	Water with cooking oil	Water with vinegar
Day 1				
Day 2				
Day 3				
Day 4				
Day 5				

9 Place an elodea plant in each cup. (Picture C)

10 Observe each plant. What does the plant look like? Record your observations in the "Day 1" row of your chart.

Predict: *How will each material added to the water affect the elodea plants?*

11 Observe the elodea plants every day for 5 days. Record your observations.

State Your Conclusions

1. How might you explain the differences in the elodea plants at the end of 5 days?

2. Use what you learned in this activity to explain how water pollution might affect living things in natural bodies of water.

Let's Experiment

What effects do different amounts of pollution have on plants? Use what you know about scientific methods to design an experiment to find out.

▼ *Water goes down the drain.*

Pollution Solutions

▶ ***How can people prevent water pollution?***

The drain in your kitchen sink might look something like the one on the left. Think about how water swirls and gurgles down the drain until it disappears. Where does the water go? Let's follow it.

From Drains to Waterways

Pipes under your sink collect the water. These pipes connect with larger pipes that carry the wastewater away from your house or building. In many places, even larger pipes, called sewers, carry the wastewater away from your neighborhood.

The wastewater in sewers contains germs that can cause disease. It also contains other harmful materials. How might dumping such wastes into rivers or lakes change the water?

▼ *How sewage is treated*

Dirty water passes through screens that keep out fish, trash, and other large objects.

Some dirt and other solids settle out of the water.

Air is bubbled through the water.

Dirty Water

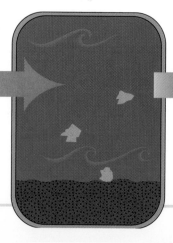

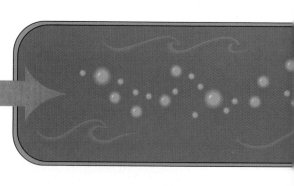

Fortunately, most cities have sewage treatment plants, like the one shown on the right. Sewage treatment plants can clean wastewater before it enters rivers and lakes. Follow the steps in the drawings below. They show how one kind of sewage treatment plant cleans water. You can see that many harmful materials are removed from wastewater as it is moved through the treatment plant. Finally, the cleaned water is piped back into a river or lake. Sewage treatment plants can help keep rivers and lakes clean and safe.

You might wonder if sewage treatment can clean all the harmful materials from water. Unfortunately, the answer is no. Some harmful materials, such as oils, cannot easily be removed from water. It's best not to pour such materials down a drain. Can treatment plants alone solve the pollution problem? No, they cannot. But they certainly can help!

▲ Sewage treatment plant

More dirt and other small solids settle out.

Water filters through materials that remove remaining solids.

Chlorine is added to the water to kill germs that cause disease.

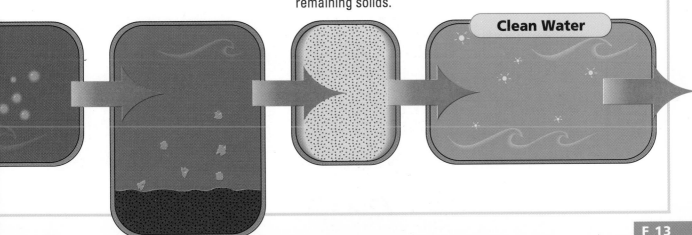

Clean Water

Preventing Water Pollution

You're part of a team! You and your teammates share a common goal—keeping water safe for living things. A joint effort can help keep waterways as clean as the lake in the picture. You learned some things you can do to get closer to the goal. You learned how communities treat wastewater. Let's see what some of the other team members are doing.

Farmers make up part of the team. Some fertilizers and pesticides used in farming can be harmful. Rain can wash these materials into waterways. Many farmers are using fewer of these materials than before. They also are trying to use fertilizers and pesticides that cause as little harm as possible.

➤ *Swimming in water that is clean and safe*

Factories are important members of the clean water team. How can they keep water clean? Many of them have stopped dumping poisonous wastes into waterways. Some factories even operate their own sewage treatment plants.

Many factories also are trying to keep heat from polluting water. The temperature of water matters more than you might think. Many plants and animals cannot survive when the water temperature changes even slightly. Much wastewater that comes from factories and power plants is very hot. Many factories store these hot wastes in towers or ponds until they cool to a temperature that is safe. Only then is this wastewater released into waterways.

Governments share the goal of the team. The United States government passed laws to limit water pollution. These laws can help keep waters safe for activities such as swimming and fishing.

Imagine splashing and swimming in the clean, cool, refreshing water of a lake. That's quite a reward for teamwork!

Checkpoint

1. How do sewage treatment plants help prevent water pollution?
2. How can farmers and factories help prevent water pollution?
3. **Take Action!** Make a poster about preventing water pollution. Show what different people can do.

SOCIAL STUDIES

Down the Drain

When you wash your hands, you might not think about the water you're using. If you're like most Americans, you use about 380 liters of water a day at home. That's 11,400 liters a month and 138,700 liters a year! How do people use all that water?

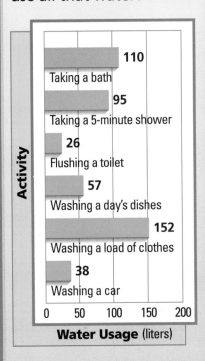

Water Usage (liters)

What Did You Find Out?
1. *How much water does it take to wash a day's worth of dishes?*
2. *How much water does it take to wash a load of clothes?*
3. *Which uses less water, a bath or a 5-minute shower?*
4. *How could your family use less water?*

Activity

How Does Groundwater Affect Food?

You might wonder how water in the ground affects food. You can observe a plant to see how groundwater gets into food.

Picture A

Picture B

Picture C

Gather These Materials

cover goggles
red food coloring
tall plastic glass of
  water

plastic knife
fresh stalk of celery
  with its leaves

Follow This Procedure

1 Make a chart like the one on the next page. Record your observations in your chart.

2 Put on your cover goggles.

3 Put several drops of red food coloring into a tall glass of water. (Picture A) The red food coloring stands for a harmful material that is contained in water in the ground.

4 Use a knife to trim the bottom of a fresh stalk of celery with its leaves. *CAUTION: Handle sharp items carefully.*

5 Place the celery into the glass with red food coloring. (Picture B)

Predict: **What will happen to the red food coloring?**

6 Observe the celery stalk over the next few hours. Record your observations.

7 Use the knife to carefully cut the celery stalk. (Picture C) What does the celery look like on the inside?

State Your Conclusions

1. Explain the color changes you see in the celery stalk.

2. Suppose the red food coloring is a harmful material. What parts of the plant would be affected by it?

3. How might polluted water from the ground affect food?

Record Your Results

Observations

Let's Experiment

How can salt contained in groundwater affect plants? Mix some salt in a glass of water and water a plant with the water. What will happen to the plant? Use what you know about scientific methods to find out.

Chapter Review

Reviewing Words and Concepts

Write the letter of the word or phrase that best completes each sentence.

1. Water is our most important ____.
2. Anything harmful that is added to water is ____.
3. Food for animals is plentiful in a water ____.
4. Harmful materials in water can travel through a ____.
5. The wastewater in sewers contains germs that can cause ____.
6. Some harmful materials, such as ____, cannot easily be removed from water.
7. Sewage treatment plants can clean ____ before it enters rivers and lakes.
8. Some fertilizers and pesticides used in ____ can be harmful to waterways.
9. Some ____ operate their own sewage treatment plants to keep from polluting water.
10. Many plants and animals cannot survive when the water ____ changes even slightly.

a. disease
b. habitat
c. factories
d. temperature
e. farming
f. wastewater
g. natural resource
h. food chain
i. oils
j. water pollution

Connecting Ideas

1. Copy the concept map. Use the terms at the right to complete the map about water pollution to show how it affects living things.

large fish   plants
small fish

A. harmful wastes

B. ____
C. ____
D. ____
E. people and other animals

2. Write a sentence or two about the ideas shown in the concept map.

Interpreting What You Learned

1. How is water important to people?
2. Describe three ways that water can become polluted.
3. Explain what happens to wastewater from buildings.
4. Explain how factories can keep heat from polluting water.
5. How can governments help keep water clean?
6. How do hot wastes from factories pollute waterways?

Performance Assessment

How can you test for water pollution?

Materials • 5 plastic cups with water samples
• 5 pieces of blue litmus paper

Collecting Data

1. Look at the five plastic cups labeled *1*, *2*, *3*, *4*, and *5*. They each contain a sample of water that your teacher prepared. You will find out which of the samples of water are polluted.
2. To test for pollution, you will use blue litmus paper. If the sample is polluted, the blue litmus paper will turn red. If the sample is not polluted, the blue litmus paper will remain blue.
3. Dip the end of one piece of litmus paper into the cup labeled *1*. Observe whether the end of the litmus paper changes color. Record your results.
4. Use the other pieces of litmus paper to test for pollution in the cups labeled *2*, *3*, *4*, and *5*. Record your results.
5. Write a short report telling which of the samples are polluted.

Analyzing Data

Describe what might happen to a fish if it were placed in each of the water samples you tested.

All About Trash

We're tracking trash.

How can you reduce trash?

Your lunch might contain different kinds of food wrappings and packages. Keep track of the things from your lunch that you throw away during one week. Then plan and put together a lunch that does not contain any trash.

yogurt

For Discussion
1. *What lunch container can you use?*
2. *How can you pack a lunch with no trash?*

2.1 *Too Much Garbage*

▶ *What happens to all my trash?*

Lunchtime is over. Like the boy in the picture, you pick up your trash. You spot the wastebasket and toss in the trash. Be careful! The can is almost overflowing.

Looking at Trash

What do people throw away? Students from the University of Arizona poked through piles and piles of trash to find out. What a surprise they got! They found that newspapers, magazines, and packaging make up about half of all trash.

The students also found that tires, cloth items, and disposable diapers make up a large part of trash. Leaves, grass clippings, wood, and food scraps make up another large part. What other things are found in trash? If you named items made of plastic, metal, and glass, you're right.

▼ *Where would you put these items?*

Removing the Trash

What might happen to a milk carton you throw in a wastebasket? Here's one way to find out. Let's follow the path the milk carton might take. Suppose the wastebasket is emptied into a large trash can or trash bags, such as the ones in the picture. Later, a garbage truck, like the one shown below, pulls up to the curb. Someone loads the trash into the truck and drives away. Where does the garbage truck go?

The truck might carry the trash to one of several places. It might carry it to a place that has many huge furnaces. Here, workers **incinerate** (in sin′ ə rāt′) the trash, or burn it in a careful way.

You may wonder if incineration is a safe way to get rid of trash. When trash is burned, some harmful materials can enter the air and cause air pollution. What can be done to help solve this problem?

▼ *Trash is moved from trash bags or cans, to a garbage truck, and then to a sanitary landfill.*

Most modern incinerators burn trash at very high temperatures. These high temperatures help burn away some harmful materials in trash. Many incinerators also put filters, called scrubbers, in their smokestacks. The scrubbers help clean some harmful materials out of smoke before the smoke enters the air. In these ways, air pollution from incineration can be reduced.

Incineration is just one way to get rid of trash. Many communities do not operate incinerators. Where else might the garbage truck take your trash?

Today, most trash ends up in a sanitary landfill, such as the one shown in the picture. A **sanitary landfill** (san′ ə ter′ ē land′ fil′) is a place where garbage is buried in as safe a way as possible. On the following pages, you'll learn a lot more about a sanitary landfill.

Burying Foods

Will potatoes break down if they are buried in the soil? Let's investigate and find out.

What to Do
A. Fill two large cups with soil. Label one cup with the number 1 and the other with the number 2.
B. Take two pieces of cooked potato and draw what they look like.
C. Bury one piece of potato in soil in cup 1. Seal the other piece of potato inside a plastic bag and bury it in soil in cup 2.
D. Keep the soil moist for the next week.
E. Remove the potatoes after a week, and draw what they look like.

Record Your Data

	Potato Appearance	
	Start	Finish
No bag		
In bag		

What Did You Find Out?
1. *Will a potato break down more readily in soil?*
2. *Do your results show that soil is needed for a potato to break down?*

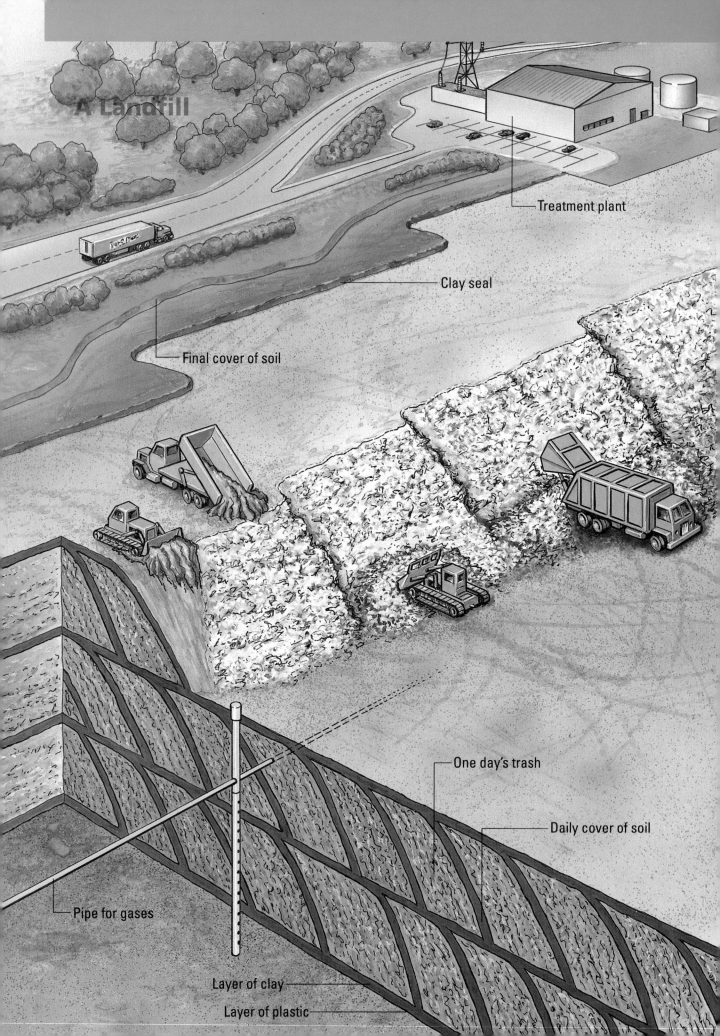

A Landfill

Treatment plant

Clay seal

Final cover of soil

One day's trash

Daily cover of soil

Pipe for gases

Layer of clay

Layer of plastic

A Look at a Landfill

Suppose your trash is buried in a landfill. One kind of sanitary landfill is shown on the left page. Let's take a closer look at it.

Every day, trucks dump tons of trash in a landfill. Bulldozers push the trash into place. Machines spread soil over the trash. This layer of soil helps control odors. Find the layers of plastic and clay at the bottom of the landfill. These layers help keep harmful materials from leaking into the ground.

As garbage **decomposes** (dē′ kəm pōs′ əs), or breaks down, it forms harmful gases. Pipes in the landfill carry these gases to a treatment plant. Here the gases are burned away or used in the process of making electricity.

When a landfill is full, it is sealed with a layer of clay and covered with soil. Then the land can be used for something else. Even airports and parks can be built on landfills.

Landfills are not the perfect answer to the trash problem. Many items in trash take years to decompose. Some places are running out of space for landfills. Can people help control the problem? Read the next lesson to find out.

Checkpoint

1. What makes up most trash?
2. How can air pollution from incinerators be reduced?
3. Describe a sanitary landfill.
4. Take Action! Draw a picture that shows what happens to all the trash from your school.

Break It Up

Most trash is buried under soil in landfills. You can find out which kinds of trash break down naturally and which do not.

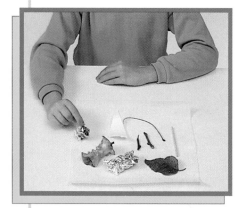

Picture A

Gather These Materials

cover goggles 👓
a stick with a leaf
  attached
8 milk cartons
scissors
soil
water
paper towels

assorted items from
  trash such as:
apple core
piece of aluminum foil
a piece of plastic bag
a piece of packing foam
a food wrapper

Follow This Procedure

1 Make a chart like the one on the next page. Record your observations in your chart.

2 Put on your cover goggles.

3 Use the scissors to cut the tops from the milk cartons. *Caution: Handle sharp items carefully.*

4 Look at several items, such as those listed above, that come from trash. (Picture A)

Predict: *Which of these objects will break down in the ground? Which will not?*

5 Fill each milk carton halfway with soil.

Picture B

Picture C

Record Your Results

Week Number 1		
Item name	Prediction	Observation

6 Place each item of trash inside a milk carton. (Picture B) Label the carton with what is inside.

7 Completely fill each carton with soil.

8 Water the soil in each carton. Place all the cartons in a warm place. (Picture C)

9 Check the cartons once a week for eight weeks. You can pour out what is inside onto a paper towel. Wash your hands after you check the cartons. Record your observations. Make a different chart for each week.

State Your Conclusions

1. Which of your predictions was correct?
2. Which items break down after eight weeks?
3. How do you think your observations compare with what you could observe at a landfill?

Let's Experiment

A compost pile contains materials that break down in soil. What materials can be added to a compost pile? Use what you know about scientific methods to find out.

2.2 Second Chances

What can I do about the garbage problem?

If you use paper plates and cups every day for six months, you might use as many as are shown here. Suppose you throw these paper products away. How would that activity affect the trash problem?

Controlling Trash

You may wonder how you can help control the trash problem. You can reduce the amount of trash you throw away. What can you use instead of paper plates and cups? The picture shows an answer. What other ideas for reducing trash are shown in the picture?

▼ People can reduce the amount of trash they throw away.

Here's another way you can help control trash. You can **recycle** (rē sī′ kəl) items, or use them over and over. Think about some of your clothes. What happens to them after you outgrow them? You might pass them on to others. When clothes get too shabby to wear, you might use them for rags. If you used paper towels, you might use the number shown here within months. You can see how using cloth rags can cut down the amount of paper trash.

Reusing containers also can help reduce trash. Using a cloth bag over and over for shopping can keep lots of paper and plastic bags out of the trash. Plastic containers and old shoeboxes come in handy for keeping your belongings. Think about some kinds of things you could store in containers like these.

Into The Field

What have you used today that can be reused?

Make a list of the items you have used. Next to each item, write down one or two ways that it could be used again.

Did You Know?

Which of the objects in this picture can be recycled? All of them!

1. Most recycling centers accept containers that are made of aluminum.

2. Some stores will collect used batteries and send them to a recycling center. There, the metals in the batteries can be recovered.

3. People can pass on clothing to others, or recycle their old clothes by using them for rags.

4. Most recycling centers will recycle glass containers. You may need to separate glass containers according to their colors.

5. Tin cans can be recycled. Workers at recycling centers separate the tin bodies of the cans from the aluminum tops and bottoms.

6. Most recycling centers accept paper. Different kinds of paper, such as newspaper, white paper, cardboard, and magazines, must be separated before recycling.

7. Most plastic can be recycled. Many labels on plastic containers give information about recycling.

8. Old tires can be recycled at many recycling centers.

9. You can recycle yard wastes. Adding such wastes to soil makes soil better for gardens.

Recycling Aluminum

You probably like to read stories with happy endings. Here's a big success story. Today, people recycle more than half the aluminum cans sold in the United States. The next time you see an aluminum can, think about this fact. The can probably came from recycled aluminum.

Suppose you rinse an aluminum can and want to recycle it. How can you recognize a recycling bin? That's easy! You look for a recycling sign like the one shown in the bottom left corner of this page.

How can used, bent aluminum cans be made into shiny, new ones? The story on these two pages will help solve that mystery. As you read, follow the numbers from one picture to another. The story begins with aluminum cans, like those shown on the left. First, the cans are put into a machine that makes a loud, clattering noise. This machine is called a hammer mill. Then, metal bars inside the hammer mill smash the cans and shred them into tiny bits.

Recycling Aluminum Cans

1. Aluminum cans
2. Tiny bits of aluminum
3. Melted aluminum
4. Aluminum bars
5. Sheets of aluminum

➤ *Symbol for recycling*

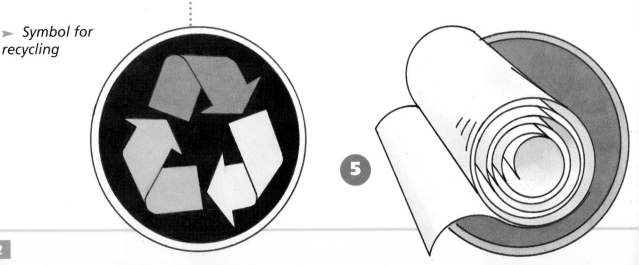

Next, the shreds of aluminum are put into a large furnace. The temperature in the furnace is so hot that it melts all the aluminum shreds into a liquid. Then, the aluminum is poured into special molds. Finally, when the aluminum cools down, it hardens into bars of metal like those shown in picture 4.

Heavy rollers press down on the aluminum bars. The rollers squeeze the bars into long, thin sheets. These sheets are rolled up until they look like the rolls in step 5. Now, here's the last chapter of the story. The thin sheets of aluminum are made into cans.

You know that recycling helps reduce the amount of trash. But there's more than one reward for recycling aluminum cans. When you recycle these cans, you are helping conserve aluminum, an important natural resource. Recycling aluminum cans also conserves energy. Making cans from recycled aluminum uses less electricity than making cans from raw aluminum. In fact, energy saved by recycling can provide you with hours of electricity in your home.

3

4

Checkpoint

1. How can you reduce the amount of trash you throw away?
2. Name items that can be recycled.
3. How can recycling aluminum cans help the environment?
4. **Take Action!** Make a poster for your classroom about recycling.

Activity

Re-use the Old News

Many old newspapers are just thrown away. Some of them are collected. Here is a way you can recycle the old news.

Picture A

Gather These Materials

cover goggles

newspapers

large, shallow pan

water

fork

2 small bowls

mixing spoon

laundry starch

masking tape

piece of window screen
 to fit into pan

plastic wrap

wooden block

Picture B

Picture C

Follow This Procedure

1 Make a chart like the one on the next page. Record your observations in your chart.

2 Put on your cover goggles.

3 Tear newspaper into tiny pieces. Place the pieces in one of the bowls. Moisten the paper with water. Use a fork to mix the paper and water into a milky pulp. Describe the mixture. (Picture A)

4 In the second bowl, add 2 spoons of laundry starch to some warm water. Stir until the starch dissolves.

Predict: **What do you think the starch will do to the pulp?**

5 Add the dissolved laundry starch to the bowl with the newspaper. Describe the mixture.

6 Tape the edges of a piece of window screen.

7 Put the screen in the pan. Scoop up some of the pulp from the bowl and place it on the center of the screen. (Picture B)

8 Carefully lift the screen containing the paper pulp and place it on a stack of newspapers. The newspapers will absorb some of the water.

9 Cover the paper pulp with plastic wrap.

10 Press a wooden block on top of the plastic wrap to squeeze out the water. (Picture C)

11 Remove the wooden block and plastic wrap. Let the paper dry. Describe the paper.

State Your Conclusions

1. Does your finished product look and feel like paper? Is it as good as paper that you buy?
2. What are some other ways in which old newspapers can be used?

Let's Experiment

How did the amount of starch you used affect the strength of the paper? Use what you know about scientific methods to find out. Use different amounts of starch.

Record Your Results

Observations	
Before adding starch	
After adding starch	
After paper is dry	

Chapter Review

Reviewing Words and Concepts

Write the letter of the word or phrase that best completes each sentence.

1. Huge furnaces _____ trash, or burn it in a careful way.
2. A place where garbage is dumped and covered with soil is called a _____.
3. Garbage in landfills forms harmful gases when it _____.
4. Air pollution from incinerators can be reduced by putting _____ in the smokestacks.
5. About half of all trash is made up of magazines, _____, and packaging.
6. Using items over and over is called _____.
7. Pipes in a landfill carry harmful gases to a _____ plant.
8. When you recycle aluminum cans, you are helping _____ aluminum, an important natural resource.
9. Some items that can be taken to recycling centers are aluminum cans, newspapers, and _____ bottles.
10. Recycling helps reduce the amount of _____.

a. scrubbers
b. conserve
c. trash
d. recycling
e. incinerate
f. decomposes
g. plastic
h. treatment
i. newspapers
j. sanitary landfill

Connecting Ideas

1. Copy the concept map. Use the terms at the right to complete the map about trash to show what happens to it.

recycle   incinerate
sanitary landfill

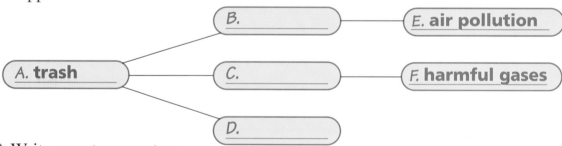

2. Write a sentence or two about the ideas shown in the concept map.

Interpreting What You Learned

1. How is trash incinerated?
2. Describe what happens to trash in a sanitary landfill.
3. How can people help control the amount of trash?
4. How are aluminum cans recycled?
5. How does recycling help conserve natural resources?

Performance Assessment

How can you group plastic objects?

Materials
- markers
- assorted plastic objects
- 7 large paper bags

Collecting Data

1. Look at the assortment of plastic objects that your teacher has gathered. Inspect each object. Find the symbol for recycling on each object (see page F32).
2. Find the number inside each recycling symbol. The different numbers represent different types of plastic.
3. Use a marker to number the paper bags from *1* to *7*.
4. Sort the plastic objects into groups. A group should contain objects that have the same number inside their recycling symbols. Place each group of objects into the paper bag with the same number.
5. Look at the plastic objects in each paper bag. Some bags may not contain any items. To record your results, make a chart that shows what is in each bag.

Analyzing Data

What do you think is the best way to sort plastic objects? Explain why you think so.

Making a Difference

Let's put the swings over here.

Discover Activity

How can you change the land?

Even building a small, new playground can change your surroundings. Imagine that you must design a playground for your school. First, think about where you would build it. Then, describe all the ways that the new playground would change the land.

For Discussion

1. *Where would you build your playground?*
2. *What parts of your design can help the land?*

3.1 *People and Nature*

▶ **How do people change the environment?**

You begin your long walk to school. Most mornings are very quiet. But this morning is different. You wonder, "What is all that noise?" Soon, your question is answered. You see trucks and bulldozers rumbling across a field. The buzzing of saws rings through the air. Let's find out what's going on.

Changing Surroundings

Once, tall trees crowded the field shown here. But workers cut down the trees and cleared the land to build this house. Soon, other houses will be built nearby. Whenever people build buildings, they change the **environment** (en vī′rən mənt). All the things that surround a living thing are called its environment.

▼ *People change the environment when they build houses.*

In the Discover Activity, you learned about changing the environment. The pictures on these pages show other ways people change the environment to meet their needs. Notice how this town grew larger. Many people needed homes. How did building these homes affect the number of trees?

Building changes the environment in other ways, too. People use natural resources, such as gas and oil, to provide heat and electricity for buildings. Workers dig pits or drill deep holes to get natural resources from the land.

Meeting People's Needs

Think about other things you need besides shelter. You know that food is an important need. Where do you get your food?

Much of your food is grown on farms. Farmers use and change the land to provide many different kinds of food for people.

Sometimes, huge forests are cleared or swamps are drained to make farmland. The paths of rivers and streams can even be changed to provide drinking water for animals or water for crops.

▼ *People cut down trees to build towns.*

You might wonder how food gets from a farm to a store. Much food is carried from place to place in trucks, or trains, or even airplanes. People need to build roads, and railroad tracks, and airports. How might such building change the environment?

People also need to build factories to process and package food. Some factories make clothing and other items people use. How can factories change the environment?

People depend on nature for the energy and materials needed to build homes and manufacture items. People are becoming more and more aware of how their activities change the environment. Many people are working to meet their needs in ways that do little, if any, harm to the environment.

Checkpoint

1. What effect does building a house have on the land?
2. What other ways do people change the environment?
3. **Take Action!** Make a drawing showing how your neighborhood might have looked 50 years ago.

DATAFILE

SOCIAL STUDIES

How Land Changes

Every year, more people live in the United States than lived in the country the year before.

From the year your parents were born to the year you were born, people have been changing the land.

The graph shows how much the land in the United States changed in less than 25 years.

Changes in the Land

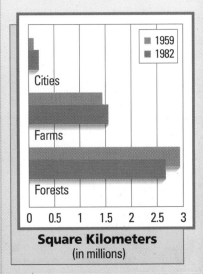

Square Kilometers
(in millions)

What Did You Find Out?
1. *What kinds of land took up more square kilometers in 1982 than they did in 1959?*
2. *How do you think the graph would look if it showed the past 200 years instead of 23 years?*

Into The Field

What do animals use as their homes?

Observe several different animals. Find out where each one lives. On a piece of paper, record the type of shelter that each animal lives in.

LESSON

3.2 *Living Things Together*

▶ **How do people affect plants and animals?**

Imagine a huge forest. Many animals get everything they need to survive from this habitat. Suppose people begin to cut down trees and build cities. What might happen to all the animals that live in the forest?

Changing Habitats

Living things need food, water, and shelter. They also need air and space to live. Many living things, such as the squirrel shown here, can still meet their needs when their habitats change. Look at the pigeons in the picture below. These animals form a **population** (pop′yə lā′shən), a group of living things of the same kind that live in the same place. This population of pigeons can meet all its needs and survive in the city.

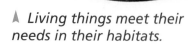

▲ Living things meet their needs in their habitats.

Most places have more than one kind of population. What populations might live in a city? You may name populations of people, or sparrows, or maple trees. All the populations that live together in the same place make up a **community** (kə myü′nə tē). Living things in a community depend on each other. How might living things in a city depend on each other?

Think again about a forest community. What animals and plants might live there? Suppose the forest environment changes. Buildings, such as this shopping mall, replace the plants of the forest. Many animals can no longer find food. Some animals, such as this deer, move to new habitats. There, they can get food and other things they need to live.

Some animals cannot meet their needs when their habitats change. They cannot move to new habitats. These animals may not be able to survive. When many living things of the same kind cannot survive, they might become **endangered** (en dān′jərd). Endangered living things are those that are few in number. Someday, they may no longer be found on the earth. Keep reading to learn about some kinds of endangered animals.

▼ *Animals' habitats are changed when the environment is changed.*

Save the Animals!

Endangered animals are few in number.

The California condor is the largest flying land bird in North America. The growth of cities has destroyed much of this bird's habitat. California condors are endangered today. In 1994, only 89 of these birds remained. Most of them were in captive breeding programs.

Giant pandas have become a symbol of endangered animals. Much of their habitat in the mountain forests of China has been destroyed. Many bamboo plants these pandas need for food have been cut down. Today, only a small number of Giant pandas live in the wild.

California condor

Giant panda

Many leopards once roamed parts of Asia and Africa. Today, few survive there. When land was changed, leopards could no longer find animals such as goats and antelope that they needed for food.

Where These Animals Live

California condor

Leopard

American crocodile

Giant panda

In the 1970s, fewer than 30 female American crocodiles lived in Florida. Building destroyed much of the animals' habitat. Because of laws, there were at least 200 American crocodiles living in Florida in 1994.

American crocodile

Becoming Extinct

The Badlands Bighorn sheep, shown below, once grazed on the prairies of North and South Dakota, Nebraska, Wyoming, and Montana. When in danger, the animals climbed steep mountains to find safety. The map on the next page shows where the Bighorn sheep once lived.

When people settled the prairies, the Badlands Bighorn sheep moved into the cliffs of the Badlands, like those shown in the picture, to find safety. Few plants grow on the dry, steep hills of the Badlands. Many of the sheep did not survive because they could not find enough food. People also hunted these sheep for their large horns. Finally, the Badlands Bighorn sheep became extinct. Plants and animals are **extinct** (ek stingkt′) when they are no longer found on the earth. The last Badlands Bighorn sheep was seen about 70 years ago.

▼ *The Badlands Bighorn sheep sought safety in the steep cliffs of the Badlands.*

The Xerces blue butterfly is another extinct animal. This insect lived only in the sand dunes near the city of San Francisco. When the city spread out over the dunes, the butterfly disappeared.

In the 1700s and 1800s, billions of passenger pigeons lived in North America. At times, flocks of these birds darkened the skies, almost shutting out the sunshine. Today, not a single passenger pigeon is alive. Some were killed by hunters. Most died when their forest habitats were destroyed.

Carolina parakeets, shown in the picture on the right, once were a common sight in parts of the United States. The map shows where one type lived. These birds had orange and yellow heads and green bodies. Hunters killed many of these parakeets for their colorful feathers. Today, they are extinct.

People are working together to keep many plants and animals from becoming extinct. In the next lesson, you will learn how people can help protect plants and animals.

Past Habitats

Carolina parakeet

Badlands Bighorn sheep

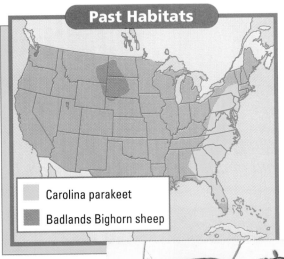

⊿ The Badlands Bighorn sheep and the Carolina parakeet, as shown above, are extinct animals that once lived in the United States.

Checkpoint

1. How do changes to a habitat affect the animals in a community?
2. Name two animals that are endangered.
3. What are three extinct animals?
4. **Take Action!** Draw a picture or cut out pictures from a magazine to show a community that lives in a pond.

Activity

A Place Called Home

Many living things live near your school. You can work with a team to find out about the plants and animals that live in this habitat.

Picture A

Picture B

Meadow

Picture C

Gather These Materials

journal
plastic bags for
  collecting
masking tape

1 meter-long string
twigs or stones
thermometer

Follow This Procedure

1 Make a chart like the one on the next page. Record your observations in your chart.

2 Prepare a journal for this project. Include pages for describing and drawing animal life and plant life.

3 Prepare several plastic bags for collecting. Put masking tape labels on each bag.

4 Go outside with your team to your assigned habitat. While one person stands still holding one end of a 1 meter-long string, another member of the team will move in a circle around the first person (Picture A). Mark off the circle using twigs or stones. The circle will be the boundary of your habitat.

5 Use the thermometer to take the temperature in different parts of your habitat. (Picture B)

Record Your Results

Location	Plant life description	Animal life description	Temperature

6 Examine all the living things within your habitat. This includes all the plants and animals you can see.

7 Collect samples of things like leaves or feathers in 2 separate plastic bags. Label each bag with the contents, the habitat and the date. If you are unsure about taking something, be sure to ask your teacher. (Picture C)

8 Write down or draw what you have seen in your journal. Include the date and time.

9 Return to your habitat another time and repeat your observations.

State Your Conclusions

1. What are the most common living things in your habitat?

2. What would happen to the animals in your habitat if all the plants died out?

Let's Experiment

How does the habitat change with the seasons? Use what you know about scientific methods to find out.

3.3 Protecting Plants and Animals

▶ **How can I help protect plants and animals?**

Suppose that one week you will not be home to water the plants in your garden. What can you do? You might ask someone to help you. When people cooperate, they often can take better care of plants and animals.

Making a Difference

The children in the picture know that these trees need water to survive. Notice how they cooperate to care for the trees.

During the summer of 1991, people in Chicago saved many trees by watering them. That summer, the city had very little rainfall. "Friends of the Parks," a group of citizens, asked people to help. Volunteers watered trees in several of the city's parks. Because people cooperated, many trees survived.

➤ *People helping trees survive*

The pictures above show some plants that are endangered. Many people throughout the world are cooperating to protect different kinds of endangered plants. People also are trying to keep some plants from becoming endangered in the future. You, too, can help some plants survive. For example, when you walk outside, you can be careful not to trample or uproot wild plants.

The best way people can protect plants and animals is to protect their habitats. The story of the monarch butterfly is a good example of how people can do this. In the autumn, some populations of monarch butterflies leave their summer homes in Canada and Alaska and fly south. They spend the winter in several southern states, where temperatures are warmer and food is easier to find. Many monarchs find their way to Pacific Grove, California. Here, thousands of these butterflies cluster together, clinging to the eucalyptus trees that grow there.

Some people in Pacific Grove wanted to build new buildings on land that has many eucalyptus trees. A group called "The Friends of the Monarch" worked to keep the land free from buildings. Now the monarchs have a safe place to spend winters.

⅄ Date palm (left)
Rafflesia (center)
Carolina Venus's Flytrap (right)

⅄ Monarch butterfly

Refuges and Laws

Governments all over the world are cooperating to protect plants and animals. In the 1970s, the United States Congress passed several laws to help keep endangered plants and animals safe.

How can people provide safe places for plants and animals? You might be interested in finding out what some people have done.

In the early 1900s, the number of brown pelicans in the United States was getting smaller. People wanted to save this pelican and preserve its habitat. A wildlife refuge is a place where wildlife is protected. The United States government opened the first wildlife refuge on Pelican Island, off the coast of Florida. The picture below shows pelicans living in this refuge.

Today, more than 350 wildlife refuges are scattered across the United States. These refuges have helped protect many kinds of animals and plants.

▼ Pelican Island

Look at the picture of the trumpeter swans. The story of these swans really has a happy ending! Many years ago, large numbers of trumpeter swans lived in the wild. As people built more and more cities, they changed the swans' habitats. Many of these swans were not able to get enough food. Each year, fewer and fewer populations of trumpeter swans were able to survive. They became an endangered animal. In fact, by 1900, the swans had almost disappeared from the earth.

Finally, in 1935, the new head of the United States Biological Survey took action. J. N. "Ding" Darling helped get enough money to buy land near Red Rocks Lake in Montana. This land was used as a wildlife refuge for the endangered trumpeter swans. Today, hundreds of these swans live in this hidden valley. Now they are no longer endangered. Thanks to the cooperation and hard work of many people, trumpeter swans made a great comeback.

▲ *Trumpeter swan*

Checkpoint

1. How can people help protect plants and animals?
2. Name some living things that have been saved from extinction.
3. **Take Action!** Work with a partner. Do a skit about saving an endangered animal or plant.

Activity

Building a Nesting House

How can you recycle a milk carton to make a nesting house for a small songbird? Try this activity to find out.

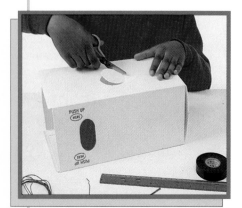

Picture A

Picture B

Picture C

Gather These Materials

cover goggles

empty milk carton

scissors

nail

wire

dried grass

masking tape

hammer

Follow This Procedure

1 Make a chart like the one on the next page. Record your observations in your chart.

2 Put on your cover goggles.

> **Predict: How can you turn this carton into a nesting house for small birds?**

3 Carefully use the scissors to cut a hole about 4 cm in size in one side of the carton. Cut the hole about 5 cm below the top of the carton. (Picture A) *CAUTION: Handle sharp items carefully.*

4 On the opposite side of the carton, make two small nail holes, one above the other. Make one hole about a third of the way down from the top. Make the other hole a third of the way up from the bottom. Thread the wire through the two holes. (Picture B)

5 Place dried grass inside the carton to make it soft for the birds. (Picture C)

6 Fold the top of the carton closed and tape it shut tightly.

7 Find a tree or pole outside that is not too close to any building, but where you can watch it. With the help of an adult, hammer the nails, one above the other, into the tree.

8 Hang the house. Wrap the two ends of the wire tightly around the two nails.

9 Watch the nesting house for four weeks.

State Your Conclusions

1. What kind of activity have you been able to observe over several weeks?

2. Why is it important to hang the nesting house in a place that is not too close to buildings or other trees?

3. What might be the best time of year to expect a house guest in your nesting house? Why?

Let's Experiment

What would happen if you made the front door of the nesting house 6 cm instead of 4 cm? Use what you know about scientific methods to find out.

Record Your Results

Date	Observations
Week 1:	
Week 2:	
Week 3:	
Week 4:	

Chapter Review

Reviewing Words and Concepts

Write the letter of the word or phrase that best completes each sentence.

1. All the things that surround a living thing are called its ____.
2. Farmers change the land to provide ____ for people.
3. Living things of the same kind that live in the same place form a ____.
4. Workers change the environment when they drill deep holes or dig pits to get ____ from the land.
5. Living things that are few in number and may someday no longer be found on the earth are ____.
6. All the populations that live together in the same place make up a ____.
7. Plants and animals that are no longer found on the earth are ____.
8. The best way for people to protect plants and animals is to protect their ____.
9. Wildlife ____ have helped protect many kinds of animals and plants.
10. Brown ____ have been saved from extinction.

a. population
b. habitats
c. food
d. endangered
e. pelicans
f. refuges
g. extinct
h. community
i. environment
j. natural resources

Connecting Ideas

1. Copy the concept map. Use the terms at the right to complete the map about living things to show how they are affected by the environment.

   community   extinct
   population   environment

   A. _____ — B. _____

   C. _____

   D. **endangered**

   E. _____

2. Write a sentence or two about the ideas shown in the concept map.

Interpreting What You Learned

1. How do people change the environment?
2. What can happen if a population cannot meet its needs in its environment?
3. What are two reasons living things become extinct?
4. What is a wildlife refuge?
5. How can governments help protect endangered plants and animals?
6. How does a community differ from a population?

 ## Performance Assessment

How does changing a habitat affect animals?

Materials • cutout egg • white construction paper
• black construction paper • pebbles and sand • aluminum foil pan
• markers or crayons • scissors

Collecting Data

1. Using the cutout egg your teacher gives you, trace an egg on the piece of white construction paper.
2. Cut out the egg you traced.
3. Spread a layer of pebbles and sand in the pan.
4. Look at the colors and shapes of the pebbles and sand. Draw the same colors and shapes on the egg so it looks like pebbles and sand.
5. Place the egg on the pebbles and sand. Observe how well it matches this habitat. Record your observations.
6. Imagine that people changed this habitat and covered it with pavement. Place the black construction paper on top of the pebbles and sand. Then place the egg on top of the black paper. Observe how well it matches the changed habitat. Record your observations.

Analyzing Data
What might happen to an animal if its habitat was changed this way?

Kids 4, Trash O

Our trash keeps piling up, and there's less and less room for it. Landfills all over the country are crammed with cans and bottles. Millions of reusable plastic items are thrown away each year. Trash dumps fill to the bursting point. To the rescue: kids and recycling!

Matthew Wilhelm, of Nashua, New Hampshire, wanted to do something to help his town. So he went into the trash business. He hauls his neighbors' cans, newspapers, and bottles to a local recycling center. To do his hauling, he uses a toy wagon that he calls a "recyclemobile." Each neighbor pays $1 a month. Matthew says, "By the end of the day, the recyclemobile is heavy."

Cafeterias in their school district were throwing out 1,250,000 plastic foam lunch trays every year!

But he knows that his hard work is helping his neighbors to solve a big problem.

Anne Linder, Joanna Keiser, and Tiffany McClain of St. Louis, Missouri, went into action because they learned a shocking fact. They found out that cafeterias in their school district were throwing out 1,250,000 plastic foam lunch trays every year! The girls were very upset by the amount of waste. They convinced their school to recycle these trays instead. In time, they persuaded eight schools, plus some local companies, to recycle. The girls' goal is to bring recycling to every school and business in their district.

The Wisconsin town of Muskego was running out of room to dump trash. The fifth-grade class at the Country Meadows School knew that recycling items kept them from ending up in the trash. So the class installed recycling bins in their classroom for glass, aluminum, and paper. They soon got every classroom in the school to do the same thing. Then they put on a play for the city council. Their play, which they had written, told about how good recycling is for the earth. It convinced the whole city to start a recycling program.

Another child, Amy Hamberry, came up with a winning suggestion in WNYW-Fox 5 TV's Kids Club environmental contest. What was her idea?

If store products came in less wrapping, we'd have less wasted paper to recycle in the first place. The next time you go to the store, you might want to compare the packaging used for different products.

Now You Do It

1. Every time you throw something away, put it in a bag instead of in a trash can. At the end of the day, weigh your bag. Write down the weight. Multiply by 365. That is how much trash you make in a year!

2. Now make a list of each item in your bag. What things could you recycle? Find out how you could recycle them.

3. Choose something you would like to recycle: aluminum cans, newspapers, bottles, or plastic. Choose a place to gather these materials. Make a plan to recycle that material. Then do it!

Helping the Environment

Cheryl Mainer

Occupation: Chemical engineer
Challenge: To make a clean and safe environment for all of us to live in

They used to dig a hole, fill it with waste, cover it, and move on. That's what Cheryl Mainer says about landfills of the past. Cheryl is a chemical engineer. Her job is to help keep the environment clean.

How can we keep the environment clean?

"For one thing we can build better landfills. They are now designed by engineers. First a site is found. Then a hole is dug. It must be slanted so that rain will not collect in the landfill.

Then a heavy layer of plastic is laid down. This keeps harmful materials from leaking out of the landfill. Finally, the landfill is ready for waste. When the landfill is full, it is covered with more heavy plastic. Then it is covered with a deep layer of dirt and planted with grass."

What else can we do?

"Companies can make an effort to make less waste. When a chemical company is making a product, some chemicals are left over. These leftovers might go out the smoke stack into the air and cause air pollution. I figure out how to change that. Reusing those chemicals can save money for the company and help save the environment for all of us."

What's the best part of your job?

"I always liked figuring out where stuff came from. Now I figure out where it goes. When I was little, I loved playing outside. I still like playing outside—but now I get paid for it. But the best part of my job is knowing that I am doing something to help the environment."

Garbage Truck: A Daily Necessity

Have you ever wondered how all the garbage from your neighborhood can fit into one garbage truck? The garbage must be compacted, or firmly packed together, in order for it to fit.

2 When the hopper is full, a lever on the side of the truck is pulled; this moves a big push-blade.

3 The push-blade pushes garbage farther into the truck, compacting it; this leaves space for more garbage.

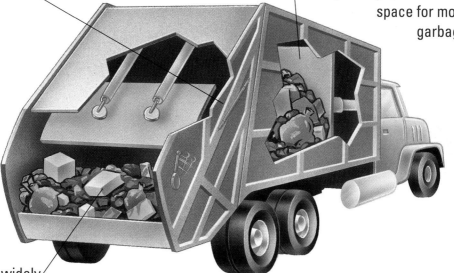

1 The most widely used garbage truck is a rear loading compactor truck; the back open part is the hopper.

Find Out On Your Own

Keep track of the number of bags of garbage your family throws away each week. Find out ways to make this number smaller.

Module Performance Assessment

Our Environment

Using what you learned in this module, help make your school aware of the importance of caring for the environment. Complete one or more of the following activities. You may work by yourself or with others in a group.

Pollution

Plan a cleanup project for your school or community. Decide what needs to be cleaned up and how you might organize volunteers to reach your goal. Post a progress chart in your school.

Art

Draw a map of your community, including all the bodies of water. Find out if any of your local waterways are polluted. Color the polluted waterways on your map. Place the map where other students can see it.

Biology

Take photographs, cut pictures out of old magazines, or draw your own pictures of the populations of animals and plants in your environment. Write sentences giving information about each picture. Prepare an exhibit for the school hallway.

Writing

Imagine that you are able to change one thing in your environment. Write a story or a poem telling what you would change and why.

Drama

Create and present a short one- or two-minute public service announcement for television that will encourage people to protect the environment.

Module Review

Reviewing Words and Concepts

Write the letter of the word or phrase that best completes each sentence.

1. The habitats of plants and animals that live in water can be changed by ____.
2. One way to get rid of trash is to ____ it.
3. When a ____ is full, it is sealed with a layer of clay and covered with soil.
4. You can conserve natural resources and energy by ____ aluminum cans.
5. Many items in trash take years to ____.
6. Cutting down trees and building houses are ways that people change the ____.
7. People, sparrows, or maple trees are ____ that might live in a city.
8. Giant pandas are ____ animals because much of their habitat has been destroyed.
9. The United States opened the first wildlife ____ to protect the brown pelican.
10. All the trees, birds, and other living things that live together in a forest make up a ____.

a. incinerate
b. recycling
c. populations
d. refuge
e. environment
f. endangered
g. decompose
h. community
i. sanitary landfill
j. water pollution

Interpreting What You Learned

1. Explain how harmful materials in water can become part of a food chain.
2. Tell about two different ways of getting rid of trash. Explain how each way can affect the environment.
3. What changes are people making to protect water from pollution?

Applying What You Learned

1. What characteristics would you use to classify endangered and extinct animals?
2. Draw a diagram that shows how an aluminum can or a piece of clothing can be recycled.
3. Think of an item of trash. Describe steps it will pass through after it is thrown away.

Using Metric

About 1 centimeter

About 1 millimeter

About 1 meter

Water boils
(100°C)

Normal body
temperature
(37°C)

Water freezes
(0°C)

Degrees Celsius

1 cm

1 cm

1 square
centimeter

1 cm

1 cm

1 cm

1 cubic
centimeter

About 1 kilogram

11 football fields
end to end is about
1 kilometer

1 liter of milk

Using Scientific Methods

Scientists ask many questions. No one may know the answers. Then scientists use scientific methods to find answers. Scientific methods include steps like the ones on the next page. Sometimes scientists use the steps in different order. You can use these steps to do the experiments in this section.

Test Hypothesis If possible, do an experiment to see if your hypothesis is correct. Then you should do the experiment again to be sure.

Collect Data Your observations from the experiment are your data.

Study Data You can understand your data better if you put it in charts and graphs.

Make Conclusions Decide if your hypothesis is correct.

Identify Problem The problem is usually a question such as, "What materials are best for blocking sound?"

Make Observations Notice many things about an object such as its size, color, or shape.

State Hypothesis Try to answer the problem.

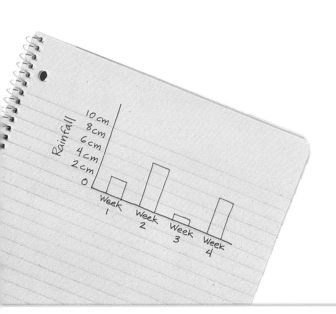

Safety in Science

Scientists are careful when they do experiments. You need to be careful too. The next page shows some rules to remember.

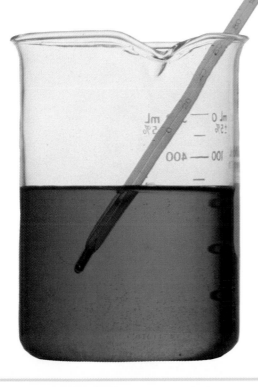

Safety Tips

- Read each experiment carefully.

- Wear cover goggles when needed.

- Clean up spills right away.

- Never taste or smell unknown things.

- Handle thermometers carefully.

- Put things away when you finish an experiment.

- Wash your hands after each experiment.

Experiment Skills
Making Observations

Experimenting with Mealworms

Tom liked visiting his uncle's farm. One day he noticed some tiny animals called mealworms. They were living in a damp sack of grain that an animal had spilled. Tom wondered if the mealworms like to live in a damp place or a dry place. He decided to do an experiment with ten mealworms to find out.

At the end of his experiment, Tom observed that only two of the ten mealworms crawled to a dry place. All the rest crawled to a wet place.

Thinking About the Experiment

1. Where did Tom first observe the mealworms?

2. What was Tom trying to find out in his experiment?

3. What materials did Tom use in his experiment? Check the materials list on the next page to find out.

Making observations means watching closely. Tom used his observations to make a conclusion.

4. How many mealworms did Tom observe at the dry place?

5. How many mealworms did Tom observe at the wet place?

6. What conclusion do you think Tom made?

Try It!

Try Tom's experiment and see if you come to the same conclusion.

Problem

Do mealworms prefer to live in a damp place or a dry place?

Hypothesis

Mealworms prefer to live in a damp place.

Materials

small cake pan	2 sponges
10 mealworms	water
cardboard	sand

Procedure

1 Fill the bottom of the pan with sand.

2 Wet 1 sponge. Then squeeze it.

3 Place the wet sponge in the sand on one side of the pan.

4 Place the dry sponge opposite the wet sponge.

5 Use a piece of cardboard to put the mealworms on the sand in the middle of the pan.

6 Observe the mealworms after 30 minutes. Write down how many are at each sponge.

Data and Observations

	Number of mealworms
Wet sponge	
Dry sponge	

Conclusion

Write your conclusion based on your data and observations.

Practice

Making Observations

1. Suppose you observed the mealworms for five days. Set up the data table that you would use.
2. Suppose you wanted to see if the mealworms grew. How could you make observations about growth?
3. What would you use to measure how much they grew?

Testing a Hypothesis

Experimenting with Heating Air

Nathan was keeping a weather chart as part of his science project. He noticed that the air seemed to get colder on clear nights than on cloudy nights. He wondered if clouds really affected the temperature of the air below them. He thought of this hypothesis as a possible answer to his question: *Covering air in some way helps keep it warm.*

Nathan did an experiment to test his hypothesis. He placed thermometers in two boxes. Then he covered both boxes and placed them in the sun for twenty minutes.

Thinking About the Experiment

Usually in an experiment, parts of the experiment take the place of things in nature. For example, the bottom of Nathan's shoe boxes act like the ground.

1. What does the plastic cover on the boxes take the place of?

2. Why did Nathan remove the cover from one of his boxes?

3. To test his hypothesis, did Nathan really need to remove the cover from one box? Why?

4. What do you think happened to the temperature of the air in each of the boxes?

Try It!

Try Nathan's experiment and see if you come to the same conclusion.

Problem

Do clouds help keep air warm?

Hypothesis

Covering air in some way helps keep it warm.

Materials

2 shoe boxes the same size

2 thermometers

plastic wrap

masking tape

60-watt bulb

Procedure

1 Place a thermometer in the bottom of 2 shoe boxes. Cover both with a double thickness of clear plastic wrap.

2 Set the boxes under a lighted bulb, about 10 cm from the bulb. Be careful, light bulbs can cause burns!

3 After 20 minutes, remove the plastic wrap from one of the boxes.

4 Record the temperature in each box every minute for the next 5 minutes. Do not remove the thermometers.

Data and Observations

Temperature of Air in Each Box

Time	Uncovered Box	Covered Box
0		
1		
2		
3		
4		
5		

Conclusion

Write your conclusion based on your data and observations.

Practice

Testing a Hypothesis

1. Suppose you wanted to do an experiment to find out if the color of the ground affects how fast air heats up. What would be your hypothesis?
2. How could you change Nathan's experiment to test your hypothesis?
3. What variable would change in testing this hypothesis?

Setting Up a Control

Experimenting with Plants

Marianne wanted to have colored glass put in her bedroom window. She had several plants in her room. She wondered if colored light coming in through the window would change how the plants grew. She decided to do an experiment with plants and red light to find out. In her experiment, Marianne found out that plants grow better in regular light than in colored light.

Thinking About the Experiment

1. Look at the materials list to find out how many cups Marianne used for her experiment.

Anything in an experiment that could change is called a variable. Only one variable should change during an experiment.

2. What variable did Marianne change between the two cups using cellophane?

3. Why was it important for the two cups to have all the same things except for the kind of cellophane?

The cup with a clear cellophane cone was the control in Marianne's experiment. It let in all light, just as clear glass would. Marianne could compare the plant from the control cup with the plant from the other cup.

4. Suppose Marianne did not have a control cup. Could she tell if the plant with red cellophane was growing any differently? Why or why not?

Try It!

Try Marianne's experiment and see if you come to the same conclusion.

Problem

How does red light affect bean seed growth?

Hypothesis

A bean plant will not grow as well in red light as in regular sunlight.

Materials

2 bean seeds
cellophane, clear and red squares
metric ruler
2 plastic cups
potting soil
stapler
tape
water

Procedure

1. Fill one of the cups with water. Soak 2 bean seeds in it overnight.

2. Empty the water from the cup. Fill both cups more than half full with potting soil.

3. Put a seed in each. Add a little soil on top of the seeds.

4. Water both cups well.

5. Make cones out of the two squares of cellophane. Use a staple to keep their shapes.

6. Tape a cone onto each cup.

7. Place the cups in a sunny spot.

8. After two weeks, measure the height of the plants. Count the number of leaves on each.

Data and Observations

	Red wrap	Clear wrap
Plant height		
Number of leaves		

Conclusion

Write your conclusion based on your data and observations.

Practice

Setting Up a Control

Plants need minerals to grow. Suppose you want to find out if plants grow better when minerals are added to the soil.

1. How would you change Marianne's experiment to find out how well plants grow with added minerals?

2. What would be the control in your experiment?

Setting Up an Experiment

Experimenting with Wedges

Jeff's father used a wedge to split wood. The hammer pushed the wedge into the wood and the wood split or cracked. Jeff wondered if the sharpness of a wedge makes a difference in how well it works. He decided to set up an experiment to find out. Jeff knew it was not safe to use his father's sharp wedge. He used wedges made out of chalk.

Thinking About the Experiment

Jeff set up his experiment carefully. He kept every part of the setup the same except for one variable. That was the variable he wanted to test.

1. What variable is Jeff testing?

2. Read the procedure to find out what variables Jeff kept the same in the experiment.

3. Predict how easy or hard it will be to push each of the chalk wedges into the clay.

Try It!

Try Jeff's experiment and see if you come to the same conclusion.

Problem

Does the sharpness of a wedge make a difference in how easily it can be pushed into something?

Hypothesis

A wedge is most useful if it has a sharp edge.

Materials

3 pieces of chalk
large ball of modeling clay
rough surface

Procedure

1 Rub one end of each piece of chalk on the rough surface to make a wedge shape. Make the ends of the wedges sharp, rounded, and flat.

2 Push each chalk wedge into the ball of clay.

3 Record how hard or easy it is to push each wedge.

Data and Observations

Wedge shape	Force needed
Rounded	
Flat-ended	
Sharp	

Conclusion

Write your conclusion based on your data and observations.

Practice

Setting Up an Experiment

Suppose you wanted to know if the material a wedge is made of affects how well it works.

1. What might be your hypothesis?
2. What variable would you test?
3. How would you set up your experiment?

Identifying Variables

MODULE D

Experimenting with Seeds

Pete was helping his mother plant seeds in the garden. He wondered if the seeds would germinate faster in warm weather than in cool weather. He did an experiment to find out.

Pete soaked 12 bean seeds in water overnight. The next day, he found a lid from a baby food jar and a lid from a peanut butter jar. He cut circles from a paper towel and put a circle in each lid. He put 10 drops of water and 4 bean seeds in the baby food lid. The peanut butter lid was much bigger, so he put 20 drops of water and 8 bean seeds in the peanut butter lid. Then Pete wrapped plastic wrap around the peanut butter lid and used a rubber band to keep the wrap in place. He put the lid in a warm, dark closet. He put the baby food lid in the refrigerator. He looked at the lids each day to see which seeds would germinate first.

Thinking About the Experiment

A variable is anything that can change in the experiment. Changing only one variable at a time tests for that variable. For example, using 20 drops of water in one lid and 10 drops of water in the other lid tests how the amount of water affects germination.

1. What did Pete first wonder about?

2. Should Pete use 20 drops of water in one lid and 10 in the other? Explain.

Pete did not set up his experiment correctly. He had too many variables that changed.

3. Explain how the lids Pete used were another variable that changed.

4. In addition to amount of water and lid size, Pete had two other variables that should not have changed. What were they?

Pete changed his experiment to keep all variables the same except one. Read Pete's new procedure on the next page.

5. How did Pete correct his procedure?

6. Which variable is Pete testing in the new procedure?

Try It!
Try Pete's experiment and see if you come to the same conclusion.

Problem
Does temperature affect how fast seeds germinate?

Hypothesis
Bean seeds will germinate faster in warm weather than in cold weather.

Materials
12 bean seeds	paper towel
cover goggles	plastic wrap
2 jar lids,	2 rubber bands
same size	scissors
dropper	water

Procedure
1 Place 12 bean seeds in water and soak them overnight.

2 Use a jar lid to trace 2 circles on a paper towel. Then cut out the circles. Make sure the circles are the same size. Put 1 circle in each of 2 jar lids.

3 Put 10 drops of water and 6 bean seeds on the paper circle in each lid.

4 Cover each lid with plastic wrap. Use the rubber bands to hold the plastic wrap in place.

5 Put 1 lid in a warm, dark place. Put the other lid in a cold, dark place.

6 Observe the seeds each day for germination. Use a chart like the one below to record your observations.

Data and Observations

Number of seeds germinated		
	Warm	Cool
Day 1		
Day 2		
Day 3		
Day 4		
Day 5		

Conclusion
Write your conclusion based on your data and observations.

Practice

Identifying Variables

1. If you wanted to do an experiment to find out if bean seeds germinate faster in the dark than in the light, what variable should you test?

2. How would you change the experiment above to test this new variable?

Collecting Data

Experimenting with Sound

Ann tapped gently with a spoon on her glass of fruit juice. She was keeping time with music on the radio. Then she drank most of the juice. When she tapped the glass again she noticed that the sound was different. The sound was higher with less juice in the glass.

Ann wondered if this would be true if she tapped bottles. She thought of this hypothesis to answer her question. The more liquid in a bottle, the lower the sound made when you tap on the bottle. She decided to set up an experiment to test her hypothesis.

Thinking About the Experiment

In an experiment, you collect data about the problem you want to solve.

1. What is the problem in Ann's experiment?

2. What did Ann collect data about?

3. Look at the experiment on the next page. How did Ann organize her data?

4. What conclusion do you think Ann made after doing the experiment?

Try Ann's experiment and see if you come to the same conclusion.

Problem
Does the amount of liquid in a bottle make a difference in the sound made by tapping on the bottle?

Hypothesis
The more liquid in a bottle, the lower the sound made when you tap on the bottle.

Materials
4 bottles of the same size
water
spoon

Procedure
1 Put four bottles on a desk or table.

2 Leave the first bottle empty. Put a little water in the second bottle. Fill the third bottle about halfway. Fill the fourth bottle almost full.

3 Tap the first and second bottles gently with a spoon. Compare the sounds. Record which is higher.

4 Tap the third bottle. Compare the sound with the sounds of the first and second bottles. Record your observations.

5 Tap the fourth bottle and compare the sounds. Record your observations.

Data and Observations

Amount of water in bottle	Sound from tapping
Empty	
A little water	
Half full	
Full	

Conclusion
Write your conclusion based on your data and observations.

Practice

Collecting Data
Suppose you wanted to do an experiment to find out if the size of the bottle makes a difference in the sound produced.
1. What might your hypothesis be?
2. How could you set up an experiment to test the hypothesis?
3. What data is important to collect in your experiment?

Setting Up an Experiment

Experimenting with Fertilizer on Plants

Lori's grandmother lived on a farm with a big pond. A garden was near the pond. Lori noticed that the water nearest the garden looked greener than the rest of the pond. This water was covered with many tiny floating duckweed plants. Her grandmother said she used fertilizer in the garden. Lori wondered if the fertilizer had washed into the pond and made the duckweed near the garden grow quickly.

She set up an experiment using pond water, duckweed, and fertilizer to find out. In her experiment, Lori found out that duckweed with fertilizer grows faster than duckweed without fertilizer.

Thinking About the Experiment

1. What could Lori's hypothesis be?

2. Read the procedure on the next page. How many cups did Lori use to set up her experiment?

Lori made sure the cups she used were the same size. She put the same amount of pond water with duckweed in each cup. Then she put the cups in the sun. Lori changed one variable. This was the variable she was testing.

3. What variable did Lori change?

The cup without fertilizer was Lori's control.

4. How did the control help Lori with her observations?

Try It!

Try Lori's experiment and see if you come to the same conclusion.

Problem

Does fertilizer change how fast duckweed grows?

Hypothesis

Fertilizer helps duckweed grow quickly in water.

Materials

gloves
2 large plastic cups
marker
phosphate fertilizer
water with duckweed
medicine dropper

Procedure

1. Fill each cup half full with water.

2. Put on the gloves. Add 10 drops of fertilizer to one of the cups. Stir the fertilizer in the water.

3. Place 20 duckweed plants in each cup.

4. Record the number of plants in your data table beside "At start."

5. Label the cups. Put them in a sunny place.

6. Observe the cups once a week for two weeks. Count the duckweed plants in each cup each time. Record the numbers on your data table.

Data and Observations

	With fertilizer	Without fertilizer
At start		
After 1 week		
After 2 weeks		

Conclusion

Write your conclusion based on your data and observations.

Practice

Setting Up an Experiment

Does the temperature of water affect how fast duckweed plants grow? Suppose you wanted to set up an experiment to find out. You could use two cups of pond water with duckweed.

1. What would be the same about each cup?
2. What would be the variable?
3. What would be the control?

Glossary

A

absorb (ab sôrb′), to take in.

algae (al′jē), a group of producers that live in water.

amplify (am′plə fī), make stronger.

antenna (an ten′ə), one of the feelers on the heads of insects and other animals.

B

blood vessel (ves′əl), any of the tubes in the body through which blood circulates.

bran (bran), the outer covering of a seed of grain.

bullhorn (bůl′hôrn′), a megaphone with a microphone that acts as a loudspeaker.

bur (bėr), a fruit that has seeds inside and hooks that cling.

C

calcium (kal′sē əm), a mineral in foods that helps keep teeth and bones strong.

carbohydrate (kär′bō hī′drāt), a nutrient that the body uses for energy.

clay soil, tightly packed soil with tiny grains.

cloud (kloud), condensed water droplets or ice particles floating in the sky.

community (kə myü′nə tē), all organisms that live in a place.

condensation (kon′den sā′shən), the changing of a gas to a liquid.

condense (kən dens′), to change from a gas to a liquid.

conductor (kən duk′tər), a material through which energy moves easily.

conserve (kən sėrv′), to save or keep from harm.

consumer (kən sü′mər), a living thing that depends on producers for food.

contract (kən trakt′), the action of a muscle becoming shorter.

control (kən trōl′), the part of an experiment that does not have the variable being tested.

convection (kən vek′shən), the flow of energy that occurs when a warm liquid or gas rises.

D

decompose (dē′kəm pōz′), break down a substance into what it is made of.

desert (dez′ərt), a dry habitat.

digest (də jest′), to change or break down food into forms the body can use.

disposable (dis pō′zə bəl), that which can be thrown away after use.

E

eardrum, the thin skin at the end of the ear canal.

echo (ek′ō), a sound that bounces back.

electric signal (i lek′trik sig′nəl), a form of energy.

embryo (em′brē ō), the tiny part of a seed that can grow into a plant.

endangered (en dān′jərd) **living things,** kinds of living things that are very few in number and might someday no longer be found on the earth.

energy (en′ər jē), the ability to do work.

environment (en vī′rən mənt), everything that surrounds a living thing.

evaporate (i vap′ə rāt′), to change from a liquid to a gas.

evaporation (i vap′ə rā′shən), the changing of a liquid into a gas.

exoskeleton (ek′sō skel′ə tən), a hard covering that supports the body of some animals.

extinct (ek stingkt′), no longer found living on the earth.

F

fat (fat), nutrient the body uses for energy.

fertilizer (fėr′tl ī′zər), a substance spread over or put into the soil to supply missing nutrients.

fiber (fī′bər), a part of foods that cannot be digested.

food chain, the way energy passes from one living thing to another in a community.

force (fôrs), a push or a pull.

forest (fôr′ist), a large area of land that gets plenty of rain and is covered with many trees.

fossil fuel (fos′əl fyü′əl), a fuel, such as oil, natural gas, or coal, that was made from living things that died millions of years ago.

fruit (früt), a covering that protects seeds made by flowering plants.

fuel (fyü′əl), any material that can be burned to produce useful heat.

G

gasoline (gas′ə lēn′), a fuel made from petroleum and used in heat engines.

germinate (jėr′mə nāt), to begin to grow and develop.

H

habitat (hab′ə tat), the place where a living thing lives.

hibernate (hī′bər nāt), to spend the winter in a state in which the body greatly slows down.

humus (hyü′məs), the decayed matter in soil.

hypothesis (hī poth′ə sis), a likely explanation of a problem.

I

incinerate (in sin′ə rāt′), to burn to ashes.

inclined (in klīnd′) **plane,** a simple machine that is a flat surface with one end higher than the other.

insulator (in′sə lā′tər), a material through which energy cannot easily flow.

iron (ī′ərn), a mineral in foods that is needed for good health.

J

joint (joint), a place where bones join together; different joints allow different movement.

L

large intestine (in tes′tən), an organ of the digestive system that removes water and stores waste material until it leaves the body.

lever (lev′ər), a simple machine made of a bar that is held up on a point called a fulcrum.

loam (lōm), soil that is a mixture of clay, sand, and humus.

M

matter (mat′ər), substance of which all objects are made.

megaphone (meg′ə fōn), a large, funnel-shaped horn or similar device, used to increase the loudness of the voice or the distance at which it can be heard.

membrane (mem′brān), a thin layer of skin that covers, separates, or connects some parts of the body.

migrate (mī′grāt), to move from one place to another when the seasons change.

mineral (min′ər əl), a material that was never alive and that can be found in soil; a nutrient the body needs in small amounts to work properly.

N

natural resource (nach′ər əl ri sôrs′), something people use that comes directly from the earth.

nerve (nėrv), a body part that carries messages to and from the brain.

nonrenewable resource (non′ri nü′ə bəl ri sôrs′), a resource that cannot be replaced once it is used up.

nutrient (nu′trē ənt), a material that plants and animals need to live and grow.

P

petroleum (pə trō′lē əm), a liquid deep in the ground that was made from living things that died millions of years ago.

photosynthesis (fō′tō sin′thə sis), the process by which plants make sugars.

pitch (pich), how high or low a sound is.

pollution (pə lü′shən), anything harmful added to the air, water, or land.

population (pop′yə lā′shən), living things of the same kind that live in the same place.

precipitation (pri sip′ə tā′shən), moisture that falls to the ground.

producer (prə dü′sər), a living thing that makes sugars.

protein (prō′tēn), a nutrient that the body uses for growth and repair.

R

recycle (rē sī′kəl), to change something so it can be reused.

reflect (ri flekt′), to bounce back.

S

saliva (sə lī′və), the fluid in the mouth that makes chewed food wet and begins digestion.

sandy soil, loose soil with large grains.

sanitary (san′ə ter′ē) **landfill,** a place where garbage is dumped and covered with soil.

screw (skrü), a simple machine used to hold objects together.

scrubber (skrub′ər), a device attached to a smokestack designed to remove harmful materials.

seed coat, the outside covering of a seed.

seedling (sēd′ling), a young plant that grows from a seed.

sewage (sü′ij), waste water and human wastes.

shelter (shel′tər), something that covers or protects from weather, danger, or attack.

simple machine, any of six kinds of tools with few or no moving parts that make work easier.

skeleton (skel′ə tən), the bones of a body.

sleet (slēt), partly frozen rain.

small intestine (in tes′tən), the organ of the digestive system in which most digestion takes place.

solar (sō′lər) **energy,** energy that comes from the sun.

sound, the energy of vibrating matter.

state of matter, the form that matter has—solid, liquid, or gas.

stomach (stum′ək), the organ of the digestive system that receives food after it is swallowed.

T

temperature (tem′pər ə chər), a measurement of how hot or cold matter is.

tendon (ten′dən), a ropelike part of the body that holds a muscle to a bone.

theory (thē′ər ē), one or more related hypotheses supported by data that best explains things or events.

thermometer (thər mom′ə tər), an instrument for measuring temperature.

transportation (tran′spər ta′shən), means of moving from one place to another.

V

variable (ver′ē ə bəl), anything in an experiment that can be changed.

vibrate (vī′brāt), to move quickly back and forth.

vitamin (vī′tə mən), a nutrient the body needs in small amounts to work properly.

vocal cords (vō kəl′ kôrdz), thin flaps at the top of the windpipe.

volume (vol′yəm), loudness or softness of a sound.

W

water cycle (sī′kəl), the movement of water by evaporation, condensation, and precipitation.

water pollution (pə lü′shən), anything harmful added to water.

water vapor (wô′tər vā′pər), water in the form of a gas.

wedge (wej), a simple machine used to cut or split an object.

wheel and axle (hwēl and ak′səl), a simple machine that has a center rod attached to a wheel.

wildlife refuge (ref′yüj), place of safety or security for wild animals and plants.

work (wėrk), the result of a force moving an object.

Index

Acknowledgments

Pupil Edition interior design
Ligature, Inc.
Rosa + Wesley Design Associates

Unless otherwise acknowledged, all photographs are the property of ScottForesman. Unless otherwise acknowledged, all computer graphics by Ligature, Inc. Page abbreviations are as follows: **(T) top, (C) center, (B) bottom, (L) left, (R) right, (INS) inset.**

Module A
Photographs
Front & Back Cover: Background: Tom Algire/Tom Stack & Associates   Children's Photos: Allan Landau for ScottForesman

Page A2(C) Larry Ulrich/DRK Photo   **A3(T)** C.Allan Morgan/Scott, Foresman   **A3(B)** Don and Pat Valenti   **A5** Mike Price/Bruce Coleman, Inc.   **A6-7** Stephen J Krasemann/Peter Arnold, Inc.   **A10** Larry Ulrich/DRK Photo   **A11** Larry Ulrich/DRK Photo   **A12** C.Allan Morgan   **A13** John Cancalosi/DRK Photo   **A14(T&B)** C.Allan Morgan   **A15(T)** Jeff Foott/Tom Stack & Associates   **A15(B)** C.Allan Morgan   **A16(T)** C.Allan Morgan   **A16(B)** John D Cunningham/Visuals Unlimited   **A17** John J.Hoffman/Bruce Coleman, Inc.   **A23** Robert & Linda Mitchell   **A24** Don & Esther Phillips/Tom Stack & Associates   **A25** Martin W Grosnick/Bruce Coleman, Inc.   **A26(T)** Robert & Linda Mitchell   **A26(B)** Breck P.Kent   **A30** T.A.Wiewandt   **A31** T.A.Wiewandt/DRK Photo   **A32(T&B)** C.Allan Morgan   **A33(T&B)** C.Allan Morgan   **A34** T.A.Wiewandt   **A35** David Muench   **A41, A42(B), A43(B), A46** Don and Pat Valenti/f/stop   **A47(T)** Rod Planck   **A48(TL)** Rod Planck   **A48(BL)** Rod Planck   **A48(R)** Don and Pat Valenti/f/stop/   **A50(TL)** Robert & Linda Mitchell   **A50(BL)** Tom Algire/Tom Stack & Associates   **A50(CR)** Nancy Adams/Tom Stack & Associates   **A50(BR)** C.Allan Morgan   **A51(T)** Tom Algire/Tom Stack & Associates   **A51(B)** Don & Pat Valenti/f/Stop Pictures, Inc.   **A56(B)** Rannels/Grant Heilman Photography   **A58(T)** Ed Kashi   **A58(B)** Allan Roberts   **A59** Courtesy of Pamela McKinnon, Goldendale, WA.   **A60** Delwin Price

Illustrations
Page A2 Carla Simmons   **A12-13** Mark Langeneckert   **A32-33** Carla Simmons   **A61** Rich Lo

Module B
Photographs
Front & Back Cover: Children's Photos: Allan Landau for ScottForesman

Page B3(BL) Alex S.MacLean/Landslides   **B11(T)** Milt & Joan Mann/Cameramann International, Ltd.   **B27** Alex S.MacLean/Landslides   **B30(ALL)** Warren Faidley/Weatherstock   **B31(L)** Warren Faidley/Weatherstock

Illustrations
Page B3(T) Karen Kluglein   **B3(B)** Rolin Graphics   **B6(T)** Rolin Graphics   **B8-9** Wild Onion Studio   **B10** Karen Kluglein   **B14-15** Elizabeth Allen   **B16-17** Elizabeth Allen   **B24-25** Ebet Dudley   **B41** Karen Kluglein   **B44-45** Ron Becker   **B52** Michael Schenk   **B61** Steve Fuller

Module C
Photographs
Front & Back Cover: Background: William J.Weber/ Visuals Unlimited   Children's Photos: Allan Landau for ScottForesman

Page C6 David Young-Wolff/PhotoEdit   **C8(ALL)** Courtesy Pittsburg Plate Glass Industries, Inc.   **C9(ALL)** Courtesy Interstate Brick Co.   **C10** Owen Franken/Stock Boston   **C11** Milt & Joan Mann/Cameramann International, Ltd.   **C15** Bruce Coleman, Inc.   **C16** Wengle/DRK Photo   **C17** Tom Ulrich/Visuals Unlimited   **C18(T)** The Granger Collection, New York   **C18(B)** Solomon D Butcher Collection/Nebraska State Historical Society   **C19(L)** Philip E Harroun/Museum of New Mexico   **C19(BR)** Jerry Jacka Photography   **C27(L)** Don and Pat Valenti/f/stop   **C27(R)** William J Weber/Visuals Unlimited   **C30(L)** Culver Pictures   **C30(R)** H. Armstrong Roberts   **C31(L)** Milt & Joan Mann/ Cameramann International, Ltd.   **C31(R)** Tony Freeman/Photo Edit   **C34(L)** Courtesy Owens-Corning   **C34(R)** Milt & Joan Mann/Cameramann International, Ltd.   **C36(L)** Fred McConnaughey/Photo Researchers   **C36(R)** Alex S. MacLean/Landslides   **C37** Paolo Koch/Photo Researchers   **C46-47(ALL)** Milt & Joan Mann/Cameramann International, Ltd.   **C50(T)** John D. Cunningham/Visuals Unlimited   **C50(B)** John D. Cunningham/Visuals Unlimited   **C51(T)** B.J. Spenceley/Bruce Coleman, Inc.   **C51(B)** S. Nielsen/DRK Photo   **C52** Oxford Scientific Films/ANIMALS ANIMALS   **C59(B)** Courtesy the FRANKLIN JOURNAL and The Farmington Maine Public Library   **C60** Courtesy San Antonio Zoo

Illustrations
Page C3 Mas Miyamoto   **C5** Blanche Sims   **C6-7** Hank Iken   **C17** Ebet Dudley   **C26** Laurie O'Keefe   **C30-31** Hank Iken   **C32-33** Steve Fuller   **C35** Peggy Tagel   **C44-45** Mas Miyamoto   **C61** Gary Torrisi

Module D
Photographs
Front & Back Cover: Background: Wayne Lankinen/DRK Photo   Children's Photos: Allan Landau for ScottForesman

Page D2(R) E.R.Degginger   **D3(T)** Culver Pictures   **D3(B)** Joe McDonald/ANIMALS ANIMALS   **D5** Kerry T. Givens/Tom Stack & Associates   **D6** E.R.Degginger   **D7** Maslowski/Visuals Unlimited   **D12(T)** Marty Snyderman/Visuals Unlimited   **D12(B)** Jeff Foott/DRK Photo   **D13(T)** Mary Clay/Tom Stack & Associates   **D13** Leonard Lee Rue III/ANIMALS ANIMALS   **D14(T)** Naval Photographic Center, Washington, D.C.   **D14(BL)** Dave B.Fleetham/Tom Stack & Associates   **D14(BR)** Supplied by Carolina Biological Supply Company   **D15** Stephen Dalton/ANIMALS ANIMALS   **D21** Michael Fogden/DRK Photo   **D22(T)** Peter Ward/Bruce Coleman, Inc.   **D22(T INS)** Daniel Gotshall/Visuals Unlimited   **D22(B)** C.C. Lockwood/DRK Photo   **D22 (B INS)** Catherine Koehler   **D23(T)** Science VU/Visuals Unlimited   **D23(T INS)** Alan & Sandy Carey   **D23(B)** Doug Allan/ANIMALS ANIMALS   **D23(B INS)** Doug Wechsler/ANIMALS ANIMALS   **D24** Wayne Lankinen/DRK Photo   **D25** E.R.Degginger   **D28** P. Armstrong/Visuals Unlimited   **D29** Joe McDonald/ANIMALS ANIMALS   **D30** Richard Ellis   **D31** Robert A Ross/E.R.Degginger   **D32(T)** Tom Edwards/Visuals Unlimited

D32B Alan & Sandy Carey   D39 Culver Pictures
D40(T) INDIAN ENCAMPMENT ON LAKE HURON -Paul
Kane 1845-50, Art Gallery of Ontario, Toronto   D40(BL) The
Bettmann Archive   D40(BR) Culver Pictures   D41 Culver
Pictures   D44(TL) Culver Pictures   D44(TR) Culver Pictures
D44(CL) The Bettmann Archive   D44(CR) The Bettmann
Archive   D44(BL) Courtesy Ford Motor Company
D44(BR) From the Collections of Henry Ford Museum &
Greenfield Village   D45(TL) Culver Pictures
D45(TR) and (CL) Milt & Joan Mann/Cameramann International,
Ltd.   D45(CR) Courtesy Ford Motor Company   D45(BL)
Courtesy Kloster Cruise Ltd.   D45(BCL) Douglas Aviation
D45(BCR) Brent Jones   D45(BR) Courtesy Chrysler Corp.
D50 Mark W. Richards/Photo Edit   D52 Takeshi Takahara/Photo
Researchers   D53 William Franklin McMahon/ScottForesman
D58 David Young-Wolff/ Photo Edit   D59 Robert
Brenner/Photo Edit   D60 Brent Jones/ Scott, Foresman

Illustrations
Page D2 Vincent Perez   D6 Wild Onion Studio
D11 Vincent Perez   D29, D30, D31, D32 JAK Graphics
D46-47 Pam Hohman   D48-49 Ron Becker
D61 George Kelvin

Module E
Photographs
Front & Back Cover: Background: John Gerlach/DRK Photo
Children's Photos: Allan Landau for ScottForesman

Page E5 Milt & Joan Mann/Cameramann International, Ltd.
E6 Milt & Joan Mann/Cameramann International, Ltd.
E7(T&B) Milt & Joan Mann/Cameramann International, Ltd.
E11 Milt & Joan Mann/Cameramann International, Ltd.
E12(T) Ben Goldstein/Don and Pat Valenti   E12(B) Alan &
Sandy Carey   E12(BR) Kevin Doyle/Visuals Unlimited
E19 John D. Cunningham/Visuals Unlimited   E25 John
Parnell/Telephoto   E27(T) Rod Planck/Tom Stack & Associates
E27(B) John Gerlach/DRK Photo   E28 Stephen J
Krasemann/DRK Photo   E29 Hans Pfletschinger/Peter Arnold,
Inc.   E34(T) Bill Everitt/ Tom Stack & Associates
E34 (T INS) Bill Everitt/Tom Stack & Associates   E34(B) Arthur
R. Hill/Visuals Unlimited   E34(B INS) Arthur R Hill/Visuals
Unlimited   E35(T) S. Maslowski/Visuals Unlimited
E35(T INS) S. Maslowski/Visuals Unlimited   E35(B) Kjell
B.Sandved/Visuals Unlimited   E35(B INS) Kjell B.Sandved/
Visuals Unlimited   E36 Vaina Chen/Bruce Coleman, Inc.
E37(T) Kjell B.Sandved/Visuals Unlimited   E37(B) Dennis
Paulson/Visuals Unlimited   E43 Bob Daemmrich   E44 Tim
Davis/Photo Researchers   E48 Sybil Shelton/Peter Arnold, Inc.
E49 Milt & Joan Mann/Cameramann International, Ltd.   E50
Milt & Joan Mann/Cameramann International, Ltd.   E51(TL)
AP/Wide World   E51(TC) AP/Wide World   E51(TR) Milt &
Joan Mann/ Cameramann International, Ltd.   E51(BL) ACME
Photo/UPI/ Bettmann   E51(BC) Milt & Joan Mann/Cameramann
International, Ltd.   E51(BR) Bob Daemmrich/Image Works
E52(T) The Bettmann Archive   E52(B) The Bettmann Archive
E53 Laura Dwight   E59 Myrleen Ferguson/Photo Edit
E60 Nathan Mandell/Scott, Foresman

Illustrations
Page E8-9 Ron Lipking   E11-12 Susan Spellman
E18 Walter Stuart   E26 Catherine Twomey
E28 Laurie O'Keefe   E29 Laurie O'Keefe
E32-33 Catherine Twomey   E50 JAK Graphics
E58-59 Carl Kock   E61 Steve Fuller

Module F
Photographs
Front & Back Cover: Background: Marty Stouffer/ANIMALS
ANIMALS   Children's Photos: Allan Landau for ScottForesman

Page F3(T) Clint Hansen   F3(B) William Peterson
F5 C.C.Lockwood/DRK Photo   F8 E.R.Degginger
F13 Milt & Joan Mann/Cameramann International, Ltd.
F14 Bob Daemmrich   F22 Brent Jones   F22(B) Tony
Freeman/Photo Edit   F23 Milt & Joan Mann/Cameramann
International, Ltd.   F39(ALL) Milt & Joan Mann/Cameramann
International, Ltd.   F40 Link/Visuals Unlimited   F42(L) James
Karales/Peter Arnold, Inc.   F42(R) Bruce Berg/Visuals Unlimited
F43(T) Milt & Joan Mann/Cameramann International, Ltd.
F43(B) Tom Edwards/ Visuals Unlimited   F44(T) Tom
McHugh/Photo Researchers   F44(B) Marty Stouffer/ANIMALS
ANIMALS   F45(T) Stephen J Krasemann/DRK Photo   F45(B)
E.R.Degginger   F46 Phil Degginger   F47 John James Audubon,
1825/The New-York Historical Society, New York City   F50
David Young-Wolff/Photo Edit   F51(TL) Dohra
Lambrecht/Visuals Unlimited   F51(TC) Peter Arnold, Inc.
F51(TR) Kerry T Givens/Tom Stack & Associates   F51(B)
Dwight R. Kuhn   F52 Wendell Metzen   F53 David R. Frazier
Photolibrary   F59 Fox5 TV/Kid City

Illustrations
Page F6-7 John Burgoyne   F24 Hank Iken   F32-33 Ron
Becker   F40-41 Clint Hansen   F46 William Peterson
F47 JAK Graphics   F61 Gary Torrisi